TM

...FOR DUMMIES

BESTSELLING BOOK SERIES

CW00953146

References Rest of Us

®

Are you intimidated and confused by computers? Do you find that traditional manuals are overloaded with technical details you'll never use? Do your friends and family always call you to fix simple problems on their PCs? Then the *...For Dummies®* computer book series from IDG Books Worldwide is for you.

...For Dummies books are written for those frustrated computer users who know they aren't really dumb but find that PC hardware, software, and indeed the unique vocabulary of computing make them feel helpless. *...For Dummies* books use a lighthearted approach, a down-to-earth style, and even cartoons and humorous icons to dispel computer novices' fears and build their confidence. Lighthearted but not lightweight, these books are a perfect survival guide for anyone forced to use a computer.

> *"I like my copy so much I told friends; now they bought copies."*
> — Irene C., Orwell, Ohio

> *"Quick, concise, nontechnical, and humorous."*
> — Jay A., Elburn, Illinois

> *"Thanks, I needed this book. Now I can sleep at night."*
> — Robin F., British Columbia, Canada

Already, millions of satisfied readers agree. They have made *...For Dummies* books the #1 introductory level computer book series and have written asking for more. So, if you're looking for the most fun and easy way to learn about computers, look to *...For Dummies* books to give you a helping hand.

® IDG BOOKS WORLDWIDE

1/99

MCSE
Windows® 2000
Directory Services

FOR

DUMMIES®

MCSE
Windows® 2000
Directory Services
FOR
DUMMIES®

by Anthony Sequeira

IDG Books Worldwide, Inc.
An International Data Group Company

Foster City, CA ◆ Chicago, IL ◆ Indianapolis, IN ◆ New York, NY

MCSE Windows® 2000 Directory Services For Dummies®

Published by
IDG Books Worldwide, Inc.
An International Data Group Company
919 E. Hillsdale Blvd.
Suite 300
Foster City, CA 94404
www.idgbooks.com (IDG Books Worldwide Web site)
www.dummies.com (Dummies Press Web site)

Library of Congress Control Number: 00-103376

ISBN: 0-7645-0710-9

Printed in the United States of America

10 9 8 7 6 5 4 3 2 1

1O/QX/QT/QR/IN

Distributed in the United States by IDG Books Worldwide, Inc.

Distributed by CDG Books Canada Inc. for Canada; by Transworld Publishers Limited in the United Kingdom; by IDG Norge Books for Norway; by IDG Sweden Books for Sweden; by IDG Books Australia Publishing Corporation Pty. Ltd. for Australia and New Zealand; by TransQuest Publishers Pte Ltd. for Singapore, Malaysia, Thailand, Indonesia, and Hong Kong; by Gotop Information Inc. for Taiwan; by ICG Muse, Inc. for Japan; by Intersoft for South Africa; by Eyrolles for France; by International Thomson Publishing for Germany, Austria and Switzerland; by Distribuidora Cuspide for Argentina; by LR International for Brazil; by Galileo Libros for Chile; by Ediciones ZETA S.C.R. Ltda. for Peru; by WS Computer Publishing Corporation, Inc., for the Philippines; by Contemporanea de Ediciones for Venezuela; by Express Computer Distributors for the Caribbean and West Indies; by Micronesia Media Distributor, Inc. for Micronesia; by Chips Computadoras S.A. de C.V. for Mexico; by Editorial Norma de Panama S.A. for Panama; by American Bookshops for Finland.

For general information on IDG Books Worldwide's books in the U.S., please call our Consumer Customer Service department at 800-762-2974. For reseller information, including discounts and premium sales, please call our Reseller Customer Service department at 800-434-3422.

For information on where to purchase IDG Books Worldwide's books outside the U.S., please contact our International Sales department at 317-572-3993 or fax 317-572-4002.

For consumer information on foreign language translations, please contact our Customer Service department at 800-434-3422, fax 317-572-4002, or e-mail rights@idgbooks.com.

For information on licensing foreign or domestic rights, please phone +1-650-653-7098.

For sales inquiries and special prices for bulk quantities, please contact our Order Services department at 800-434-3422 or write to the address above.

For information on using IDG Books Worldwide's books in the classroom or for ordering examination copies, please contact our Educational Sales department at 800-434-2086 or fax 317-572-4005.

For press review copies, author interviews, or other publicity information, please contact our Public Relations department at 650-653-7000 or fax 650-653-7500.

For authorization to photocopy items for corporate, personal, or educational use, please contact Copyright Clearance Center, 222 Rosewood Drive, Danvers, MA 01923, or fax 978-750-4470.

About the Author

Anthony Sequeira has been a professional speaker and writer in the IT industry for the past seven years. He holds every major Microsoft certification, including MCT, MCSE+I, MCDBA, MCSE 2000, and MCSD. Anthony has written many books, including titles on Internet Information Server and Windows 2000 Server. He has also written for several important industry magazines and newsletters. He currently speaks about Active Directory technologies for KnowledgeNet.com. When he is not speaking or writing about computer technologies, Anthony is flying his plane in the skies above Arizona. How did he learn to fly? Microsoft Flight Simulator, of course!

ABOUT IDG BOOKS WORLDWIDE

Welcome to the world of IDG Books Worldwide.

IDG Books Worldwide, Inc., is a subsidiary of International Data Group, the world's largest publisher of computer-related information and the leading global provider of information services on information technology. IDG was founded more than 30 years ago by Patrick J. McGovern and now employs more than 9,000 people worldwide. IDG publishes more than 290 computer publications in over 75 countries. More than 90 million people read one or more IDG publications each month.

Launched in 1990, IDG Books Worldwide is today the #1 publisher of best-selling computer books in the United States. We are proud to have received eight awards from the Computer Press Association in recognition of editorial excellence and three from Computer Currents' First Annual Readers' Choice Awards. Our best-selling ...*For Dummies*® series has more than 50 million copies in print with translations in 31 languages. IDG Books Worldwide, through a joint venture with IDG's Hi-Tech Beijing, became the first U.S. publisher to publish a computer book in the People's Republic of China. In record time, IDG Books Worldwide has become the first choice for millions of readers around the world who want to learn how to better manage their businesses.

Our mission is simple: Every one of our books is designed to bring extra value and skill-building instructions to the reader. Our books are written by experts who understand and care about our readers. The knowledge base of our editorial staff comes from years of experience in publishing, education, and journalism — experience we use to produce books to carry us into the new millennium. In short, we care about books, so we attract the best people. We devote special attention to details such as audience, interior design, use of icons, and illustrations. And because we use an efficient process of authoring, editing, and desktop publishing our books electronically, we can spend more time ensuring superior content and less time on the technicalities of making books.

You can count on our commitment to deliver high-quality books at competitive prices on topics you want to read about. At IDG Books Worldwide, we continue in the IDG tradition of delivering quality for more than 30 years. You'll find no better book on a subject than one from IDG Books Worldwide.

John Kilcullen
Chairman and CEO
IDG Books Worldwide, Inc.

*Eighth Annual
Computer Press
Awards ≥ 1992*

*Ninth Annual
Computer Press
Awards ≥ 1993*

*Tenth Annual
Computer Press
Awards ≥ 1994*

*Eleventh Annual
Computer Press
Awards ≥ 1995*

IDG is the world's leading IT media, research and exposition company. Founded in 1964, IDG had 1997 revenues of $2.05 billion and has more than 9,000 employees worldwide. IDG offers the widest range of media options that reach IT buyers in 75 countries representing 95% of worldwide IT spending. IDG's diverse product and services portfolio spans six key areas including print publishing, online publishing, expositions and conferences, market research, education and training, and global marketing services. More than 90 million people read one or more of IDG's 290 magazines and newspapers, including IDG's leading global brands — Computerworld, PC World, Network World, Macworld and the Channel World family of publications. IDG Books Worldwide is one of the fastest-growing computer book publishers in the world, with more than 700 titles in 36 languages. The "...For Dummies®" series alone has more than 50 million copies in print. IDG offers online users the largest network of technology-specific Web sites around the world through IDG.net (http://www.idg.net), which comprises more than 225 targeted Web sites in 55 countries worldwide. International Data Corporation (IDC) is the world's largest provider of information technology data, analysis and consulting, with research centers in over 41 countries and more than 400 research analysts worldwide. IDG World Expo is a leading producer of more than 168 globally branded conferences and expositions in 35 countries including E3 (Electronic Entertainment Expo), Macworld Expo, ComNet, Windows World Expo, ICE (Internet Commerce Expo), Agenda, DEMO, and Spotlight. IDG's training subsidiary, ExecuTrain, is the world's largest computer training company, with more than 230 locations worldwide and 785 training courses. IDG Marketing Services helps industry-leading IT companies build international brand recognition by developing global integrated marketing programs via IDG's print, online and exposition products worldwide. Further information about the company can be found at www.idg.com.   1/26/00

Dedication

This book is dedicated to my father, David Sequeira. When I was very young, he bought me a personal computer that I am sure he couldn't really afford at the time. I remember that old thing had to plug into the television and used a cassette player for storage. Dad was kind and loving enough to pretend he knew what I was talking about when I showed him my first BASIC program. Thank you for everything, Dad.

Author's Acknowledgments

I would like to thank my agent, James Conrad, for getting me this opportunity. I also want to thank my project editor, John Pont, and my technical reviewer, Doug Bassett, for their thorough work. John's incredible editing job improved this book tenfold, and Doug's technical knowledge and insight regarding Microsoft technologies never ceases to amaze me. Thanks to everyone behind the scenes at IDG Books Worldwide for making this book possible. I also would like to thank Tom Graunke, Ted Hernandez, Chris Dragon, and Mark Rukavina, of KnowledgeNet for all their help with my career throughout the years. Thanks most of all to my incredible wife, Joette. This book simply would not have been possible without her many sacrifices.

Publisher's Acknowledgments

We're proud of this book; please send us your comments through our IDG Books Worldwide Online Registration Form located at www.dummies.com.

Some of the people who helped bring this book to market include the following:

Acquisitions, Editorial, and Media Development

Project Editor: John W. Pont

Acquisitions Manager: Judy Brief

Proof Editor: Mary SeRine

Technical Editor: Douglas Bassett, MCSE 2000

Senior Permissions Editor: Carmen Krikorian

Media Development Specialist: Brock Bigard

Media Development Coordinator: Marisa Pearman

Editorial Manager: Constance Carlisle

Media Development Manager: Laura Carpenter

Media Development Supervisor: Richard Graves

Editorial Assistants: Amanda Foxworth, Jean Rogers

Production

Project Coordinators: Regina Snyder, Leslie Alvarez

Layout and Graphics: Amy Adrian, Joe Bucki, Jacque Schneider, Brian Torwelle, Jeremey Unger, Joyce Haughey, Betty Schulte, Erin Zeltner

Proofreaders: Laura Albert, Jennifer Mahern, Charles Spencer

Indexer: Richard Shrout

General and Administrative

IDG Books Worldwide, Inc.: John Kilcullen, CEO; Bill Barry, President and COO; John Ball, Executive VP, Operations & Administration; John Harris, CFO

IDG Books Technology Publishing Group: Richard Swadley, Senior Vice President and Publisher; Mary Bednarek, Vice President and Publisher, Networking and Certification; Walter R. Bruce III, Vice President and Publisher, General User and Design Professional; Joseph Wikert, Vice President and Publisher, Programming; Mary C. Corder, Editorial Director, Branded Technology Editorial; Andy Cummings, Publishing Director, General User and Design Professional; Barry Pruett, Publishing Director, Visual

IDG Books Manufacturing: Ivor Parker, Vice President, Manufacturing

IDG Books Marketing: John Helmus, Assistant Vice President, Director of Marketing

IDG Books Online Management: Brenda McLaughlin, Executive Vice President, Chief Internet Officer; Gary Millrood, Executive Vice President of Business Development, Sales and Marketing

IDG Books Packaging: Marc J. Mikulich, Vice President, Brand Strategy and Research

IDG Books Production for Branded Press: Debbie Stailey, Production Director

IDG Books Sales: Roland Elgey, Senior Vice President, Sales and Marketing; Michael Violano, Vice President, International Sales and Sub Rights

◆

The publisher would like to give special thanks to Patrick J. McGovern, without whom this book would not have been possible.

◆

Contents at a Glance

Cartoons at a Glance

By Rich Tennant

page 25

page 243

page 143

page 177

page 7

page 289

page 65

page 279

page 95

Cartoon Information:
Fax: 978-546-7747
E-Mail: richtennant@the5thwave.com
World Wide Web: www.the5thwave.com

Table of Contents

Introduction

. . . .

So, you want to conquer exam 70-217, Implementing and Administering a Microsoft Windows 2000 Directory Services Infrastructure? This book is exactly what you need. It covers every objective needed for success on this challenging Windows 2000 certification exam.

Get ready to forget much of what you know to be true regarding the so-called directory services of Windows NT 4.0. Much has changed in the new directory services of Windows 2000 — and much has been added. As I explain throughout this book, you must master an extensive vocabulary of directory service terminology and techniques.

About This Book

This book has only one purpose: to help you prepare completely for exam 70-217. It is that simple. Everything in this book — every word and every practice question — relates directly to potential exam questions.

Each chapter contains elements designed to help you pass this certification exam, including

- A concise listing of the exam objectives covered in the chapter
- A Quick Assessment test to see what you might already know
- To-the-point, easy-to-read text on the subject. You do not have to wade through every detail of Active Directory Services — just the information you need to know to have great success on exam day
- Lab exercises that help to reinforce exam topics
- A Prep Test at the end of the chapter to further get you in the mood for the real thing

You'll also find two full-length practice tests in the book's appendixes, and the CD-ROM that accompanies this book includes hundreds of additional practice questions.

Foolish Assumptions

Because you are reading this book, I assume you are going to take exam 70-217 someday — hopefully, someday very soon. I also assume that you possess the following:

- A mastery of the Windows interface, including the ability to locate, create, and manipulate folders and files and to configure the desktop environment
- General knowledge of computer hardware components, including memory, hard disks, and central processing units
- General knowledge of networking concepts, including network operating systems, client-server relationships, and local area network (LAN) technologies
- The ability to install Windows 2000 Server or Advanced Server
- The ability to use the administrative tools of Windows 2000 Server
- A basic understanding of the TCP/IP protocol, including the knowledge necessary to install this protocol's components in Windows 2000 Server

How to Use This Book

Remember, this book helps you get ready for exam 70-217. Here are some tips for getting the very most from this book:

- Study every question in this text, including the Quick Assessment and the Prep Test in each chapter, the practice exams at the end of the book, and the practice questions on the CD-ROM that comes with this book.
- Be sure to practice the labs that appear in each chapter. If necessary, create a test system for this purpose. Running through the labs helps to ensure you have mastered the concepts you need to know for the test.
- Carefully review the lists and tables in each chapter. They present information that you need to memorize for the exam.
- Take advantage of the icons used in this book to help you study. The icons help you to focus on key facts.

How This Book Is Organized

This book has nine parts, and each part has two or more chapters. The first part of the book deals with the exam and Windows 2000 track specifics. Parts II through VII focus on the exam objectives that you must know before you take the exam. Part VIII is the Part of Tens, which provides valuable tips and Q&A regarding specifics about taking this exam. Part IX comprises the practice tests, a glossary, and details about this book's CD-ROM.

Here is more detail on each of the different parts of the book.

Part I: The Wonderful World of ADS

In Part I, you get familiar with the details of the Windows 2000 certification track and exam 70-217 in particular. Part I also provides a helpful overview of directory services and the specific features of Windows 2000 Active Directory Services (ADS).

Part II: Installing, Configuring, and Troubleshooting ADS

For the exam, you need to know quite a bit about properly installing and configuring Active Directory. This part of the book details all this information for you, including installing Active Directory and installing and configuring its components.

Part III: DNS and Active Directory

An Active Directory installation requires DNS. This part of the book reviews all you need to know about properly installing and configuring DNS for Active Directory.

Part IV: Configuration Management

After you have Active Directory properly installed and configured, you can really begin to do some awesome work with it. Perhaps most impressive is the control ADS gives you over users' desktops. This part of the book tells you what you need to know about using ADS and Group Policy to effectively manage your entire network.

Part V: Remote Installation Services

Installing client systems has never been easier thanks to Windows 2000's Remote Installation Services. The chapters in Part V give you all you need to know about these services for the exam.

Part VI: Managing and Optimizing ADS

In this part of the book, you review how to manage your Active Directory configuration to ensure that you have it properly optimized for your network. The chapters in this part of the book also cover Active Directory maintenance tasks such as moving, defragmenting, and caring for the database itself.

Part VII: Active Directory Security Solutions

In Part VII, you focus on ADS security mechanisms that greatly simplify your security job. Many of these tools revolutionize the way in which you approach security in your Windows network, and you can expect to see some exam questions about these tools.

Part VIII: The Part of Tens

One chapter in the Part of Tens offers tips about how to succeed on the exam. I also answer ten common questions regarding the exam.

Part IX: Appendixes

In Part IX, you have a chance to do some more great practice for the real exam. Here, you find two full-length practice exams. I also provide a glossary of key terms used in this book, and I tell you all about the CD that accompanies this book.

About the CD-ROM

The CD-ROM that accompanies this book includes hundreds of additional practice exam questions and the Dummies Test Engine. The CD also includes a links page, a nifty screensaver, and demo versions of helpful test-prep tools. Be sure to utilize this important resource.

Conventions Used in This Book

Use this book to get the knowledge you need to pass the exam. To help you get this knowledge quickly and efficiently, I employ the following features throughout this book:

✔ A Quick Assessment at the beginning of each chapter helps you target the specific topics that you need to study in that chapter.

✔ Lab exercises give you hands-on experience with various ADS-related tasks that you need to know for the exam.

✔ A special font helps to identify Web addresses that you can use to find out more information — for example, www.hungryminds.com.

✔ Command arrows enable you to list a series of menu commands in the most concise manner possible. For example, here's how I would tell you to start the DHCP Management console: Click Start➪Programs➪ Administrative Tools➪DHCP.

✔ Tables and lists throughout the book summarize key information that you need to memorize for the exam.

✔ The Cheat Sheet contains key information you must have memorized to succeed come exam day. Take it with you on your way to the exam and look it over prior to entering the "little square room."

✔ The practice questions presented in this book will help you master information covered on the exam. At the end of each chapter, you'll find Prep Test questions that review the topics covered in that chapter. And in the appendixes, you will find two full-length practice exams and a glossary of important terms.

Icons Used in This Book

To help you master the topics of Active Directory more quickly and efficiently, I use several icons throughout this book:

The Tip icon points out useful information regarding Active Directory that many often overlook. This information really helps you get the most out of Windows 2000's Active Directory Services, often saving you time or money or both! Typically, this information is also game for the exam.

The Remember icon points out important nuggets of information that you need to tuck away in your memory for future reference.

The Warning icon points out information that could cause disaster if you do not heed the advice given. Once again, this information is often exam relevant.

The Instant Answer icon helps you pinpoint exam content covered in this book. Pay extra attention when you see this icon — you are in exam territory for sure.

The Time Shaver icon points out information that can save you valuable time in your study efforts. Who doesn't need that?

Where to Go from Here

If you are familiar with the Windows 2000 track and have a solid fundamental knowledge of directory services and ADS in particular, go ahead and jump right to Part II. This part begins the coverage of the exam objectives. If you are new to the Windows 2000 track and to directory services, simply turn the page!

Part I

The Wonderful World of ADS

The 5th Wave   By Rich Tennant

"We sort of have our own way of mentally preparing our
people to take the MCSE network infrastructure exam."

In this part . . .

Welcome (back) to the wonderful world of Windows 2000 certification testing. Maybe you have been forced here thanks to the expiration of previous Microsoft certifications, or perhaps you are just beginning your quest for certification. No matter why you are here, I believe you will find this book a welcome solution to the problems presented to you on exam 70-217, Implementing and Administering a Windows 2000 Directory Services Infrastructure. You can start by getting familiar with this exam and the Windows 2000 certification track in general.

In Chapter 1, I explore the Windows 2000 certification track and the objectives for the administering ADS exam. In Chapter 2, I review directory service technologies and the specific features of Active Directory.

If you are familiar with the requirements for Windows 2000 certification, and you have a solid background in directory services, you may be okay with skipping this part of the book.

Chapter 1

The Administering ADS Exam

●●●

In This Chapter

▶ Exploring the Windows 2000 exam track

▶ Reviewing the objectives for exam 70-217

▶ Deciding whether you are ready

●●●

*T*he Microsoft Certified Professional (MCP) program has undergone massive changes thanks to the release of Window 2000. Current NT 4 MCSEs (Microsoft Certified Systems Engineers) face perhaps the most stunning change, because their certification expires at the end of 2001. Be sure you stay ahead of the curve and get the new Windows 2000 exams knocked out in plenty of time.

This chapter explores the overall requirements of the Windows 2000 MCSE track. I also detail the objectives for exam 70-217, Implementing and Administering a Microsoft Windows 2000 Directory Services Infrastructure — a very important exam because it represents a core requirement for the Windows 2000 MCSE certification.

Exploring the Windows 2000 MCSE Track

Before I tell you about the directory services exam, take a look at how exam 70-217 fits into the overall Windows 2000 MCSE track. To earn certification as a Windows 2000 MCSE, you must pass these four core exams:

✔ Exam 70-210, Installing, Configuring, and Administering Microsoft Windows 2000 Professional

✔ Exam 70-215, Installing, Configuring, and Administering Microsoft Windows 2000 Server

✔ Exam 70-216, Implementing and Administering a Microsoft Windows 2000 Network Infrastructure

✔ Exam 70-217, Implementing and Administering a Microsoft Windows 2000 Directory Services Infrastructure

Instead of these four core exams, candidates who have passed three Windows NT 4.0 exams — 70-067, 70-068, and 70-073 — can take this single exam: 70-240, Microsoft Windows 2000 Accelerated Exam for MCPs Certified on Microsoft Windows NT 4.0. This option exists until December 31, 2001. This exam is free to qualified candidates, but you can attempt it only once.

In addition to the four core exams in the Windows 2000 MCSE track, you must pass one of the following exams:

✔ Exam 70-219, Designing a Microsoft Windows 2000 Directory Services Infrastructure

✔ Exam 70-220, Designing Security for a Microsoft Windows 2000 Network

✔ Exam 70-221, Designing a Microsoft Windows 2000 Network Infrastructure

Finally, you need to pass two elective exams. For the most up-to-date list of potential elective exams (and Microsoft has plenty of them), see www. microsoft.com/trainingandservices.

Examining the Administering ADS Exam

Before you start studying for the exam, spend some time reviewing Microsoft's list of exam objectives. These objectives may change at any time, so check out the latest information by visiting www.microsoft.com/ trainingandservices. At this very useful site, search for exam 70-217 and review the latest information about its content.

Reviewing the objectives for exam 70-217

The following sections in this chapter provide a complete list of the exam objectives as of the time of this writing. You will be happy to note that this book completely prepares you for the exam by taking an objective-by-objective approach to the topics Microsoft expects you to know.

Use these exam objectives to help you study! As you master a topic, cross it off the list. You should also highlight areas in which you need more work. As I mention in the introduction, the chapters in this book map directly to these objectives to help you in this endeavor. Also, note my chapter references in the following list of exam objectives. Use all these features to ensure that you are ready come test time.

The following sections list all the tasks you must know for the exam.

Installing, configuring, and troubleshooting Active Directory

✔ Install, configure, and troubleshoot the components of Active Directory. (See Chapter 3.)

- Install Active Directory.
- Create sites.
- Create subnets.
- Create site links.
- Create site link bridges.
- Create connection objects.
- Create global catalog servers.
- Move server objects between sites.
- Transfer operations master roles.
- Verify Active Directory installation.
- Implement an organizational unit (OU) structure.

✔ Back up and restore Active Directory. (See Chapter 4.)

- Perform an authoritative restore of Active Directory.
- Recover from a system failure.

Installing, configuring, managing, monitoring, and troubleshooting DNS for Active Directory

✔ Install, configure, and troubleshoot DNS for Active Directory. (See Chapter 5.)

- Integrate Active Directory DNS zones with non-Active Directory DNS zones.
- Configure zones for dynamic updates.

✔ Manage, monitor, and troubleshoot DNS. (See Chapter 6.)

- Manage replication of DNS data.

Installing, configuring, managing, monitoring, optimizing, and troubleshooting change and configuration management

✔ Implement and troubleshoot Group Policy. (See Chapter 7.)

- Create a Group Policy object (GPO).

- Link an existing GPO.

- Delegate administrative control of Group Policy.

- Modify Group Policy inheritance.

- Filter Group Policy settings by associating security groups to GPOs.

- Modify Group Policy.

✔ Manage and troubleshoot user environments by using Group Policy. (See Chapter 8.)

- Control user environments by using administrative templates.

- Assign script policies to users and computers.

✔ Manage and troubleshoot software by using Group Policy. (See Chapter 9.)

- Deploy software by using Group Policy.

- Maintain software by using Group Policy.

- Configure deployment options.

- Troubleshoot common problems that occur during software deployment.

✔ Manage network configuration by using Group Policy. (See Chapter 8.)

✔ Deploy Windows 2000 by using Remote Installation Services (RIS). (See Chapter 10.)

- Install an image on a RIS client computer.

- Create a RIS boot disk.

- Configure remote installation options.

- Troubleshoot RIS problems.

- Manage images for performing remote installations.

✔ Configure RIS security. (See Chapter 11.)

- Authorize a RIS server.

- Grant computer account creation rights.

- Prestage RIS client computers for added security and load balancing.

Managing, monitoring, and optimizing the components of Active Directory

✔ Manage Active Directory objects. (See Chapter 12.)

  • Move Active Directory objects.

  • Publish resources in Active Directory.

  • Locate objects in Active Directory.

  • Create and manage accounts manually or by scripting.

  • Control access to Active Directory objects.

  • Delegate administrative control of objects in Active Directory.

✔ Manage Active Directory performance. (See Chapter 13.)

  • Monitor, maintain, and troubleshoot domain controller performance.

  • Monitor, maintain, and troubleshoot Active Directory components.

✔ Manage and troubleshoot Active Directory replication. (See Chapter 14.)

  • Manage intersite replication.

  • Manage intrasite replication.

Configuring, managing, monitoring, and troubleshooting Active Directory security solutions

✔ Configure and troubleshoot security in a directory services infrastructure. (See Chapter 15.)

  • Apply security policies by using Group Policy.

  • Create, analyze, and modify security configurations by using Security Configuration and Analysis and security templates.

  • Implement an audit policy.

✔ Monitor and analyze security events. (See Chapter 16.)

Checking out the exam format

As of the time of this writing, exam 70-217 is a standard, multiple-choice type Microsoft exam. You have 110 minutes to complete approximately 45 questions of varying length. Many questions feature exhibits, and you may see some select-and-place question formats. These select-and-place questions have you drag text labels to appropriate locations in a Window during the exam. To practice with these new question types, be sure to visit www.microsoft.com/trainingandservices to download a sample.

The current passing score for this exam is approximately 665 out of 1,000 points. This low required passing score should give you an idea of how many students struggled with the very difficult Beta version of this exam. Have no fear — if you follow the tips for successful study mentioned in the next section, you will have no problem!

Finding tips for successful study

If you want to pass the exam, you are in the right place. Cover to cover, this book zeroes in on the exam objectives. Each chapter focuses on a different area of the exam objectives (with the exception of the chapters in Parts I and VIII).

Each chapter begins with a look at the exam objectives the chapter covers. This makes studying in conjunction with the official exam objectives a real breeze! Next, a Quick Assessment test helps you determine how much you already know about the topics covered in that chapter. You then launch into the chapter. At the end of each chapter, a special Prep Test provides multiple-choice questions to help you review the information you studied in that chapter.

In the appendixes, you get even more exam practice. You can work through two full-length practice exams. And your preparation does not stop there. Be sure to install the tools on the CD-ROM and get more practice!

Watch out for Instant Answer icons throughout this book. These icons flag tricky information that may appear on the exam.

This book does not offer complete coverage of Active Directory implementations. It gets close to this objective but would fall short in some areas. This book concentrates on the information you need to know to pass the exam — plain and simple.

Are You Ready?

I want to help you make sure you are ready for the exam. A big key to achieving this goal is to answer all the practice questions that this book provides. And you'll find lots of them! Be sure you complete all the Quick Assessments, Prep Tests, and practice exams to ensure you are ready.

You also need to set up a practice system if at all possible to truly wrap your hands around Active Directory. To practice the tasks you need to know for the exam, use your practice system to work through the labs in each chapter. In order to build this practice system, you should have an Intel-compatible computer system with the following:

- A copy of Windows 2000 Server or Windows 2000 Advanced Server

  Evaluation copies of Windows 2000 are available from the Microsoft Web site. These copies are typically very inexpensive and work just fine for your practice system.

- 133 MHz or higher Pentium-compatible CPU

- 128MB of RAM

- 2GB hard drive with at least 1GB of free space

- The other typical system components, including a mouse, a monitor, and a CD-ROM drive

In addition to taking advantage of all the review questions and labs, check out the information in the Part of Tens. The chapters in that part of the book contain important information regarding the exam, answering many questions you might have and providing plenty of tips for success!

Chapter 2

Exam Prep Roadmap: Understanding Active Directory Services

*I*n my opinion, Active Directory Services (ADS) represent the most significant enhancement to the NT operating system. With ADS, Microsoft enters into the arena of robust, scalable directory services — an extremely important step for the continued success of Microsoft's operating systems.

But just what is a directory service and why are they so important? This chapter tackles those issues, giving you an understanding of directory services and fundamental ADS concepts.

If you are confident in your understanding of directory services and ADS basics, you may skip this chapter and dig right in to the other chapters in this book. On the other hand, by spending some time on this chapter, you may uncover a nugget or two of information that could solidify your understanding of material I cover elsewhere in the book.

What Is a Directory Service?

You can find lots of different definitions out there for the phrase *directory service.* This demonstrates the complexity of the topic. Here's my definition:

A directory service is a customizable information store that functions as a single point from which users can locate resources and services distributed throughout the network. This customizable information store also gives administrators a single point for managing its objects and their attributes. Although this information store appears as a single point to the users of the network, it is actually most often stored in a distributed form.

A genuine directory service is much more than a database technology that stores users and groups. This is a really important point — one that you should keep in mind as you review the topics I cover throughout this book.

The database that forms a directory service is not designed for transactional data. (For this reason, I prefer to use the phrase "information store" in my definition of a directory service.) The data stored in your directory service should be fairly stable and should change only as frequently as the objects in your network. For example, the data that forms a directory service changes much less frequently than a sales database. Data that changes very frequently would be stored in another type of database on the network. (Of course, Microsoft would suggest Access or SQL Server for storing your transactional data.)

What all good directory services should offer

Microsoft claimed to have a directory service in previous Windows NT versions, but it fell quite short of most industry standards. To be considered a genuine enterprise directory service, a system should meet the following criteria:

- ✔ If necessary, the information store can be distributed among many different physical locations. However, for the purposes of searches and administration, it appears as a single database.

- ✔ The information store can accommodate new types of objects, as necessary, to meet the network's changing needs.

- ✔ Users and administrators can easily search for information from various locations throughout the network.

- ✔ The system has no dependency upon physical location.

- ✔ The information store is accessible from many different operating systems. Typically, this is possible thanks to nonproprietary communication standards utilized in the system.

Does Windows 2000 meet these criteria with Active Directory Services? You bet it does!

Many Windows 2000 Servers host Active Directory Services. You create these machines by installing the information store services and promoting the computer to the role of domain controller. These domain controllers exist, strategically placed by you, the network administrator, across the enterprise network. Even though they are distributed, network users access Active Directory as if it resides on a single server. In fact, network users are shielded completely from the actual complexities of the system — and they like it that way!

Active Directory Services rely on a "blueprint" that defines the types of objects stored in the information store. The official term for this "blueprint" in Active Directory is the *schema*. The great news for you as an administrator is that this schema is *extensible* — a fancy way of saying that you (or other authorized personnel) can add objects and their attributes to the schema to define additional components in your network. In fact, just about any information you want to store in Active Directory can be accommodated. For example, you may want to include Employee ID Number information for each user account in your Active Directory information store. Although the schema already has dozens of attributes for users, no such attribute exists, but it is one you should add! Just remember that you do not store transactional information here — leave that to a full-fledged database system.

Active Directory offers robust search capabilities for users of the network. You can search for any object stored in the directory, using any of the object's attributes in the search criteria. Following the previous example, you could search for all users in the network whose Employee ID Numbers are greater than a certain value. This is all so simple and flexible thanks to a special service in ADS called the global catalog. This special subset of the information store resides on select domain controllers called global catalog servers. These servers store the portion of the full information store that are most likely to be used in searches. They are very efficient at fulfilling the requests of network users (including administrators). Global catalog servers locate resources quickly and efficiently, regardless of their actual location in the network.

Thanks to a complex and robust system for replication of information store information throughout the distributed system, no reliance on physical location exists within Active Directory Services. In Windows 2000, you actually define the physical topology of your network in the directory service, so domain controllers can notify themselves effectively and efficiently of changes to the information.

Microsoft made sure to adhere to nonproprietary technologies in the design of Active Directory. This design makes integration with many other computer systems possible and even encouraged. ADS coexists well with Novell networks, UNIX networks, and many others.

Other directory services

Active Directory is not the only directory service in town. Novell has Novell Directory Services (NDS), or Edirectory, as Novell likes to call it these days. Banyan has StreetTalk, and we are bound to see more from Sun Microsystems, Netscape, and others.

The key to the success of these competing directory services will depend on support for LDAP (Lightweight Directory Access Protocol). LDAP specifies a standard, vendor-independent syntax for querying a directory service. Microsoft's ADS provides robust support for LDAP.

Key Active Directory Service Features

Windows 2000's Active Directory offers several key features that make ADS a suitable directory service for a small or large network implementation. These key features also help Active Directory attain true directory service status! Here is a summary of these key features:

- ✔ **DNS integration:** Active Directory relies on DNS for its location services — a great idea because DNS is a standard used by Internet technologies everywhere.

- ✔ **Kerberos security:** For logon purposes, Windows 2000 uses the industry-standard Kerberos security service, which replaces the much weaker and proprietary NT LAN Manager protocols of previous NT versions.

- ✔ **LDAP:** Yet another standard! This one makes it easy to get information out of Active Directory using a standard syntax.

- ✔ **Replication:** Active Directory sports a very sophisticated system for replication. This helps to distinguish Windows 2000 from previous versions of NT, which simply do not offer these replication features.

DNS integration

DNS is an incredibly popular Internet technology that resolves TCP/IP Internet addresses to "friendly" host names. This service makes it easy for users to find resources in the huge network that is the Internet. For example, assume that Microsoft is hosting its Web site on a computer with the Internet address of 290.30.45.67. Having to use this address in the browser is much too cumbersome for users. DNS is the technology that resolves the friendly `www.microsoft.com` name to the address of 290.30.45.67.

Active Directory relies on this very service heavily in Windows 2000. Computers in your Windows 2000 network use DNS to locate domain controllers, global catalog servers, and other key systems. For example, if one of your users needs to change her password, the user's computer initiates a search of DNS to locate a nearby domain controller so the password change can be made.

In addition to location services, DNS does what it does best for you in the network: It resolves friendly names to IP addresses. Also, the system serves as a naming convention for your Active Directory domains. For example, you may have a domain named `sales.acme.com` in your Active Directory forest and this name exists exactly that way in the DNS system.

I cannot overemphasize the reliance on DNS. Because Active Directory relies on DNS in this manner, you need to install and configure DNS properly in your network before you implement Active Directory. Chapters 5 and 6 of this book provide all the information you need to know about this subject.

It is easy to get confused about DNS and Active Directory because the latter relies so heavily upon DNS. Remember, they are still separate and distinct in their roles. For example, DNS stores resource records that resolve TCP/IP addresses, while Active Directory stores objects that define your network.

Kerberos security

Including Kerberos in Windows 2000 was a smart move by the Microsoft development folks. By opting for nonproprietary technologies rather than Microsoft's own solutions, Windows 2000 offers much better integration with other network operating systems (NOSs).

Kerberos is a cross-platform network authentication protocol. Using very strong encryption, clients verify their identity to servers thanks to this protocol. This design provides much-needed strong security for a critical event in the network: a user logging on to a remote system to access network resources.

Under the Kerberos system, tickets provide the needed authentication information. A ticket provides the necessary authentication, but only for a limited time period — yet another mechanism that helps protect the network. Key Distribution Centers (KDCs) provide the tickets that power this security system. As you may expect, KDCs are your domain controllers of Active Directory Services.

LDAP

All domain controllers in Windows 2000 provide the Lightweight Directory Access Protocol (LDAP) service. This service provides an industry-standard method for accessing the information stored in the directory. Using LDAP, you can perform a wide variety of functions against the directory service, including searches, modifications, additions, and deletions.

LDAP specifies that Active Directory objects be represented in a very special and standard way. Active Directory uses domain components, OUs, and common names to create a unique path to the object in the information store. Again, remember that all this information follows the LDAP standard.

These unique paths take two forms: a distinguished name and a relative distinguished name. These names identify each and every object in Active Directory. The distinguished name identifies the exact location of the object in the overall directory and takes the form shown in the following example:

```
CN=Anthony Sequeira,OU=Marketing,DC=acme,DC=com
```

The relative distinguished name is a mere portion of this full path and uniquely identifies the object only within a given container. For example, in the context of the Marketing organizational unit (OU) within the acme.com domain, the relative distinguished name for the object in the preceding example is simply Anthony Sequeira.

Replication

Because Active Directory is stored in a distributed fashion across domain controllers, it needs to have a mechanism in place for keeping these distributed information stores up to date with each other. *Replication* is the name of this process. Active Directory features a complex, multimaster replication model, enabling Active Directory information to be modified on any domain controller in the network. This design provides plenty of benefits, including network efficiency, fault tolerance, and simplified administration.

To make replication more efficient and effective than ever before, Windows 2000 implements some new features for Microsoft operating systems. For one, network administrators can now define the physical topology of the network in Active Directory to better control how and when replication occurs. Also, change replication is much more efficient now, as only attributes are replicated through the system when changes to objects are made.

Domain Trees and the Forest

Multiple domains in a large enterprise installation of Windows 2000 form what is called an Active Directory *forest*. In a small installation, a single domain makes up the forest. As I explain throughout this book, much of the multiple domain management headaches from previous versions of Windows NT are gone — and good riddance!

The core administrative unit in Active Directory is still the domain. The domain functions as a security boundary and unit of replication, as it does in previous versions of the NT operating system. New to Windows 2000, however, is the organizational unit (OU). These highly flexible containers can often eliminate the need for multiple domain structures and serve as a boundary for the delegation of administrative controls and the assignment of important Group Policies.

If you decide that you still want to use a multiple domain model in your Windows 2000 network, you build your domains to form Active Directory *trees*. A tree is a hierarchical arrangement of Windows 2000 domains that share a contiguous namespace. For example, you may begin a new ADS forest by creating the initial domain of acme.com. Later, you may build upon this domain by adding sales.acme.com and marketing.acme.com. Notice how these additional domains continue to reflect the acme.com namespace. Notice also how they conform to DNS standards, as I discuss in previous sections of this chapter.

You can always add Active Directory trees to your forest. For example, perhaps acme.com also owns an organization named xyzco.com. This domain can be created in the forest and give rise to additional domains such as sales.xyzco.com and marketing.xyzco.com. This is an example of an additional Active Directory tree in the acme.com forest. Incidentally, you refer to the sales and marketing subdomains in these examples as *child domains*. The parent domain in the xyzco example is xyzco.com. As these examples demonstrate, domain trees and the forest provide a very flexible manner in which you define the logical structure of Active Directory.

Part II
Installing, Configuring, and Troubleshooting ADS

The 5th Wave   By Rich Tennant

Despite its inclusion on the Hardware Compatibility List, Martin shuddered at the thought of having to install Windows 2000 on the workstation from the early 1950s.

©RICHTENNANT

In this part . . .

*A*DS has many components, and the exam expects you to know how to install and configure these components for a successful Active Directory implementation. In this part of the book, you review the critical skills necessary for building the foundation of your Windows 2000 network, including disaster recovery procedures that could help save your job someday!

In Chapter 3, you review how to install and configure the many components of Active Directory. In Chapter 4, you study how to back up and restore Active Directory.

Chapter 3

Installing the Components: We're Off to See the Wizard

Exam Objectives

▶ Installing Active Directory and verifying the installation

▶ Creating sites and subnets

▶ Moving server objects between sites

▶ Creating site links and site link bridges

▶ Creating connection objects and preferred bridgehead servers

▶ Creating global catalog servers

▶ Transferring Flexible Single-Master Operations (FSMO) roles

▶ Implementing an organizational unit (OU) structure

▶ Understanding trusts

. . . .

*W*indows 2000 Active Directory Services introduce a whole host of new components that you must install and configure properly. Foremost among these components is AD itself. A proper implementation begins with a successful installation of Active Directory using the Active Directory Installation wizard.

For the exam, you must know how to install and *uninstall* Active Directory Services using the Active Directory Installation wizard. You also need to know how to properly configure and troubleshoot the main components of ADS, including sites, subnets, site links, and bridges. To help you prepare for the installation-related questions on the exam, this chapter focuses on the following topics:

    ✔ Installing Active Directory Services

    ✔ Installing and configuring sites, subnets, and site links

    ✔ Implementing an organizational unit (OU) structure

    ✔ Mastering the Flexible Single-Master Operations (FSMO) roles

    ✔ Understanding Windows 2000 trusts

Quick Assessment

Installing Active Directory and verifying the installation

1   In a Windows 2000 network, the _____ wizard installs and removes ADS.

2   In a Windows 2000 network, the executable named _____ installs and removes ADS.

Creating sites and subnets

3   You define TCP/IP subnets in Active Directory using _____ objects.

Moving server objects between sites

4   If you do not create sites first in Active Directory, all server objects are placed in _____.

Creating site links and site link bridges

5   Site links control _____ between Active Directory sites.

Creating connection objects and preferred bridgehead servers

6   _____ servers facilitate replication between sites.

Creating global catalog servers

7   The _____ server maintains universal group information and responds to user queries.

Transferring FSMO roles

8   The _____ master is responsible for creating unique SIDs in the Active Directory forest.

Implementing an OU structure

9   An alternative to a multiple domain model is made possible thanks to _____.

Understanding trusts

10 If users complain about slow access to resources in another domain in your forest, you can speed access times by using a(n) _____ trust.

Answers

1 *Active Directory Installation.* See "Installing Active Directory."

2 *DCPROMO.* See "Installing Active Directory."

3 *Subnet.* Study "Creating Sites and Subnets."

4 *Default-First-Site-Name.* Review "Moving server objects between sites."

5 *Replication.* See "Creating Site Links and Site Link Bridges."

6 *Bridgehead.* Review "Creating Connection Objects."

7 *Global catalog.* Read "Reviewing Flexible Single-Master Operations Roles."

8 *RID.* See "The RID master."

9 *Organizational units.* See "Implementing Organizational Units."

10 *Shortcut.* Examine "Understanding Trusts."

Installing Active Directory

The amazing Active Directory Installation wizard performs many functions, including the initial installation of ADS in Windows 2000 Server. Commonly referred to by its executable name of DCPROMO, the Active Directory Installation wizard also handles the following tasks:

- ✔ Creating a new Active Directory forest
- ✔ Adding a domain controller to an existing domain
- ✔ Creating the first domain controller for a new domain
- ✔ Creating a new child domain
- ✔ Creating a new domain tree
- ✔ Installing DNS
- ✔ Creating the directory service database and associated log files
- ✔ Creating the shared system volume
- ✔ Removing Active Directory Services

When you first run DCPROMO in your Windows network, you use it to create a new Active Directory forest and simultaneously create the first domain controller for a new domain. You can run the Active Directory Installation wizard again as many times as necessary to perform other tasks such as adding new domain controllers and building new domains.

Notice that you use DCPROMO to remove Active Directory Services from a server. This represents a much-needed improvement over previous versions of Windows NT. In previous NT versions, you must reinstall the operating system in order to remove the directory service components. Because you can accomplish this task without having to reinstall Windows 2000 Server, you have tremendous flexibility when managing computer roles in your Windows 2000 network.

When you use the Active Directory Installation wizard, it asks whether you want to add a domain controller to an existing domain or create the first domain controller for a new domain. You add a domain controller to an existing domain in order to create multiple peer domain controllers for fault tolerance and load balancing.

If you are creating the first domain controller for a new domain, you choose to create a new child domain, or create the first domain of a new domain tree. If your organization will maintain two discontinuous namespaces (for example, acme.com and acmedev.com), you end up creating different domain trees that can participate in Active Directory together in a forest.

Because Windows 2000 requires DNS services in order to function properly, the Active Directory Installation wizard can install and configure Microsoft's DNS service for use with Active Directory. DCPROMO creates an Active Directory-integrated forward lookup zone. However, it does not create a reverse lookup zone. You can also manually install and configure the DNS service. See Chapter 5 for all the details.

The Active Directory Installation wizard also creates the database, database log files, and the shared system volume needed by Active Directory. The default location for the Active Directory database and its log files is *systemroot*\ NTDS. For the best possible performance, however, you should place the database and the log files on separate physical hard drives on the domain controller.

 The shared system volume stores scripts and some Group Policy objects for the domain. By default, Windows 2000 stores the shared system volume in *systemroot*\SYSVOL. You can change this location, but you must format the partition with Windows 2000's NTFS V5 file system.

Replication of the shared system volume occurs on the same schedule as replication of the Active Directory. Consequently, file replication to or from a newly created SYSVOL may not occur until two replication periods have elapsed. This time interval is typically 10 minutes — two standard five-minute replication intervals. For everything you need to know about replication within Active Directory, see Chapter 14.

 Windows 2000 Server Active Directory Services have two domain modes: native mode and mixed mode. Mixed mode is the default domain mode and permits Windows 2000 integration with earlier versions of Windows NT. After you have Windows 2000 running on all the domain controllers in the organization, you can switch from mixed mode to native mode. After you make this change, you can never select mixed mode again. In order to realize many of the advantages of Windows 2000 Server Active Directory Services, you should strive for native mode in your organization as soon as possible during the installation and upgrade process.

Notice that only the existence of down-level *domain controllers* keeps you from moving to native mode. You can have all the down-level Windows *client* and *server* systems in the network that you want and still move to native mode. Only domain controllers are of concern here. For this reason, you should concentrate on upgrading NT 4 domain controllers first in a migration from NT 4 to Windows 2000.

Lab 3-1 lists the steps for installing ADS. To complete this lab, and all other labs in this book, you must log on to the system with an account that has administrative rights on the network. Notice that you can also refer to installing ADS as promoting a standalone server to the role of domain controller. Also notice that this lab creates a new forest. How exciting!

Lab 3-1	Installing Active Directory Services (Promoting a Standalone Server to Domain Controller)

1. **Click Start⇨Run.**

2. **In the Run dialog box, type** dcpromo **and click OK.**

   DCPROMO launches the Active Directory Installation wizard. This is only going to work on one of the three versions of Windows 2000 Server.

3. **In the wizard's Welcome dialog box, click Next.**

   The wizard displays the Domain Controller Type dialog box, as shown in Figure 3-1.

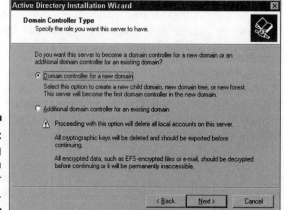

Figure 3-1: Configuring the domain controller type.

4. **Select Domain Controller For A New Domain and then click Next.**

   With this option, you are creating a new domain. Alternatively, you could create a redundant domain controller in an existing domain. Creating redundant domain controllers with additional systems is always a great idea. After all, you do not want Active Directory to be reliant on a single system! On these additional servers, simply run DCPROMO and choose the option to add a domain controller to an existing domain.

5. **In the Create Tree or Child Domain dialog box, select Create A New Domain Tree and then click Next.**

   This option specifies that you want to create a new domain tree. Alternatively, you could create a child domain in an existing tree. Child domains enable you to extend the logical structure of Active Directory to encompass another domain in a contiguous namespace. (See Chapter 2 if you need more information.)

6. **Select Create A New Forest Of Domain Trees in the Create or Join Forest dialog box and then click Next.**

   You have just created a new Windows 2000 Active Directory forest. This dialog box also enables you to join an existing forest.

7. **In the New Domain Name dialog box, type a unique name for your new domain — for example,** fordummies.com **— and click Next, as shown in Figure 3-2.**

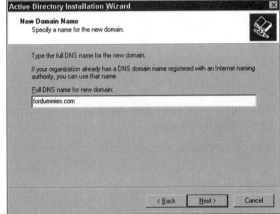

Figure 3-2:
Configuring
the full DNS
name for
your
domain.

8. **In the NetBIOS Domain Name dialog box, click Next to accept the default NetBIOS name for your domain.**

   You must have a unique Windows 2000 domain name as well as a unique NetBIOS domain name for your domain. Often times, Windows 2000 barks at you here and indicates that your name is already in use on the network. You look at the Windows 2000 domain name and confirm it is not in use. What you have failed to consider is that Windows 2000 automatically creates a down-level NetBIOS name using the last 15 characters of the Windows 2000 name — *and this is the name that is causing the conflict.*

9. **Accept the default database and log file locations for Active Directory Services by clicking Next in the Database and Log Locations dialog box.**

10. **Accept the default location for the shared system volume by clicking Next.**

    You must put the shared system volume on an NTFS Version 5 volume.

11. **Click OK, indicating that you understand your DNS configuration does not currently support the namespace you specified in Steps 7 and 8.**

12. **In the Configure DNS dialog box, select Yes, Install And Configure DNS On This Computer (Recommended) and then click Next.**

    In Chapter 5, you review how to configure DNS for Active Directory.

13. **In the Permissions dialog box, select Permissions Compatible Only With Windows 2000 Servers and click Next.**

    From a security perspective, this is the best way to configure your Remote Access Server settings — as long as you no longer have Windows NT 4 RAS servers in your network.

14. **In the Directory Services Restore Mode Administrator Password dialog box, type and confirm a password and then click Next.**

    Note that this is not your administrator password. This additional password exists in the system to protect the restoral of Active Directory. As I explain in Chapter 4, the restoral of Active Directory is a very powerful feature that could be used to do irreversible harm to the network.

15. **Review the information you have provided in the Summary dialog box and click Next when finished.**

16. **Click Finish in the Completing dialog box.**

17. **To complete the installation, click Restart Now in the Active Directory Installation Wizard dialog box.**

Congratulations! You have just installed an Active Directory forest that consists of one domain. This domain consists of a single domain controller. Remember, in a "real" Windows 2000 network, you would run DCPROMO on other systems as appropriate to create additional, redundant domain controllers and perhaps additional domains in the forest.

Verifying the Installation

To verify the successful installation of Active Directory Services, you can use the following methods:

- Verify that the SRV records needed in DNS were properly created. Perhaps the easiest way to do this is by using the NSLOOKUP utility. Simply follow these steps:

  1. **Open a command prompt window.**

  2. **Type** NSLOOKUP **and press Enter.**

  3. **Type** ls -t SRV *domain* **and press Enter.**

     The SRV records in DNS are listed in the command prompt.

  4. **Close the command prompt session.**

✔ Verify that the SYSVOL directory was created properly. You can locate SYSVOL in %systemroot%\SYSVOL.

✔ Verify that the database and associated log files were created properly on your system. You find them in %systemroot%\NTDS.

✔ Examine the event logs to check for any errors reported during installation. Check the following logs:

- System Log
- Directory Services
- DNS Server
- File Replication service

Creating Sites and Subnets

Every domain controller in your Windows 2000 network maintains a read and write copy of the Active Directory database. These computers must constantly update each other with changes to the database through a process called *replication*.

Windows 2000 must know the physical structure of your network so you can work with the system to schedule and maintain efficient replication. Windows 2000 uses the concept of sites to develop the physical structure of Active Directory.

Active Directory sites

Site objects consist of TCP/IP subnet objects and define a group of well-connected computers in your environment. Using TCP/IP subnets to define sites works out quite well because subnets are almost always groups of well-connected computers. *Well-connected* in this case means computers that have at least a 10MBps connection between them. Please note that the 10MBps connection refers to available bandwidth in this case. For example, if you install 10MBps Ethernet in your network and you have considerable traffic in one area saturating a link, this area does not qualify as a site because it does not have a suitable level of available bandwidth.

Intrasite replication — that is, replication between domain controllers in a site — occurs frequently. (Thank goodness you have the high available bandwidth.) As the Windows 2000 administrator, you schedule replication *between* sites — that is, *intersite replication.* Your scheduling of the replication is critical because these sites are typically connected by slower bandwidth connections, by definition.

Moving server objects between sites

When you install Active Directory on the first server in the enterprise, Windows 2000 creates a site object named Default-First-Site-Name, as shown in Figure 3-3. You should rename this site to make the name more meaningful, and add additional sites (and subnet objects) for the different areas of high-bandwidth connectivity in your network. As you add systems to the Windows 2000 network, Windows 2000 places these systems in the appropriate sites based on the TCP/IP (subnet) addresses they possess. If you do not create the sites that define your network early on, you are forced to move server objects from the Default-First-Site-Name to the appropriate sites later on. Moving a server object from one site to another is as simple as right-clicking the object in Active Directory Sites and Services and choosing Move, but why go through all this work when you can have Windows 2000 do it for you?

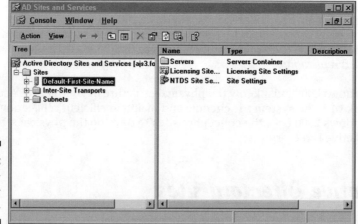

Figure 3-3:
Default-First-Site-Name.

Lab 3-2 spells out the steps for creating a new site. As you can see, this procedure is incredibly simple. However, a site is really quite useless until you populate it with the appropriate subnet objects. You review subnet objects and their creation in the next section of this chapter.

Lab 3-2   Creating a New Site

1. **Click Start⇨Programs⇨Administrative Tools⇨Active Directory Sites and Services.**

2. **In the Active Directory Sites and Services console, expand the Sites container to view the existing sites.**

   Notice the Default-First-Site-Name that Windows 2000 creates automatically.

3. **Right-click the Sites container and choose New Site from the shortcut menu.**

4. **In the New Object – Site dialog box, shown in Figure 3-4, type a name for the new site you're creating.**

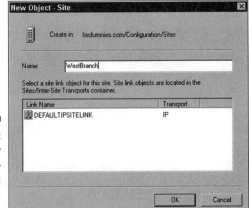

Figure 3-4:
The New
Object –
Site dialog
box.

5. **In the Site Link objects area, select the DEFAULTIPSITELINK.**

    For more information about site links, see the section "Creating Site Links and Site Link Bridges," later in this chapter.

6. **Click OK.**

7. **Click OK in the Active Directory information dialog box.**

Congrats! You have just created an Active Directory site object.

Active Directory subnets

You must associate one or more subnets with each site. Subnets are derived from the IP address and subnet mask of a computer in the subnet. Thus, subnet objects in Active Directory correlate directly with the TCP/IP subnets in your network.

Subnets associated with sites are critical for determining the site in which a particular computer is located, and Windows 2000 uses this information to find a domain controller in the same site as the computer that is authenticated during logon. Subnets associated with sites are also used during Active Directory replication to determine the best route between domain controllers.

It only makes sense that sites should consist of one or more subnet objects, because, by definition, Active Directory sites are areas where computers share a high-bandwidth connection with each other. If you look at your own TCP/IP subnets in your network, you typically see areas of high-bandwidth connectivity.

Lab 3-3 lists the steps for creating a subnet object and then adding it to a site.

Lab 3-3	Creating a Subnet Object and Adding It to a Site

1. **Click Start⇨Programs⇨Administrative Tools⇨Active Directory Sites and Services.**

2. **In the Active Directory Sites and Services console, expand the Sites container.**

3. **Right-click the Subnets container and choose New Subnet from the shortcut menu.**

4. **In the New Object – Subnet dialog box, shown in Figure 3-5, complete the Address and Mask fields with the appropriate values for your subnet.**

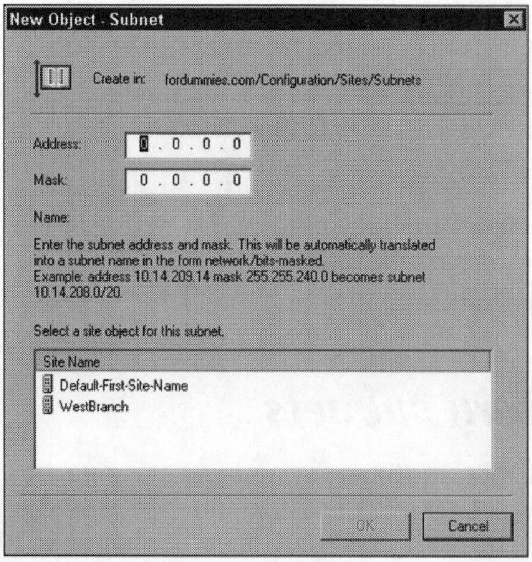

Figure 3-5:
The New
Object –
Subnet
dialog box.

5. **Select the site you want to associate with this subnet and then click OK.**

Now you have given your site object a purpose in life. Great work!

Creating Site Links and Site Link Bridges

You create site links in Windows 2000 Active Directory Services in order to facilitate and configure replication between sites (intersite replication). These site link objects represent the lower available bandwidth connections you have in your network between certain areas. Each site link contains the schedule and cost that determines how and when replication occurs between sites.

Site links use IP (Internet protocol) or the SMTP (Simple Mail Transfer Protocol) protocols in order to transport the replication information between sites. IP replication uses RPCs (remote procedure calls) for intersite and intrasite replication. SMTP replication can be used only for intersite replication and for replication between different domains.

Lab 3-4 describes the steps for creating a site link.

Lab 3-4   Creating a Site Link

1. **Click Start⇨Programs⇨Administrative Tools⇨Active Directory Sites and Services.**

2. **In the AD Sites and Services console, expand the Inter-Site Transports container.**

3. **Right-click the IP container and choose New Site Link from the shortcut menu.**

4. **In the New Object – Site Link dialog box, shown in Figure 3-6, type a name for your new site link.**

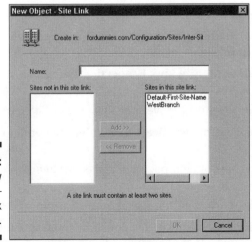

Figure 3-6:
The New
Object –
Site Link
dialog box.

5. **Specify which sites you want to link, using the Add and Remove buttons to move sites between the two lists in the bottom half of the dialog box, and then click OK.**

Configuring a site link

After you create a site link, you must configure it. As Lab 3-5 demonstrates, you can configure the following settings for your new site link:

✔ **Cost:** Site link costs are useful when you have redundant network connections between sites. You should assign a lower cost to high-bandwidth connections, because Windows 2000 always uses a lower cost network connection whenever possible.

✔ **Replication frequency:** This integer value dictates how many minutes AD waits before using a connection to check for replication updates between sites. The range of acceptable values for replication frequency is 15 to 10,080 (one week).

✔ **Replication schedule:** This setting determines when a site link is accessible for replication. Typically, you do not schedule replication availability for SMTP site links.

Lab 3-5	Configuring a Site Link

1. **Click Start➪Programs➪Administrative Tools➪Active Directory Sites and Services.**

2. **In the AD Sites and Services console, expand the Inter-Site Transports container.**

3. **Expand the IP container.**

4. **Right-click the site link that you want to configure and then choose Properties from the shortcut menu.**

5. **On the General tab in the Site Link Properties dialog box, use the Cost field to configure a site link cost.**

   Leave the default cost of 100. (I cover site link cost in Chapter 14.)

6. **On the General tab, use the Replicate Every field to configure replication frequency.**

   This setting defines how often replication can occur in a given schedule window. More on this in Chapter 14.

7. **On the General tab, click the Change Schedule button.**

   In the Schedule For dialog box, you can configure a block of time for which the connection is either available or unavailable, as shown in Figure 3-7. Again, more on this in Chapter 14.

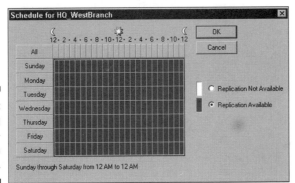

Figure 3-7:
Scheduling
the avail-
ability of a
site link.

8. **Click OK.**

9. **Click OK in the Site Link Properties dialog box.**

10. **Right-click the IP container in the AD Sites and Services console and choose Properties.**

11. **In the IP Properties dialog box, note the Ignore Schedules check box on the General tab.**

    What a nice way to quickly override all the scheduling components pre-
    sented in site links. You may need to do this periodically when managing
    your Windows 2000 network. See Chapter 14 for more information.

12. **Click OK.**

Building site link bridges

You can link two or more site links together for replication purposes using a
site link bridge. In a fully routed IP network, however, you have no need for site
link bridges because all site links are transitive by default. Therefore, most of
us will never utilize site link bridges because most of us work in fully routed IP
networks!

If your network is not a fully routed IP network, you can disable this transitive behavior and create site link bridges as necessary. Use the Active
Directory Sites and Services console to create site link bridges. Figure 3-8
shows a sample network that consists of two sites, three subnets, and two
site links.

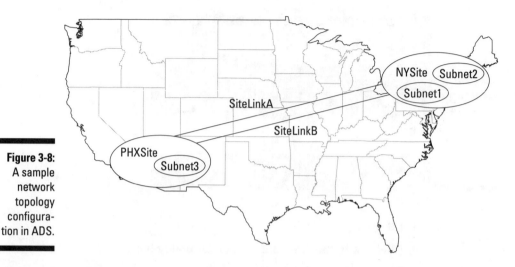

Figure 3-8:
A sample
network
topology
configura-
tion in ADS.

Creating Connection Objects

Windows 2000's Knowledge Consistency Checker (KCC) automatically creates the actual connections for replication between domain controllers. This utility actually made its first appearance in Microsoft Exchange Server for handling replication in that complex e-mail server system.

Microsoft recommends that you simply let the KCC do its job, even though Windows 2000's AD Sites and Services console provides tools for manually creating and configuring your own connection objects. You should only create your own Active Directory connection object if you are certain that you need one and you want it to persist until you manually remove it.

In addition to manually creating connection objects, you can also manually specify the systems that replicate information between sites. Microsoft refers to these domain controllers as *bridgehead servers.* Once again, Windows 2000 should do a good job of handling these assignments automatically for you.

You may have to configure a preferred bridgehead server if your design incorporates a firewall that protects one of your Windows 2000 sites. In this case, you typically configure your firewall proxy server as the preferred bridgehead server to ensure the complete replication of information between sites. Use the AD Sites and Services console to configure preferred bridgehead servers.

Creating Global Catalog Servers

Global catalog servers represent a very important component of the Active Directory Services in Windows 2000. These servers store a portion of the attribute values for every object in the forest. These attributes represent the properties that should be used most frequently in searches by users of the Active Directory. In this regard, global catalog servers permit users to search the Active Directory for information regardless of which domain in the forest actually contains the data. Global catalog servers also facilitate user logons by providing universal group membership to a domain controller.

Every major site in your Active Directory implementation should have at least one global catalog configured within it. By default, a global catalog server is created automatically on the initial domain controller in the forest. You can easily create the others that you need. Lab 3-6 describes the procedure.

Lab 3-6   Creating a Global Catalog Server

1. **Click Start⇨Programs⇨Administrative Tools⇨Active Directory Sites and Services.**

2. **In the AD Sites and Services console, expand the Sites container.**

3. **Expand the site that contains the domain controller you want to enable as a global catalog server.**

4. **Expand the Servers container.**

5. **Double-click the appropriate domain controller.**

6. **Right-click NTDS Settings and choose Properties.**

7. **Select the Global Catalog check box, as shown in Figure 3-9.**

8. **Click OK.**

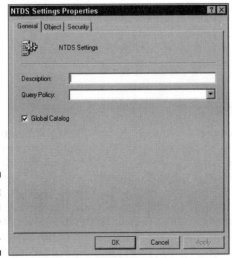

Figure 3-9:
Creating a
global cata-
log server.

You can add additional attributes to the global catalog for objects in your forest, but doing so causes a full replication of the global catalog information throughout your forest. You do not want to do this often because the increased replication load could really begin to slow things down.

Reviewing Flexible Single-Master Operations Roles

Windows 2000 Active Directory Services feature a multimaster replication model. In other words, all domain controllers contain a read/write copy of the directory, and any domain controller can accept changes to the directory. Essentially, under this multimaster replication model, all domain controllers are considered equal. However, you must understand that certain functions performed by these domain controllers necessitate a different replication model. Specifically, these functions require that you have a master replication model in place to avoid problems resulting from replication in the forest-wide Active Directory environment.

Active Directory addresses the need for these special functions using the Flexible Single-Master Operations (FSMO) roles — commonly pronounced as the *fizmo* roles. These roles are

- ✔ Schema master
- ✔ Domain naming master
- ✔ PDC emulator
- ✔ RID master
- ✔ Infrastructure master

The schema master

The schema master is the domain controller (DC) that permits modifications to the Active Directory schema (for example, adding Active Directory attributes or classes). The forest can contain only one schema master. By default, the first DC installed in the forest is the schema master.

You should always try to place the schema master and the domain naming master on the same DC, and place this DC close to the individuals that are responsible for schema modifications and the creation of new domains. As Lab 3-7 demonstrates, you use the Active Directory Schema Manager to change the DC acting as the schema master in a forest. As you might guess, you need administrative privileges in the network to accomplish any FSMO role management tasks.

Lab 3-7   Transferring the Schema Master

1. **Click Start⇨Settings⇨Control Panel.**

2. **Double-click Add/Remove Programs.**

3. **Select the Windows 2000 Administration Tools program and click Change.**

   Run the Windows 2000 Administration Tools application to add *all* the possible administration tools.

4. **Click Start⇨Run, type** mmc, **and then click OK.**

5. **Choose Console⇨Add/Remove Snap-in and then click Add.**

6. **Under Snap-in, double-click Active Directory Schema, and then click Close.**

7. **Click OK.**

8. **In the console tree, right-click Active Directory Schema and then choose Change Domain Controller.**

9. **Select the Any DC option to let Active Directory select the new schema master, or click Specify Name and type the name of the new schema master computer.**

10. **In the console tree, right-click Active Directory Schema and then choose Operations Master to open the dialog box shown in Figure 3-10.**

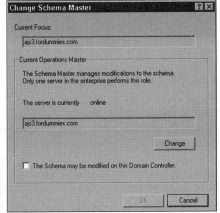

Figure 3-10:
Changing
the schema
master.

11. **Click Change.**

The resulting dialog box permits you to select your new schema master. That is all there is to it!

The domain naming master

The domain naming master controls changes to the domain namespace, such as adding and removing domains or adding or removing cross-references to external directory services. The forest can have only one domain naming master. This system also must be a global catalog server.

Lab 3-8 describes the steps for transferring the domain naming master role to another system.

Lab 3-8	Transferring the Domain Naming Master

1. **Click Start⇨Programs⇨Administrative Tools⇨Active Directory Domains and Trusts.**

2. **In the console tree, right-click the domain controller node that will become the new domain naming master and then choose Connect to Domain.**

3. **In the dialog box that's displayed, type the domain name or click Browse, and then select the domain from the list.**

4. **In the console tree, right-click Active Directory Domains and Trusts and then choose Operations Master.**

5. **Click Change.**

The resulting dialog box permits you to select your new domain naming master.

The PDC emulator

The PDC emulator services the replication requests of down-level backup domain controllers (BDCs). As its name implies, it basically pretends to be a PDC for these down-level systems. In native-mode Windows 2000 environments, the PDC emulator also is the first machine to receive password changes in the domain to ensure users can log on successfully and do not become victims of *excessive replication latency.* (This fancy phrase means the domain controller they are trying to authenticate against has not yet learned of the password change via the replication process. More on this in Chapter 14!)

You can have one PDC emulator per domain in a Windows 2000 forest. The Group Policy Editor also uses the PDC emulator computer to ensure uniqueness when editing a Group Policy object. The PDC emulator also synchronizes the time on all domain controllers in the domain with its time.

Typically, place this FSMO role on the same computer that functions as the RID master. Lab 3-9 details the procedure for transferring the PDC emulator role to the desired computer.

Lab 3-9	Transferring the PDC Emulator

1. Click Start⇨Programs⇨Administrative Tools⇨Active Directory Users and Computers.

2. In the console tree, right-click the domain controller node that will become the new PDC emulator master and then choose Connect to Domain.

3. In the resulting dialog box, type the domain name or click Browse, and select the domain from the list.

4. In the console tree, right-click Active Directory Users and Computers and then choose Operations Masters.

5. On the PDC tab in the dialog box that's displayed, click Change.

The RID master

The RID master manages the Relative Identifiers (RIDs) pool for a domain. Of course, you have one RID master per domain. The RID pool creates new security identifiers (SIDs) for users, groups, and computers. The RID master allocates these RIDs in groups of 512 to other domain controllers in the domain. The RID master is also called upon when an object is moved from one domain to another.

Typically, you need to place this FSMO role on the same machine that holds the PDC emulator role. You transfer this role to another domain controller by using the Active Directory Users and Computers console, much like transferring the PDC emulator role (see Lab 3-9).

The infrastructure master

Each domain has an infrastructure master. This system is critical for updating SIDs and distinguished name changes in multiple domain environments. It ensures consistency of objects for interdomain operations — for example, to ensure that the renaming of a user account is accurately reflected throughout the forest, in all the groups to which the user account belongs.

Do not place this role on the same system that is a global catalog server unless you are in a single-domain environment. You can transfer this role to another domain controller by using the Active Directory Users and Computers console, much like transferring the PDC emulator and RID master roles (see Lab 3-9).

In many cases, if a domain controller fails and the failure seems permanent, you must transfer the FSMO role to a functional domain controller. You can easily do so using the NTDSUTIL command at a command prompt. I cover the NTDSUTIL command in Chapter 4.

Implementing Organizational Units

The organizational unit (OU) is a very important object in the Windows 2000 Active Directory. Organizational units are containers in which you can place users, groups, computers, and other organizational units. Organizational units not only enable you to organize objects in the Active Directory, they also form a structure that can function as the basis for the assignment of Group Policy objects and the delegation of administrative control. Using organizational units, you create containers within a domain that represent the hierarchical, logical structures within your organization. In this way, you can manage the configuration and use of accounts and resources based on your organizational model.

In many cases, you can opt for a single domain model using a well-designed organizational unit structure instead of a more complex multiple domain model.

Lab 3-10 describes the procedure for creating an organizational unit.

Lab 3-10   Creating an Organizational Unit

1. Click Start➪Programs➪Administrative Tools➪Active Directory Users and Computers.

2. In the console tree, double-click the domain node.

3. Right-click the domain node or the container in which you want to add the organizational unit.

4. In the shortcut menu that's displayed, choose New➪Organizational Unit.

5. In the resulting dialog box, type the name of the organizational unit and then click OK.

Understanding Trusts

Windows 2000 automatically creates trusts between Windows 2000 domains in your forest. These utilize the Kerberos standard instead of early NTLM technology. They are also two-way and transitive by default, similar to the complete trust model used in previous Windows NT multiple-domain environments. This is great news for those NT 4 administrators that are tired of spending precious hours troubleshooting trust relationships in large installations.

Windows 2000 also has explicit trusts that you must create yourself. Fortunately, you do not often have to do so. You create and manage explicit trusts using Active Directory Domains and Trusts. Windows 2000 has two kinds of explicit trusts: external trusts and shortcut trusts. External trusts enable user authentication to a domain outside a forest. Shortcut trusts optimize the trust path in a complex forest consisting of many domains.

Prep Test

1 **Which tasks can the Active Directory Installation wizard perform? (Choose all that apply.)**

A ○ Create a new domain tree.

B ○ Install DNS.

C ○ Create the database and database log files.

D ○ Create the shared system volume.

E ○ Remove Active Directory Services.

2 **Your network consists of Windows 2000 Servers running as domain controllers, as well as NT 4.0 Servers running as backup domain controllers. In what mode should you set your Windows 2000 network?**

A ○ Native

B ○ Mixed

C ○ Legacy

D ○ Advanced

3 **Which statements are true regarding sites and subnets? (Choose all that apply.)**

A ○ Sites can contain one or more subnet objects.

B ○ Each subnet object should belong to only one site.

C ○ Replication traffic between sites is referred to as intrasite replication.

D ○ To be considered a site, the computers in that network area should have at least a 10MBps connection.

4 **You should assign lower costs to site links that represent which of the following?**

A ○ Lower-bandwidth connections

B ○ Medium-bandwidth connections

C ○ Higher-bandwidth connections

D ○ You do not assign costs to site links

5 **You plan to add a child domain in your Windows 2000 forest. Which FSMO role system must be available for this change to take place?**

A ○ PDC emulator

B ○ Domain naming master

C ○ Schema master

D ○ RID master

6 **Which component of Active Directory must be stored on an NTFS 5 partition?**

A ○ The database itself

B ○ The log files for the database

C ○ The shared system volume

D ○ The Active Directory schema

7 **You are installing a new Windows 2000 domain named thisismycooldomain.com. You receive an error during the installation indicating that the domain name is already in use. You have not installed that exact domain name in your network. What is the most likely problem?**

A ○ A DNS configuration error exists for the root domain.

B ○ The NetBIOS name for your domain is in use.

C ○ You have a corrupt Active Directory database.

D ○ You have a WINS configuration problem.

8 **You are installing a Windows 2000 network and have added several domain controllers in your domain. You have not configured any sites or subnets. Where do the domain controllers appear in Active Directory Sites and Services?**

A ○ They are in Default-First-Site-Name.

B ○ They are in the Domain Controllers organizational unit.

C ○ They are not displayed in Sites and Services.

D ○ They are in Non-Placed Domain Controllers.

9 **Users complain about very slow access to resources in a domain in your forest. The users are in a separate domain in the forest. What should you do?**

A ○ Add domain controllers to the respective domains.

B ○ Add additional sites and encompass the two domains.

C ○ Migrate to a single domain model.

D ○ Implement a site link bridge.

E ○ Use an explicit trust.

10 **You want to configure a pair of specific servers to carry out the replication between sites in your network. What should you do?**

A ○ Configure the REPLICATION parameter in the Registry of each system.

B ○ Configure each system as a preferred bridgehead server.

C ○ Use DCPROMO to reinstall Active Directory Services on the two systems.

D ○ Use NTDSUTIL to enable replication on the two servers.

Answers

1 **A, B, C, D,** and **E.** You perform many tasks with the Active Directory Installation wizard, including creating new domain trees, installing DNS, removing ADS, creating the shared system volume, and creating the database and log files. *Review "Installing Active Directory."*

2 **B.** Mixed. You use mixed mode in networks that contain a mix of Windows 2000 and Windows NT 4.0 domain controllers — for example, during a gradual upgrade to Windows 2000 from NT 4. *Review "Installing Active Directory."*

3 **A, B,** and **D.** Sites consist of one or more subnets. Subnets must only belong to one site, and to be considered a site, computers should share at least 10MBps connections. *Study "Creating Sites and Subnets."*

4 **C.** Higher-bandwidth connections. Windows 2000 always tries to use the site link with the lowest cost. Therefore, you typically assign a lower cost to your higher speed connections. *See "Creating Site Links and Site Link Bridges."*

5 **B.** Domain naming master. The domain naming master is responsible for changes to the namespace of Active Directory. A perfect example of such a change is the adding or removal of domains from the forest. *See "The domain naming master."*

6 **C.** The shared system volume. The only component of Active Directory that must be stored on an NTFS 5 partition is the shared system volume. Although not recommended, you could store all other components on FAT or FAT32 as well. *Review "Installing Active Directory."*

7 **B.** The NetBIOS name for your domain is in use. In all likelihood, the NetBIOS name that is being generated for your Windows 2000 domain name is conflicting with another NetBIOS domain name in your network. *Review "Installing Active Directory."*

8 **A.** They are in Default-First-Site-Name. If you do not create your sites soon in your Active Directory installation, you must move servers out of Default-First-Site-Name, where they are placed automatically by default. *Study "Active Directory sites."*

9 **E.** Use an explicit trust. In this case, a shortcut explicit trust helps optimize resource access domains. *See "Understanding Trusts."*

10 **B.** Configure each system as a preferred bridgehead server. You can specify certain domain controllers in sites as preferred bridgehead servers, although this is typically not required. Preferred bridgehead servers are used for replication between sites before other servers are attempted. *See "Creating Connection Objects."*

Chapter 4

Backing Up and Restoring ADS: Disaster Protection

Exam Objectives

▶ Performing an authoritative restoral of Active Directory

▶ Recovering from a system failure

*B*acking up the important system state data is critical for a healthy Windows 2000 network. Fortunately, as you review in this chapter, the operating system includes a new and improved backup program that simplifies the process of backing up Active Directory. In addition to the backup process, the exam expects you to know the two types of restoral processes: authoritative and nonauthoritative.

In this chapter, you review the following topics:

✔ The elements of system state data

✔ The procedure for backing up the system state data

✔ The difference between nonauthoritative and authoritative restores

✔ The many functions of the NTDSUTIL utility

Quick Assessment

1 The _____ restore process marks the Active Directory information as the most current so it is not overwritten.

2 You use the _____ utility in order to perform an authoritative restore.

3 You press the _____ key at startup in order to access the Advanced Startup Options menu.

4 Use the _____ command with NTDSUTIL to perform an authoritative restore.

5 You can back up Active Directory as part of the _____.

6 The system state data includes Active Directory, the Registry, the COM+ Class Registration database, boot files, the certificate services database, cluster service information, and _____.

7 Do not _____ the computer after you restore the system state data.

8 Start the computer in _____ in order to begin restoring Active Directory.

Answers

1   *Authoritative*. See "Performing Authoritative Restores."

2   *NTDSUTIL*. See "Performing Authoritative Restores."

3   *F8*. Review "Performing Authoritative Restores."

4   *Authoritative restore*. Read "Reviewing NTDSUTIL commands."

5   *System state data*. See "Backing Up Active Directory."

6   *SYSVOL*. Review "Backing Up Active Directory."

7   *Restart*. Study "Performing Authoritative Restores."

8   *Directory Services Restore Mode*. Study "Performing Authoritative Restores."

Backing Up Active Directory

Any good administrator knows the importance of backing up any information that is needed by an organization. Active Directory is certainly important information, and you need to back it up regularly to avoid network downtime. Windows 2000 includes a new and improved backup utility with which you can back up and restore the *system state data,* which includes Active Directory and other important system information.

Reviewing the elements of system state data

The system state data on a domain controller includes

- Active Directory
- SYSVOL
- The Registry
- System startup files
- Class registration database
- The certificate services database

You cannot back up these individual components of the system state data. Backing up system state data is an all-or-nothing process. However, you can restore the system state data to another system. When you do so, only the Registry files, SYSVOL directory files, cluster database information files, and system boot files are restored to the alternate location.

Running the backup program

The Windows 2000 backup program makes backing up Active Directory a breeze. Lab 4-1 lists the steps for backing up the system state data.

Lab 4-1	Backing Up the System State Data

1. **Click Start⇨Programs⇨Accessories⇨System Tools⇨Backup.**
2. **Click the Backup tab.**

3. **On the Backup tab, expand My Computer and then select the System State check box, as shown in Figure 4-1.**

   Notice that you cannot deselect any of the system state data components.

4. **Select the desired backup media and then click the Start Backup button.**

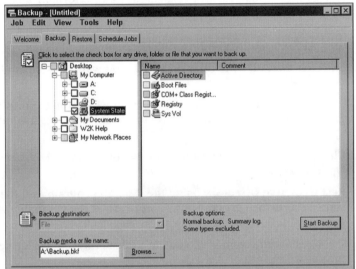

Figure 4-1:
Backing up
the system
state data.

Performing Authoritative Restores

Windows 2000 has two types of system state restore processes: authoritative and nonauthoritative. The exam focuses on authoritative restores.

Understanding the difference between nonauthoritative and authoritative restores

When you perform an authoritative restore, an important Windows 2000 utility named NTDSUTIL marks the restored AD information as the most current to ensure that it is not overwritten by other domain controllers during the replication process. This step is critical, especially if you are attempting to restore Active Directory information that was inadvertently or maliciously deleted.

When you perform a nonauthoritative restore of Active Directory, the information is not marked, so it has the potential to be overwritten by any Active Directory modifications occurring after the backup. In many cases, you perform a nonauthoritative restore if you have a server failure and you want to replace the failed server with a new one. In this case, you do not care if the restored data is updated from other servers. In fact, you want it to be!

For the exam, you must know the exact steps for performing an authoritative restore. Lab 4-2 describes this process.

Lab 4-2   Performing an Authoritative Restore

1. **Start the domain controller on which you want to perform the restore and press F8 during bootup.**

   Pressing F8 at bootup displays the Advanced Startup Options menu. This menu includes options you can use for troubleshooting a Windows 2000 system.

2. **Choose Directory Services Restore Mode from the Advanced Startup Options menu.**

3. **Restore Active Directory using the Backup program and the system state data restore process but *do not* restart the computer when prompted following the restore.**

   If you restart the computer, you have effectively just performed a nonauthoritative restore.

4. **Open a command prompt and run NTDSUTIL.EXE, as shown in Figure 4-2.**

   See the next section for more information about NTDSUTIL.

5. **At the NTDSUTIL prompt, type** authoritative restore.

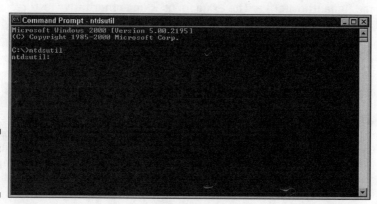

Figure 4-2:
Running
NTDSUTIL.

6. **At the authoritative restore prompt, type** restore *subtree distinguished_name_of_object.*

   For example, to restore an OU named Marketing which is located at the first level of the acme.com hierarchy, use this command:

   ```
   restore subtree OU=Marketing,DC=acme,DC=com
   ```

7. **Type** quit **and press Enter.**

8. **Type** quit **and press Enter to exit NTDSUTIL.**

9. **Restart the domain controller.**

Reviewing NTDSUTIL commands

As I explain in the preceding section, you can use NTDSUTIL to perform an authoritative restore. However, NTDSUTIL also performs many other important functions in Windows 2000. You need to know about some of the commands NTDSUTIL can use to help manage Windows 2000 directory services. Table 4-1 details this information.

Table 4-1	NTDSUTIL Commands
Command	*What It Does*
Authoritative restore	Performs an authoritative restore of Active Directory
Domain management	Prepares for new domain creation
Files	Manages Active Directory database files
Metadata cleanup	Cleans up objects from decommissioned domain controllers
Roles	Manages FSMO roles
Security account management	Manages the security account database and cleans up duplicate SIDs

For the exam, you also need to know the following details about some commands I describe in Table 4-1:

✔ **Authoritative restore:** After completing this chapter, you should be very familiar with this one! An authoritative restore enables you to bring your Active Directory database back to a particular point in time. Typically, you use this command after accidental or malicious deletions from the information store. For the exam, be sure to know the exact steps for performing an authoritative restore of Active Directory.

✔ **Domain management:** You need to be a member of the Enterprise Administrators group in order to have the permissions necessary to add domains to your forest. Now, perhaps you want to delegate this ability without adding Enterprise Administrators. You can use the NTDSUTIL utility to precreate the domain in the forest.

✔ **Files:** From within Directory Services Restore mode, you can use NTDS to move the Active Directory database file, NTDS.DIT. You can also use NTDSUTIL to move the Active Directory database log files.

✔ **Roles:** You can seize operations master roles (which I review in Chapter 3) using this feature of NTDSUTIL. In Chapter 3, I discuss transferring roles from one system to another using the various administration tools at your disposal in Windows 2000. This is all fine and good if the system possessing the role and the system that wants to take on the role are both operational and online. But what if the current role holder has blown up and is unavailable? Seizing the role might be your only answer. The Roles mode of NTDSUTIL enables you to do this.

Prep Test

1 You have inadvertently deleted several objects from Active Directory. Fortunately, you recently backed up your Active Directory installation. What is the correct order for restoring Active Directory in this case?

A ○ Use Backup to restore Active Directory; restart the domain controller; select Directory Services Restore Mode; run NTDSUTIL; restart the domain controller.

B ○ Restart the domain controller; select Directory Services Restore Mode; use Backup to restore Active Directory; run NTDSUTIL; restart the domain controller.

C ○ Restart the domain controller; select Directory Services Restore Mode; run NTDSUTIL; restart the domain controller; use Backup to restore Active Directory.

D ○ Run NTDSUTIL; restart the domain controller; use Backup to restore Active Directory; restart the domain controller; select Directory Services Restore Mode.

2 Several OUs in your Active Directory domain were maliciously deleted. You want to get these OUs restored as quickly and painlessly as possible. What type of restore should you perform?

A ○ A nonauthoritative restore

B ○ An authoritative restore

C ○ A restore of a full backup of a domain controller

D ○ A restore of a full backup of the infrastructure master

3 You need to clean up duplicate SIDs in your Windows 2000 network. Which NTDSUTIL command do you use?

A ○ Files

B ○ Metadata cleanup

C ○ Security account management

D ○ Roles

4 You need to seize a FSMO role in your Windows 2000 network. Which NTDSUTIL command do you use?

A ○ Domain management

B ○ Metadata cleanup

C ○ Security account management

D ○ Roles

5 Which of the following components are part of the system state data in Windows 2000? Choose all that apply.

A ○ The Registry

B ○ SYSVOL

C ○ Active Directory

D ○ The SYSTEM directory

6 You want to restore the system state data to another computer in your Windows 2000 network. When you do so, which components of the system state data are actually restored? Choose all that apply.

A ○ The Registry

B ○ The SYSTEM directory

C ○ The certificate services database

D ○ SYSVOL

7 Which utility do you use in order to perform an authoritative restore?

A ○ MOVEDOM

B ○ SIDWalker

C ○ NETDIAG

D ○ NTDSUTIL

8 You want to perform a backup of Active Directory in your Windows 2000 installation. How do you do this?

A ○ Choose Backup ADS in Computer Management.

B ○ Run BACKUPADS.VBS.

C ○ Back up the system state data.

D ○ Use NTDSUTIL to back up NTDS.DIT.

9 To restore Active Directory, you must restart your Windows 2000 system in which mode?

A ○ Safe Mode

B ○ Safe Mode with Networking Support

C ○ Directory Services Restore Mode

D ○ Normal Mode

10 How do you access the Advanced Startup Menu options in Windows 2000?

A ○ Press F8.

B ○ Press F10.

C ○ Press F12.

D ○ Press Alt+Del.

Answers

1 **B.** Restart the domain controller; select Directory Services Restore Mode; use Backup to restore Active Directory; run NTDSUTIL; restart the domain controller. In this case, you need to perform an authoritative restore. You use an authoritative restore to restore individual Active Directory objects in a domain with multiple domain controllers. *Read "Performing Authoritative Restores."*

2 **B.** An authoritative restore. If you have more than one domain controller in your organization, and the Active Directory service is replicated to any of these other servers, you may have to authoritatively restore any Active Directory data that you want to restore. *Study "Performing Authoritative Restores."*

3 **C.** Security account management. The security account management feature of NTDSUTIL enables you to manage the security account database and clean up duplicate SIDs. *Study "Reviewing NTDSUTIL commands."*

4 **D.** Roles. The roles command of NTDSUTIL enables you to manage FSMO roles in your Windows 2000 network. *Study "Reviewing NTDSUTIL commands."*

5 **A, B,** and **C.** The Registry, SYSVOL, and Active Directory. The SYSTEM directory is not part of the system state data. *Read "Backing Up Active Directory."*

6 **A** and **D.** The Registry and SYSVOL. The SYSTEM directory is not part of the system state data, and the certificate services database is not restored to a different computer. *Read "Backing Up Active Directory."*

7 **D.** NTDSUTIL. You use NTDSUTIL to perform an authoritative restore of Active Directory. *Study "Performing Authoritative Restores."*

8 **C.** Back up the system state data. You back up Active Directory as part of the system state data. You can easily back up the system state data by using the Backup wizard. *Read "Backing Up Active Directory."*

9 **C.** Directory Services Restore Mode. To restore Active Directory, you must restart the server in Directory Services Restore Mode. You also perform this step for a nonauthoritative restore. The big difference between the two is the use of NTDSUTIL. *Study "Performing Authoritative Restores."*

10 **A.** Press F8. By pressing the F8 key at startup, you access the Advanced Startup Options menu. This menu enables you to access Directory Services Restore mode. *Study "Performing Authoritative Restores."*

Part III
DNS and Active Directory

The 5th Wave   By Rich Tennant

"You know, this was a situation question on my network infrastructure exam, but I always thought it was just hypothetical."

In this part . . .

*1*t used to be that you *might* implement DNS in your Windows network. For example, you would need DNS if you were interested in hosting an internal Web server, or you were doing lots of integration with UNIX systems. Now, with the introduction of Active Directory, you *must* implement DNS in your Windows 2000 network. Installation of Active Directory requires a DNS service that supports SRV resource records. The chapters in this part of the book cover DNS as it relates to Active Directory, with a focus on Microsoft's favorite topics come exam time.

In Chapter 5, you examine the different zone types in Microsoft's DNS service, as well as how to install and configure DNS. In Chapter 6, you review DNS replication using Microsoft's DNS service.

Chapter 5

DNS, Meet ADS

● ●

Exam Objectives

▶ Installing, configuring, and troubleshooting DNS for Active Directory

▶ Configuring zones for dynamic updates

● ●

*T*he Domain Name System (DNS) resolves a human-readable computer
name (like www.dummies.com) to a TCP/IP address. Using DNS, systems
can find each other in local area networks (LANs) and wide area networks
(WANs), including the greatest of all WANs — the Internet. Microsoft wisely
decided to use this popular DNS technology as the location service for
Windows 2000's Active Directory.

Because Active Directory requires a DNS implementation in your network,
you can expect to see numerous DNS-related questions on the exam. To help
you ace these questions with a minimum of difficulty, this chapter and the
next one cover all you need to know about DNS. This chapter reviews the following DNS topics:

✔ Key DNS-related terminology, including server, zone, and record types

✔ Procedures for installing and configuring DNS

✔ Steps for configuring dynamic DNS

Quick Assessment

1 You install DNS via _____ in Control Panel.

2 To support Active Directory, the DNS service used must be able to store _____ records.

3 A(n) _____ lookup zone resolves from an IP address to a friendly name.

4 A(n) _____ record is used for a host in a reverse lookup zone.

5 A(n) _____-only DNS server does not actually host any records.

6 With a standard _____ zone, a single server hosts and loads the master copy of the zone.

7 To reduce administration, you can configure your zone for _____ updates.

8 The _____ service can assist with dynamic updates.

9 To take advantage of _____ dynamic updates, you must use an Active Directory-integrated zone.

Answers

1   *Add/Remove Programs.* See "Installing and Configuring DNS."

2   *SRV, or Service.* Review "DNS record types."

3   *Reverse.* Study "DNS zone types."

4   *PTR, or Pointer.* Review "DNS record types."

5   *Caching.* Study "DNS server types."

6   *Primary.* Study "DNS zone types."

7   *Dynamic.* Review "Configuring Dynamic DNS."

8   *DHCP.* Review "Configuring Dynamic DNS."

9   *Secure.* Study "Configuring Dynamic DNS."

What Is DNS?

The Domain Name System (DNS) is an Internet and TCP/IP standard name service. The DNS service enables client computers on your Windows 2000 network to register and resolve DNS domain names. You use these names to find and access resources offered by other computers on your network or other networks — even the Internet.

The Domain Name System is actually a network itself. Typically, if one DNS server does not know the answer to a request for its services (a query), it can ask another DNS server in the DNS network. You need a pretty good understanding of how all this works to succeed on the exam. Most especially, you need to understand the types of servers, zones, and records that make up the DNS namespace.

How does Active Directory use DNS?

Active Directory uses DNS to help locate the resources that it defines in the network. For example, here's how DNS comes into play when a client logs on to a Windows 2000 AD network:

1. A user attempts to log on to the Active Directory domain.

2. The NetLogon service on the client collects information about the client and sends this information to the DNS server.

3. The DNS server checks its zone database for a system running an appropriate service. (For more information about the zone database, see "DNS zone types," later in this chapter.) In this case, the DNS server is looking for a domain controller. It does this by looking for appropriate Service (SRV) records in its zone. More on this in "DNS record types," later in this chapter.

4. The DNS server returns a list of potential servers to the client.

5. The NetLogon service sends a message to the domain controllers in the list to find one that is online and fully functional in the network.

6. The NetLogon service gives the client the address of the first domain controller to respond.

7. The client sends the logon request to the domain controller.

As you can see from this example, DNS plays an important role for Active Directory. In the following sections, you can review the main components of the Domain Name System.

DNS server types

You can set up different kinds of DNS servers in your environment. Each server has a specific function that helps to ensure friendly names are resolved to IP addresses. And for the purposes of ADS, DNS helps to ensure that users can quickly and efficiently locate network resources.

You can set up the following DNS server types:

- ✔ **Primary name server:** You create a primary name server in a traditional DNS implementation. By *traditional,* I mean a non-Active Directory-integrated zone. (I cover DNS zone types in the next section of this chapter.) This very important server maintains the single read/write copy of the zone database. All changes to the database must be funneled through this server. In pure DNS terminology, this system is "authoritative" for its zone.

- ✔ **Secondary name server:** You should definitely install one or more of these servers in your traditional DNS implementation. They maintain a read-only copy of the DNS database and can be quite helpful in resolving client queries. Secondary servers provide a means for offloading DNS query traffic in areas of the network where a zone is heavily queried and used. Additionally, if a primary server is down, a secondary server provides some name resolution in the zone until the primary server is available.

- ✔ **Caching-only server:** These servers do not have a copy of the DNS database! As their name implies, they cache the results of these queries in the event that another client should come along and ask the same query. You use these servers in your network to speed up DNS resolution times. Although all DNS name servers cache queries that they have resolved, caching-only servers only perform queries, cache the answers, and return the results. They have no database records of their own.

- ✔ **Forwarding server:** You can configure your DNS servers with the addresses of other DNS servers. If your DNS server cannot resolve a query, it can forward the request on to another DNS server for help. You refer to the helper as a *forwarder server.* As shown in Figure 5-1, you can configure forwarder servers using the Properties sheet for your DNS server.

  You should configure these forwarder servers with a root hints table of addresses. Root hints point to the big kahuna of all DNS servers: the main Internet DNS servers. Windows 2000 DNS servers are equipped with a root hints database by default, as shown in Figure 5-2.

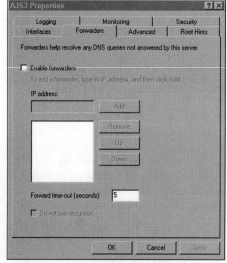

Figure 5-1:
Configuring
forwarders
in
Microsoft's
DNS.

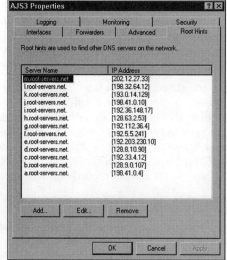

Figure 5-2:
The
Windows
2000 DNS
root hints.

✔ **Slave server:** If you configure a server to do nothing but use forwarder servers for name resolution, you have a slave server. These servers depend entirely upon their list of forwarders.

✔ **Active Directory-integrated server:** You can store the DNS database in Active Directory itself! Chapter 6 reviews the many advantages that this capability provides.

DNS zone types

A DNS database is commonly referred to in TCP/IP-speak as a zone table or, more simply, a zone. And just as you have several types of servers that make DNS function, you can configure several types of DNS zones:

- **Forward lookup zone:** You refer to a standard DNS zone table as a forward lookup zone. When clients query the DNS servers that maintain a forward lookup zone, a DNS server searches the table for the hostname of the system, using the TCP/IP address provided by the client.

- **Reverse lookup zone:** You should create a reverse lookup zone in case you (or one of your software applications) knows the TCP/IP address of a system and you want to query DNS for the *name* of the system. Figure 5-3 shows a DNS server configured with both forward and reverse lookup zones.

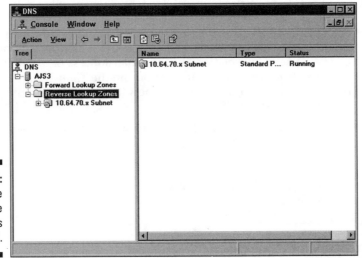

Figure 5-3:
A reverse lookup zone in Windows 2000 DNS.

- **(Standard) primary zone:** You create a standard primary zone when you create your primary name server. This zone database is a read/write copy that can be updated. You also refer to this zone as the Zone of Authority.

- **(Standard) secondary zone:** You create this zone as a backup to the primary zone. It maintains a read-only copy of the database and is created by implementing a secondary name server.

- **Active Directory-integrated zone:** Storing the zone database in Active Directory is a nifty trick possible in Windows 2000. When you do this, you create what is called an *Active Directory-integrated zone.* You either do this, or stick with your standard primary zone. As I detail in Chapter 6, you realize many benefits when you convert to an Active Directory-integrated zone.

Typically, you install a forward lookup, standard primary zone for use with Active Directory. You then enable dynamic updates on the zone, install Active Directory using DCPROMO, and then switch to an Active Directory-integrated zone type. Lost? Don't worry. I walk you through all the steps in the section "Installing and Configuring DNS," later in this chapter, and you can find even more information in Chapter 6.

In the following section, you take a look at all the record types that this very special database can store.

DNS record types

What are the typical entries in the DNS database you might ask? Here they are:

- ✔ **Start of Authority (SOA):** The SOA record identifies the location of the primary name server. As shown in Figure 5-4, it also provides additional and very useful information like the e-mail address of the administrator responsible for the zone configuration and the Time To Live (TTL) for query responses. The TTL dictates how long a query resolution can be cached by another DNS server.

- ✔ **Host (A):** The A record resolves the most common of queries: a request for the TCP/IP address of a computer system.

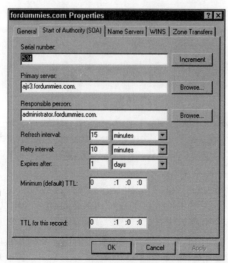

Figure 5-4:
The SOA
record.

✔ **Pointer (PTR):** The PTR record resolves queries of the reverse lookup zone. Thanks to the PTR records in DNS, the reverse lookup zone can sort the DNS listings by IP addresses as opposed to friendly names.

✔ **Canonical Name (CNAME):** The CNAME record maps an aliased or alternate DNS domain name to a host system in the network. This record type is often used to implement simple load balancing. For example, assume that you have three Web servers set up to host your Internet site. Each server is hosting an identical copy of the site. These Web servers have the following DNS names configured in the forward lookup zone:

- webserv1.acme.com

- webserv2.acme.com

- webserv3.acme.com

You create three CNAME records in the zone: www.acme.com, pointing to webserv1.acme.com; www.acme.com, pointing to webserv2.acme.com; and www.acme.com, pointing to webserv3.acme.com. DNS cleverly uses a round-robin approach as clients request name resolution for www.acme.com, resolving the first request to webserv1.acme.com, the second to webserv2.acme.com, and so on.

✔ **Service Locator (SRV):** To install Active Directory in a network, you must have a DNS system in place that supports SRV records. Figure 5-5 shows one of these important SRV records in the DNS interface. These relatively new record types enable a system to find services running in the network. For example, these SRV records come into play when a client logs on and uses DNS to find a domain controller, as I describe in the section "How does Active Directory use DNS?" earlier in this chapter.

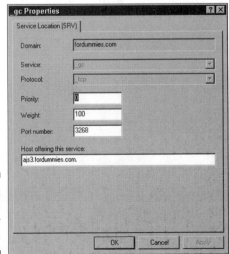

Figure 5-5:
The Service
Locator
record.

DNS systems use plenty of other record types, but you should study and know these five for the exam.

Installing and Configuring DNS

As I explain in Chapter 3, the Active Directory Installation wizard offers to install DNS if the wizard does not detect a proper DNS zone configuration during the installation of Active Directory. However, you should not rely on the wizard for these tasks. Many bug reports have been submitted regarding installation bases that relied on the wizard. Also keep in mind that the Active Directory Installation wizard does not install a reverse lookup zone.

The Windows 2000 DNS service can coexist with or migrate other DNS services, including the popular Berkeley Internet Name Domain (BIND) DNS service. One great place to find BIND information is the Internet Software Consortium Web site, shown in Figure 5-6. For more information regarding coexistence with BIND, see Chapter 6. To migrate from BIND, you must transfer the BIND zone and boot files to the Microsoft DNS service.

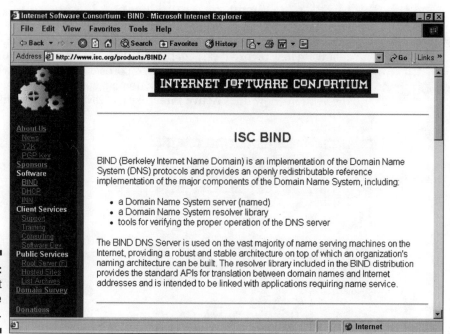

Figure 5-6:
The Internet
Software
Consortium.

Windows 2000 DNS can also upgrade or coexist with Windows NT 4.0 DNS servers.

For the exam, you should know how to configure DNS for Active Directory. Lab 5-1 describes the procedure. If you installed ADS by following the steps I describe in Lab 3-1, you cannot perform Lab 5-1 on the same computer. You can perform all the other labs in this chapter, however.

Lab 5-1   Installing DNS

1. **Click Start⇨Settings⇨Control Panel.**

2. **Double-click Add/Remove Programs and then click Add/Remove Windows Components.**

3. **In Components, select Networking Services and then click Details.**

4. **In Subcomponents of Networking Services, select the Domain Name System (DNS) check box, click OK, and then click Next.**

5. **In Copy Files From, type the full path to the Windows 2000 distribution files and then click OK.**

To host Active Directory, you must properly configure DNS with a zone for the Active Directory namespace. You should create both zone types for a proper DNS implementation for your Active Directory namespace — that is, a forward lookup zone and a reverse lookup zone. Labs 5-2 and 5-3 show you how.

Lab 5-2   Creating a Forward Lookup Zone

1. **Click Start⇨Programs⇨Administrative Tools⇨DNS.**

   Windows 2000 launches the DNS Microsoft Management Console, from which you can perform your DNS administration.

2. **Expand the DNS server.**

3. **Right-click the Forward Lookup Zone folder and choose New Zone.**

4. **Click Next to continue when the New Zone wizard appears.**

   The wizard takes the pain out of DNS administration.

5. **Ensure that Standard Primary is selected and click Next, as shown in Figure 5-7.**

6. **Ensure that Forward Lookup Zone is selected and click Next.**

7. **At the New Zone page, type the name of your zone (for example, fordummies.com) and click Next.**

8. **Select Create a New File With This File Name and click Next.**

9. **Click Finish.**

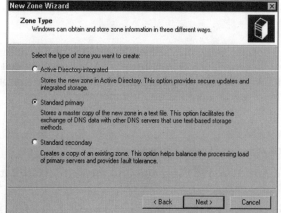

Figure 5-7:
Configuring
the standard
primary
forward
lookup zone.

Lab 5-3   Creating a Reverse Lookup Zone

1. **Click Start⊅Programs⊅Administrative Tools⊅DNS.**

2. **Expand the DNS server.**

3. **Right-click your server and choose New Zone.**

4. **Click Next to continue when the New Zone wizard appears.**

5. **Ensure that Standard Primary is selected and click Next.**

6. **Ensure that Reverse Lookup Zone is selected and click Next.**

7. **Ensure that Network ID is selected, type your network ID in the Network ID field, and click Next.**

8. **Select Create a New File With This File Name and click Next.**

9. **Click Finish.**

As far as Active Directory is concerned, your DNS server is almost ready. You should now configure the forward and reverse lookup zones for dynamic updating so that you do not get stuck creating all the records required for Active Directory yourself!

Configuring Dynamic DNS

The DNS service in Windows 2000 Server can accept dynamic updates to its database. This Dynamic DNS (DDNS) feature dramatically reduces the administrative burden you face as the network administrator. You no longer have to manually update the DNS database with client host (A) records. Windows 2000 clients can update themselves.

DDNS also permits DNS to work well in networks that utilize DHCP for the dynamic configuration of client systems.

You can configure a list of authorized DHCP servers within DDNS. Then, these servers can dynamically update the DNS database. For example, after you specify a DHCP server as an authorized server, a client updates its own host (A) record in the database, and the DHCP service adds the appropriate PTR (reverse lookup) record. You can even configure DHCP to update non-Windows 2000 clients in DNS, handling both parts of the registration process.

If you use the Active Directory-integrated zone feature with your DNS implementation, you can take advantage of a Dynamic DNS setting called *secure updates.* Chapter 6 covers secure dynamic updates.

Lab 5-4 describes the procedure for configuring DDNS.

Lab 5-4	**Configuring DDNS**

1. **Click Start➪Programs➪Administrative Tools➪DNS.**

2. **In the DNS console tree, expand your server.**

3. **Right-click your zone and choose Properties.**

4. **In the Allow Dynamic Updates area on the General tab, select Yes, as shown in Figure 5-8.**

5. **Click OK.**

Complete this same procedure to configure the reverse lookup zone for dynamic updates as well.

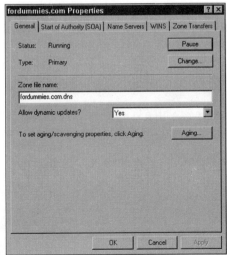

Figure 5-8:
Configuring
DDNS.

Prep Test

1 You are using DHCP and DNS together for dynamic update capabilities with Windows 2000 clients. What is the default configuration method these services will use for the dynamic update behavior?

A ○ The client updates the host (A) record, and DHCP updates the reverse lookup (PTR) record.

B ○ DHCP updates the host (A) record, and the client updates the reverse lookup (PTR) record.

C ○ DHCP updates the host (A) record and the reverse lookup (PTR) record.

D ○ The client updates the host (A) record and the reverse lookup (PTR) record.

2 During the installation and configuration of DNS, the Active Directory Installation wizard does not perform which of the following steps?

A ○ Enabling of secure dynamic updates

B ○ Active Directory-integrated zone configuration

C ○ Reverse lookup zone configuration

D ○ Forward lookup zone configuration

3 Which of the following choices is a traditional DNS zone that permits changes to be written to the DNS table?

A ○ Active Directory-integrated zone

B ○ Secondary zone

C ○ Reverse lookup zone

D ○ Primary zone

4 David is installing Active Directory in his corporate WAN. He is currently using BIND 8.2.1 servers for DNS name resolution. What are his options for the DNS portion of his installation? Choose all that apply.

A ❑ Coexist with the existing DNS servers.

B ❑ Migrate from the existing DNS servers.

C ❑ Upgrade the existing DNS servers with a Windows 2000 DNS installation.

D ❑ Remove the existing DNS servers and use WINS for name resolution.

5 **You want to ensure that your DNS installation can resolve names for systems located on the Internet. What should you do?**

A ○ Configure a caching-only server and place it just inside the corporate firewall.

B ○ Configure a Windows 2000 DNS forwarding server.

C ○ Have your internal DNS servers engage in zone transfers with your Internet Service Provider's (ISP's) DNS service.

D ○ Migrate to BIND's DNS service.

6 **You want to enable secure dynamic updates in your Windows 2000 DNS implementation. What must you configure?**

A ○ An Active Directory-integrated DNS configuration

B ○ A DNS configuration running BIND

C ○ A Windows NT 4.0 DNS configuration

D ○ A standard primary zone configuration

7 **You want to configure the DHCP service to assist in the registration of Windows 2000 and non-Windows 2000 client systems in your Active Directory-integrated zone. What must you do?**

A ○ No additional configuration is necessary.

B ○ Authorize the DHCP service in Active Directory.

C ○ Register the DHCP service with the DNS server.

D ○ You cannot configure this setup in Windows 2000.

8 **Which record is used to find services running in your Active Directory network?**

A ○ PTR

B ○ A

C ○ SRV

D ○ SOA

9 **Which of the following choices is a traditional DNS zone that makes DNS resolution more available but cannot be updated with database changes?**

A ○ Active Directory-integrated zone

B ○ Secondary zone

C ○ Reverse lookup zone

D ○ Primary zone

10 **Which service is required for an Active Directory client to log on?**

A ○ DHCP

B ○ WINS

C ○ DNS

D ○ NAT

Answers

1 **A.** The client updates the host (A) record, and DHCP updates the reverse lookup (PTR) record. The DHCP service can assist in dynamic updates for Windows 2000 and non-Windows 2000 clients. By default, for Windows 2000 clients, DHCP will register the reverse lookup record. *Study "Configuring Dynamic DNS."*

2 **C.** Reverse lookup zone configuration. The Active Directory Installation wizard can install and configure DNS for you. It does not create a reverse lookup zone, however. *Review "Installing and Configuring DNS."*

3 **D.** Primary zone. This is the zone that can perform updates. You also refer to this zone as the Zone of Authority. *Review "DNS zone types."*

4 **A and B.** Coexist with the existing DNS servers. Migrate from the existing DNS servers. You can use Windows 2000's DNS service to migrate from BIND, or it can coexist with BIND servers. *Read "Installing and Configuring DNS."*

5 **B.** Configure a Windows 2000 DNS forwarding server. By default, Windows 2000 DNS servers contain root hints for the Internet. *See "DNS server types."*

6 **A.** An Active Directory-integrated DNS configuration. Secure dynamic updates are also possible when using an Active Directory-integrated zone configuration. *See "Configuring Dynamic DNS."*

7 **C.** Register the DHCP service with the DNS server. Registering the DHCP service with DNS permits DHCP to assist with dynamic update functionality, which further reduces your administrative workload. *See "Configuring Dynamic DNS."*

8 **C.** SRV. This new record type enables a system to find services running on the network. *Read "DNS record types."*

9 **B.** Secondary zone. A secondary zone maintains a read-only copy of the DNS database. *See "DNS zone types."*

10 **C.** DNS. DNS is used to find resources in an Active Directory network. For example, a client needs DNS in order to find a nearby domain controller. *See "How does Active Directory use DNS?"*

Chapter 6

DNS Replication: Servers, Servers, Everywhere

Exam Objectives

▶ Integrating Active Directory DNS zones with non-Active Directory DNS zones

▶ Managing replication of DNS data

▶ Managing, monitoring, and troubleshooting DNS

*U*sing Windows 2000 DNS servers offers many advantages over using other DNS server products in Windows 2000. For example, when you use the Windows 2000 DNS service, you can configure your DNS zones as Active Directory-integrated. In this chapter, you gain many important benefits as an administrator by using Active Directory-integrated zones. Microsoft also provides many advanced tools and processes that enable the successful replication of the DNS database throughout your network, and you can review them in this chapter.

This chapter covers the information you need to know for the exam regarding Active Directory-integrated zones and zone replication. This chapter helps you to review the following topics:

✔ Active Directory-integrated zones

✔ Secure dynamic updates

✔ Zone transfers

✔ DNS troubleshooting

Quick Assessment

Integrating
Active
Directory
DNS zones
with
non-Active
Directory
DNS zones

1 _____ is a popular UNIX-based DNS system.

2 Active Directory-integrated zones enable support for _____ dynamic updates.

3 Active Directory-integrated zones take advantage of the Active Directory _____ system.

Managing
replication
of DNS
data

4 Windows 2000 DNS servers can engage in _____ zone transfers.

5 Windows NT 4 DNS servers must use _____ zone transfers.

6 DNS _____ implements a push mechanism for change notifications in the DNS system.

Managing,
monitoring,
and trouble-
shooting DNS

7 You use the _____ to manage your Windows 2000 DNS server.

8 You can use the _____ utility in interactive mode to help troubleshoot DNS issues.

Answers

1 *BIND.* See "Why Active Directory-integrated zones?"

2 *Secure.* Review "Secure dynamic updates."

3 *Replication.* Study "Why Active Directory-integrated zones?"

4 *Incremental.* See "Incremental Zone Transfers and Other Cool Stuff."

5 *Full.* See "Incremental Zone Transfers and Other Cool Stuff."

6 *Notify.* Review "Incremental Zone Transfers and Other Cool Stuff."

7 *DNS Microsoft Management Console.* See "Troubleshooting DNS."

8 *NSLOOKUP.* Study "Troubleshooting DNS."

Active Directory-Integrated Zones

Active Directory-integrated zones are DNS zones stored in the Active Directory database. Currently, only Windows 2000 DNS servers support the Active Directory-integrated configuration. Because of all the benefits this zone configuration offers, the exam is very hot on the topic.

Why Active Directory-integrated zones?

You achieve many benefits from storing the DNS zone information in Active Directory. These benefits include

- Multimaster updates in which each DNS server can accept updates to the DNS database stored in Active Directory. This capability solves tremendous fault-tolerance issues associated with the DNS system.

- Enhanced security.

- Automatic replication and synchronization of zones to new DNS servers that are domain controllers.

- Simplified planning and administration for both DNS and Active Directory.

- Faster, more efficient replication.

Also, Active Directory-integrated zones can easily interoperate with other, non-Windows 2000 DNS implementations. For example, you can configure a Windows 2000 Active Directory-integrated zone to engage in zone transfers with a UNIX BIND installation.

Active Directory-integrated DNS zones ease your administrative workload because you do not have to worry about managing a replication strategy for DNS. Also, the methods used to synchronize directory-stored information offer performance improvements over standard zone update methods, which may require transfers of the entire zone database.

If you store and replicate the DNS and Active Directory namespaces separately, the namespaces must be administered separately. For example, if you use standard DNS zone storage and Active Directory together, you need to accommodate two different database replication technologies.

Another great advantage to Active Directory-integrated DNS zones is performance. Because Active Directory replication processing is performed on a per-property basis, only relevant changes are propagated. Consequently, less data is used and submitted in updates for directory-stored zones.

Secure dynamic updates

After you configure an Active Directory-integrated zone in your network, you can take advantage of the secure dynamic updates feature of Windows 2000 DDNS. Quite simply, after you store the DNS database in Active Directory, you can then place security restrictions on the records just as if they were files stored on a hard drive. You place these security restrictions using the old, faithful Access Control Lists.

Lab 6-1 reviews the simple procedure for permitting only secure updates in your DDNS setup.

Lab 6-1	Configuring Secure Dynamic Updates

1. **Click Start▷Programs▷Administrative Tools▷DNS.**

2. **In the left pane, select the zone you want to configure.**

3. **Right-click the zone and choose Properties.**

4. **On the General tab, verify that the zone type is Active Directory-integrated and then click OK, as shown in Figure 6-1.**

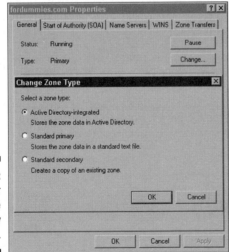

Figure 6-1:
Checking for Active Directory integration.

5. **In the Allow Dynamic Updates drop-down list, click Only Secure Updates and then click OK.**

Incremental Zone Transfers and Other Cool Stuff

You need to configure multiple servers for a zone or multiple zones for a DNS implementation. By doing so, you build fault tolerance into the design and ensure that DNS name resolution does not rely on a single DNS server. In order for additional servers to host a zone, zone transfers must replicate and synchronize all copies of the zone at each server configured to host the zone.

When you add a new DNS server to the network and configure it as a secondary server for an existing zone, it performs a full initial transfer of the zone to obtain and replicate a full copy of resource records for the zone. With DNS server implementations prior to Windows 2000's, replication of any changes to the zone requires a full zone transfer. In Windows 2000 Server, however, the DNS service supports incremental zone transfers, thereby enabling instant replication of intermediate changes throughout the DNS system.

Incremental zone transfers are an additional DNS standard for replicating DNS zones. By including support for incremental transfers on both a DNS server acting as the source for a zone and any servers that copy the zone from it, Windows 2000's DNS service provides a more efficient method for propagating zone changes and updates.

Windows 2000 DNS servers also support DNS Notify, an update to the original DNS protocol specification (RFC 1996). DNS Notify provides a means for initiating notification to secondary servers when zone changes occur. DNS Notify implements a push mechanism for notifying a select set of secondary servers when a zone is updated. Servers that are notified can then initiate a zone transfer to pull zone changes from their master servers and update their local replicas of the zone.

Troubleshooting DNS

Windows 2000 Server includes an excellent DNS troubleshooting tool called NSLOOKUP. This diagnostic tool specializes in displaying diagnostic information as provided by a DNS service.

You run the NSLOOKUP utility from a command prompt, and it features two modes: interactive and noninteractive. Use noninteractive mode if you want to look up only a single piece of data. Interactive mode is preferable if you need to retrieve multiple pieces of information from a DNS service. Figure 6-2 shows NSLOOKUP running in interactive mode.

Figure 6-2:
NSLOOKUP
in interac-
tive mode.

Table 6-1 explains several useful NSLOOKUP subcommands that you should know for the exam. Lab 6-2 describes the steps for using NSLOOKUP.

Table 6-1	Some NSLOOKUP Subcommands
Command	*What it Does*
help	Displays a summary of the NSLOOKUP commands.
exit	Exits NSLOOKUP when running in interactive mode.
ls	Lists information for a DNS domain. The default output contains computer names and their IP addresses.
lserver	Changes the default server to the specified DNS domain. The lserver command uses the initial server to look up the information about the specified DNS domain.
root	Changes the default server to the server for the root of the DNS domain namespace. Currently, the computer ns.nic.ddn.mil is used.
server	Changes the default server to the specified DNS domain. The server command uses the current default server to look up the information about the specified DNS domain.
set	Changes configuration settings that affect how lookups function.
view	Sorts and lists the output of previous ls command or commands.

Lab 6-2   Using NSLOOKUP

1. **Click Start⇨Programs⇨Accessories⇨Command Prompt.**

2. **At the command prompt, type** nslookup **and press Enter to launch NSLOOKUP in interactive mode.**

3. **Type** ls –t SRV *domain* **(where** *domain* **is your domain name) and then press Enter.**

   NSLOOKUP lists your SRV resource records, as shown in Figure 6-3.

4. **Type** exit **and press Enter to exit NSLOOKUP.**

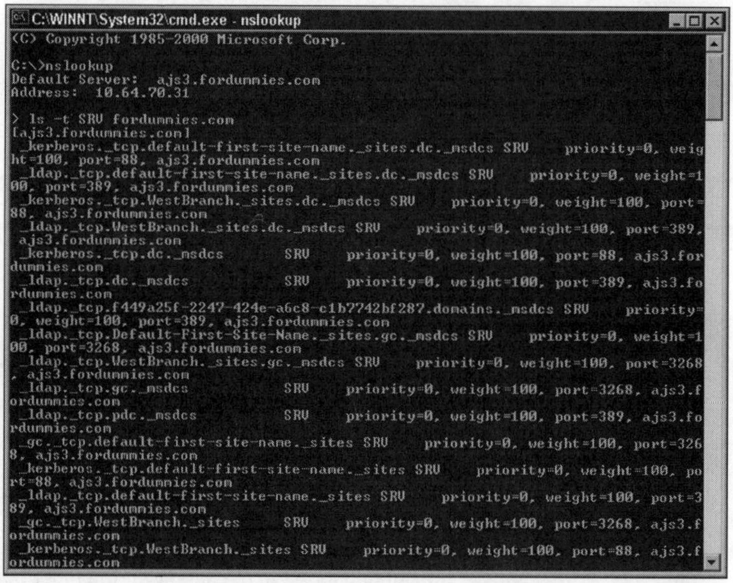

Figure 6-3:
Using
NSLOOKUP
to view the
SRV
records.

Prep Test

1 Which is not considered an advantage of Active Directory-integrated zones?

A ○ Multimaster updates

B ○ Enhanced security

C ○ Faster, more efficient replication

D ○ Enhanced Windows 2000 stability

2 Which of the following utilities is a DNS troubleshooting tool included in Windows 2000 Server?

A ○ PING

B ○ NSLOOKUP

C ○ FINGER

D ○ FTP

3 John has a network that consists of a Windows NT 4.0 domain. DNS is implemented in the network using BIND 8.2.1 servers. John wants to upgrade the domain to Windows 2000, and he wants to take advantage of secure dynamic updates. Which type of zone should he create on his Windows 2000 DNS server?

A ○ A standard primary zone

B ○ A standard secondary zone

C ○ An Active Directory-integrated zone

D ○ A delegated domain

4 You want to display the SRV records stored in your Windows 2000 Active Directory-integrated domain. You decide to use the NSLOOKUP utility in a command prompt session. What command should you use?

A ○ root

B ○ server

C ○ lserver

D ○ ls

5 Your boss is determined to keep the existing BIND 8.2.1 DNS servers used in your organization for Internet name resolution. You want to implement Windows 2000 DNS servers for your Active Directory implementation. What should you do?

A ○ Configure the Windows 2000 DNS servers to integrate with the BIND DNS servers.

B ○ Talk your boss into replacing the BIND DNS servers with Windows 2000 servers running DNS.

C ○ Upgrade the BIND servers to the latest version of BIND.

D ○ Use Windows NT 4 DNS servers to integrate with the BIND DNS servers.

6 **Which of the following choices represents a valid reason why Active Directory-integrated DNS replication is more efficient than standard DNS transfers?**

A ○ Active Directory-integrated replication is more stable.

B ○ Active Directory replication processing is performed on a per-property basis — only relevant changes are propagated.

C ○ Standard DNS transfers must use the NetLogon service.

D ○ Active Directory-integrated zones take advantage of SYSVOL.

7 **What is the key to secure dynamic updates in Windows 2000 DNS?**

A ○ Only administrators can update the DNS database.

B ○ Only the DHCP service can update the DNS database.

C ○ Only Enterprise Administrators can update the DNS database.

D ○ You can place security restrictions on the DNS database using Access Control Lists.

8 **What is the primary benefit of configuring multiple servers for each of your DNS zones?**

A ○ Fault tolerance

B ○ Stability

C ○ Enhanced replication

D ○ Network traffic

9 **When you configure a secondary zone in your network, which type of zone transfer initially occurs?**

A ○ Incremental zone transfer

B ○ Full zone transfer

C ○ Property-based transfer

D ○ No transfer occurs

10 **What is the main advantage of incremental zone transfers?**

A ○ Reduced administration

B ○ Less network traffic

C ○ DHCP integration

D ○ Fault tolerance

Answers

1 **D.** Enhanced Windows 2000 stability. Creating an Active Directory-integrated zone does not directly affect the stability of your Windows 2000 installation. Review *"Why Active Directory-integrated zones?"*

2 **B.** NSLOOKUP. When you're troubleshooting DNS problems, you can use NSLOOKUP to display DNS server information from the command prompt. *See "Troubleshooting DNS."*

3 **C.** An Active Directory-integrated zone. In order to support secure dynamic updates, John must use an Active Directory-integrated zone. *Review "Why Active Directory-integrated zones?"*

4 **D.** ls. You use the ls command to list information for a DNS domain. *Study "Troubleshooting DNS."*

5 **A.** Configure the Windows 2000 DNS servers to integrate with the BIND DNS servers. Windows 2000 DNS servers, even when using Active Directory-integrated zones, can integrate with existing DNS servers. *See "Why Active Directory-integrated zones?"*

6 **B.** Active Directory replication processing is performed on a per-property basis — only relevant changes are propagated. Active Directory replication is very efficient because it functions on a per-property basis. When you store the DNS zone in Active Directory, you take advantage of this efficiency. *See "Why Active Directory-integrated zones?"*

7 **D.** You can place security restrictions on the DNS database using Access Control Lists. Secure dynamic updates function because ACLs can be created for DNS information. The zone must be Active Directory-integrated in order for this to happen. *Review "Secure dynamic updates."*

8 **A.** Fault tolerance. Adding additional servers to your DNS setup improves the fault tolerance of the design and guards against a single point of failure in your network. *Study "Incremental Zone Transfers and Other Cool Stuff."*

9 **B.** Full zone transfer. A full transfer takes place when you add a secondary zone to your installation. Earlier DNS systems must do full zone transfers whenever changes occur in the DNS database. Windows 2000 eliminates this problem with incremental zone transfers. *Study "Incremental Zone Transfers and Other Cool Stuff."*

10 **B.** Less network traffic. Incremental zone transfers reduce the amount of network traffic in your infrastructure due to the smaller amount of information that is transferred when DNS updates occur. *See "Incremental Zone Transfers and Other Cool Stuff."*

Part IV
Configuration Management

In this part . . .

Here you review one of the more powerful features in Windows 2000 Active Directory Services: Group Policy objects (GPOs). Using GPOs, you can control just about every aspect of your Windows 2000 network, and all from a central location — for example, the Windows 2000 Server in your home office! GPOs help to lower the TCO (total cost of ownership) for your systems and enable you to maximize your weekend time. You will soon marvel at all that you can accomplish using these powerful Windows 2000 components.

In this part, you review the procedures for using Group Policy objects to manage your users' computing environments and network access capabilities. You also review how to use GPOs to distribute and maintain the software applications used in your Windows 2000 network.

In Chapter 7, you review all the mechanics of using Group Policy objects. In Chapters 8 and 9, you put those mechanics to use managing your network from the comfort of your easy chair.

Chapter 7

Implementing Group Policy

● ●

Exam Objectives

▶ Creating and linking Group Policy objects (GPOs)

▶ Modifying GPOs

▶ Delegating administrative control of GPOs

▶ Filtering GPOs

● ●

*Y*ou use Group Policy objects (GPOs) in Windows 2000 to control a user's desktop environment, distribute and maintain software, control access to networking settings, and manage security. Before you can take advantage of all these wonderful capabilities, you must know how to create and link these GPOs to container objects in the Active Directory. You should also know how to manage and modify default Group Policy behaviors.

For the exam, you should know as much as possible regarding the implementation of Group Policy objects. To help you, this chapter focuses on the following topics:

   ✔ Creating, editing, and linking GPOs

   ✔ Delegating control over GPOs

   ✔ Modifying Group Policy inheritance

   ✔ Filtering GPOs

Quick Assessment

Creating and linking GPOs

1 Associating a GPO with a container object is called _____.

2 You can link GPOs to sites, domains, or _____.

Modifying GPOs

3 A typical Group Policy setting has three states: Enabled, Disabled, or _____.

4 By default, Group Policy settings flow down through the Active Directory hierarchy through a process known as _____.

Delegating administrative control of GPOs

5 You should delegate the administrative control over GPOs by using security _____.

6 To permit a group of administrators to modify GPOs, you should grant them _____ permissions on the objects.

Filtering GPOs

7 To filter GPOs, you restrict permissions on security _____ in Windows 2000.

8 To filter a GPO, you deny the group the _____ or Apply Group Policy permission for the GPO.

Answers

1 *Linking.* See "Creating GPOs."

2 *Organizational units.* Review "Creating GPOs."

3 *Not Configured.* Study "Editing GPOs."

4 *Inheritance.* See "Managing GPO Inheritance."

5 *Permissions.* Review "Delegating Control Over GPOs."

6 *Write.* Study "Delegating Control Over GPOs."

7 *Groups.* See "Filtering GPOs."

8 *Read.* Study "Filtering GPOs."

Creating GPOs

Windows 2000 stores Group Policy settings that control a system in a Group Policy object. In an Active Directory environment, these GPOs are referred to as *nonlocal GPOs.* You store these GPOs on a domain controller.

The Group Policy settings apply to users and computers in the site, domain, or organizational unit to which you link them. If you disable or remove a GPO from the container object to which it is linked, the settings no longer apply. This is the simplest way to reverse Group Policy restrictions you have placed on a container.

As a user in the Active Directory structure, you may receive your settings from several GPOs that act together to configure your computer and desktop environment. By default, Group Policy settings flow down through the Active Directory hierarchy via a process known as *inheritance.* Later in this chapter, you review the order and precedence rules of inheritance. (See the section "Managing GPO Inheritance.") As you might guess, you can control the order in which GPOs affect a user.

In most cases, you link GPOs to domains or organizational units. For this task, you use the Active Directory Users and Computers snap-in. As Lab 7-1 demonstrates, when you use Active Directory Users and Computers to create a GPO, you actually accomplish two steps simultaneously: You create the GPO and link it to the selected container.

Lab 7-1   Creating and Linking a GPO

1. **Click Start⇨Programs⇨Administrative Tools⇨Active Directory Users and Computers.**

2. **Expand your domain in the left pane and then right-click the domain or organizational unit to which the newly created Group Policy object will be linked.**

   The GPO will be stored in the current domain.

3. **Choose Properties and then click the Group Policy tab, as shown in Figure 7-1.**

4. **Click New and then type a name for the Group Policy object.**

5. **Click Edit to launch the Group Policy snap-in shown in Figure 7-2.**

6. **Explore the many options for Group Policy settings in the Group Policy snap-in.**

7. **When you finish exploring the Group Policy snap-in, close the snap-in by clicking the close button in the top-right corner of the window.**

8. **Click OK to close the Properties dialog box and create the GPO.**

To create a GPO linked to a site object, you use Active Directory Sites and Services. Much like the steps in Lab 7-1, you simply right-click the site, choose Properties, and use the Group Policy tab to create the GPO.

Some GPO settings function properly only when linked at the domain level. For example, using the Account Policies section of the Security Settings node under Computer Configuration, you set the Password and Account Lockout policies for a domain.

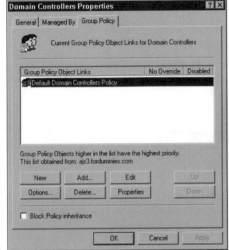

Figure 7-1:
The Group Policy tab in a container's Properties dialog box.

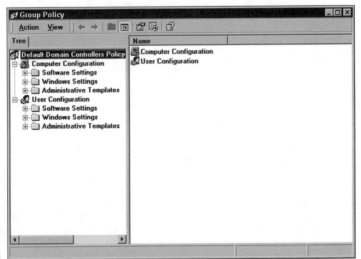

Figure 7-2:
The Group Policy snap-in.

Editing GPOs

To edit a GPO, you simply access the GPO (typically using the Group Policy tab of a container's Properties sheet), click the Edit button, and then make configuration changes. Most Group Policy settings have three states that you may set:

- ✔ Not Configured
- ✔ Enabled
- ✔ Disabled

Not Configured is the default state for most settings, as shown in Figure 7-3. Windows 2000 simply ignores settings that have this state. Of course, you choose Enabled to apply a particular setting, or Disabled to prevent a policy setting from applying.

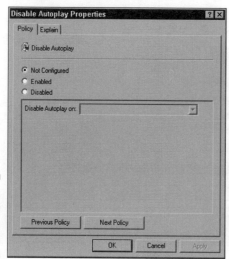

Figure 7-3:
The default
GPO state
setting.

Linking an Existing GPO

Typically, you link a GPO to the site, domain, or OU in which you create the GPO using either the Active Directory Users and Computers snap-in or the Active Directory Sites and Services snap-in. However, you can link a single GPO to multiple entities in the Active Directory structure. Lab 7-2 describes the simple procedure for linking an existing GPO.

Lab 7-2	Linking an Existing Group Policy Object

1. **Click Start⊏⟩Programs⊏⟩Administrative Tools⊏⟩Active Directory Users and Computers.**

2. **Expand your domain in the left pane and then right-click the domain or OU you want to link to an existing GPO.**

3. **Choose Properties and then click the Group Policy tab.**

4. **If the GPO does not already appear in the Group Policy Object Links list, click Add.**

5. **In the Add a Group Policy Object Link dialog box, click the All tab.**

    By default, this tab lists all the Group Policy objects in your forest, as shown in Figure 7-4.

6. **Select the GPO you want to link to the object you have selected and click OK.**

7. **In the Properties dialog box for the domain or OU you have selected, click OK.**

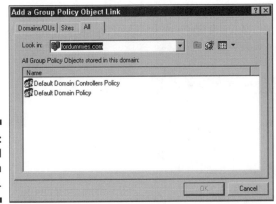

Figure 7-4:
Viewing all the GPOs in a domain.

You can easily repeat these steps to link the same GPO to other containers in Active Directory. Make the most of this feature to save yourself administration effort.

Delegating Control Over GPOs

You may want other network administrators, or even nonadministrative personnel, to assist you in managing Group Policy objects in your Active Directory forest. This management could include creating, deleting, and modifying the many GPOs you need for a properly configured network.

You can assign Read and Write permissions on Group Policy objects for any group or user account in Active Directory. This group or user will now have administrative capabilities over the GPO. Lab 7-3 describes the steps for setting permissions on GPOs.

Lab 7-3   Setting Permissions on Group Policy Objects

1. **Click Start ➪Programs➪Administrative Tools➪Active Directory Users and Computers.**

2. **Expand your domain in the left pane and then right-click the domain or OU that has a linked GPO on which you want to set permissions.**

3. **Choose Properties and then click the Group Policy tab.**

4. **Select the GPO you want to set permissions for and click Properties.**

5. **In the Properties dialog box, click the Security tab, as shown in Figure 7-5.**

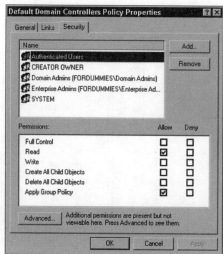

Figure 7-5:
Setting
security on
GPOs.

6. **Set the security options you want to use and then click OK.**

7. **Click OK in the Properties dialog box for the object you had selected in Active Directory Users and Computers.**

To allow other administrators to create GPOs for sections of the Active Directory, you use the Delegation of Control wizard. You review the use of this tool in Chapter 12.

Managing GPO Inheritance

You can assign GPOs at various levels in the Active Directory hierarchy. These Group Policy objects act together to provide the user and computer settings for a particular system. The GPOs apply to a user or computer in the following order:

1. **Local GPO.** Each Windows 2000 computer has a local Group Policy object assigned to it, and this is the first GPO to be processed.

2. **Site GPOs.** Next, Windows 2000 processes any Group Policy objects that are linked to the site in which the system or the user is located. If multiple site GPOs exist, they process in the order that you specify.

3. **Domain GPOs.** Next, Windows 2000 processes any GPOs linked to the domain in which the system or the user is located. If multiple domain GPOs exist, they process in the order that you specify.

4. **OU GPOs.** Next , Windows 2000 processes any GPOs linked to OUs above the GPO that contains the user or computer. These are called parent GPOs. Finally, Windows 2000 processes any GPOs linked to the OU in which the system or the user is located. If multiple OU GPOs exist, they process in the order that you specify.

A GPO inheritance example

GPO settings are cumulative for a user account or computer. If a conflict exists with the settings of GPOs that affect a user or computer account, the last GPO applied will win the conflict. The following example demonstrates how this process works:

John's user account is located in the Sales OU. This OU is within the North America (NA) OU, which is located in the Northwind.com domain.

The following GPOs exist with the settings described:

✔ **Domain GPO:**

- Minimum password length: eight characters
- Disable Display in Control Panel

✔ **NA OU GPO:**

- Disable addition of printers
- Disable Add/Remove Programs

✔ **Sales OU:**

- Enable addition of printers
- Enable Display in Control Panel

Here's the effect of these GPOs:

✔ Minimum password length: eight characters

✔ Disable Add/Remove Programs

✔ Enable addition of printers

✔ Enable Display in Control Panel

This example shows you not only the cumulative effect that these GPOs have, but also the process for resolving conflicts by examining the order in which GPOs apply to an object.

Overriding the default behavior

The example in the preceding section demonstrates the default behavior for handling inheritance of GPO settings. You can override this default behavior of GPOs by using the following settings:

✔ **No Override:** With this option, another GPO cannot overwrite the GPO's settings. If more than one GPO has this setting, the GPO higher in the Active Directory hierarchy wins conflicts.

✔ **Block Policy Inheritance:** You can set this option for any site, domain, or OU. It prevents all GPOs above in the hierarchy from affecting the object. Any GPOs configured with the No Override option represent an exception to this setting. No Override forces the policy to take effect on all child objects.

✔ **Loopback setting:** This setting is useful if you do not want user settings in GPOs to have an effect on specific systems. For example, you may use the loopback setting for computers in a special location like a kiosk, classroom, or reception area. When you enable the loopback setting, you set it in one of two modes: Replace or Merge. With Replace, the computer GPO settings completely replace any user GPO settings that would ordinarily apply. With Merge, the user configurations are applied first and then the computer configurations are applied. The computer GPO settings win any conflicts that may exist.

Use these features sparingly in your Windows 2000 network. They add overhead and make troubleshooting Group Policy assignments much more difficult!

Filtering GPOs

Perhaps you do not want a particular GPO to apply to specific users in an OU, domain, or site. You can easily configure this exception through a process called *filtering* of group policies. You simply deny the Apply Group Policy or Read permissions to a user or group, and the GPO does not affect that entity.

Of course, as in any case that involves permissions, you can best configure this setting by using groups. Create a security group that represents the individual(s) you want to exclude from the GPO's settings and then deny the permissions to this group.

Lab 7-4 lists the steps for filtering GPOs.

Lab 7-4	Filtering Group Policy

1. Click Start⇨Programs⇨Administrative Tools⇨Active Directory Users and Computers.

2. Expand your domain in the left pane and then right-click the domain or OU that has a linked GPO you want to filter.

3. Choose Properties and then click the Group Policy tab.

4. Select the GPO you want to filter and click Properties.

5. In the Properties dialog box, click the Security tab and then click the security group that you want to filter. If you need to change the list of security groups through which to filter this GPO, you can add or remove security groups by clicking Add or Remove.

6. To filter the group from receiving the GPO settings, set Apply Group Policy to Deny and set Read to Deny. Click OK to close the GPO's Properties dialog box.

7. Click OK to close the Properties dialog box for the object you selected in Active Directory Users and Computers.

Prep Test

1 Amy has configured a password policy for her domain so that all users must
have passwords with a minimum length of four characters. These passwords
are also set to expire every 90 days. Amy's boss has also indicated that the
members of the Accounting OU should have their passwords expire every 30
days, and their passwords should be forced into a minimum length of seven
characters.

To achieve these design requirements, Amy creates a GPO at the OU level for
the Accounting department. This GPO includes a password policy so that all
accounts within Accounting must have a password of seven characters or
more, and passwords expire every 30 days.

To test the policy, she logs on as a user from the Accounting OU and attempts
to change the password to a password of less than seven characters.
Unfortunately, the system permits her to change the password to one of less
than seven characters. What is the most likely problem?

A ○ You cannot apply Group Policies to OUs.

B ○ Group Policies do not refresh until you restart the system.

C ○ You can only set Group Policies for password settings at the domain
level.

D ○ Group Policies do not refresh until a user logs off and logs back on.

2 You have created an OU named Team 1 within the Sales OU. You have linked a
GPO to the Sales OU that enforces certain security requirements of your company. What will be the result for the Team 1 OU if you have not modified the
default GPO inheritance rules?

A ○ The OU inherits the security settings.

B ○ Users in the OU are presented with a choice for accepting the security
settings.

C ○ The OU does not inherit the security settings.

D ○ Not enough information is provided to determine the result.

3 After making configuration changes to the desktops of several users in your
network using a GPO, you decide that you want these changes to stop taking
effect. What should you do?

A ○ Manually reconfigure the registries on the effected machines.

B ○ Disable or unlink the GPO.

C ○ Remove the systems from the OU.

D ○ Remove the systems from the domain.

4 You want to enable another administrator to change an important GPO in your Windows 2000 network. What should you do?

A ○ Allow the administrator to take ownership of the GPO.

B ○ Assign the administrator Read permissions to the GPO.

C ○ Assign the administrator Read and Write permissions to the GPO.

D ○ Place the administrator in the Enterprise Admins security group.

5 You need to configure a very restrictive GPO on the Accounting OU. You do not want these restrictions to affect the Accounting Managers of that department, however. What should you do? Choose all that apply.

A ❑ Place the Accounting Managers in a child OU.

B ❑ Place the Accounting Managers in a global security group.

C ❑ Remove the Read permission on the GPO for the Accounting Managers group.

D ❑ Place the Accounting Managers in the Domain Admins security group.

E ❑ Use the Block Policy Inheritance setting.

6 What is the default setting for a Group Policy object setting?

A ○ Enabled

B ○ Disabled

C ○ Not Configured

D ○ Static

7 In what order are GPOs applied?

A ○ Local, Site, Domain, Parent OU, Child OU

B ○ Site, Domain, Parent OU, Child OU

C ○ Domain, Site, Parent OU, Child OU

D ○ Local, Child OU, Parent OU, Domain, Site

8 You want to ensure that a Group Policy's settings are enforced throughout your domain. Which feature should you use?

A ○ Block Policy Inheritance

B ○ Loopback

C ○ Disable the User Configuration section

D ○ No Override

9 You need to associate security settings with an entire site in your network. Which tool should you use?

A ○ Active Directory Domains and Trusts

B ○ Active Directory Users and Computers

C ○ Active Directory Sites and Services

D ○ Computer Configuration

10 **Which statements regarding Group Policy objects are true? Choose all that apply.**

A ❑ You should use Block Policy Inheritance whenever possible.

B ❑ Settings flow from parent OUs to child OUs by default.

C ❑ The Local GPO is the first to be processed.

D ❑ GPOs cannot be linked to the Active Directory forest.

Answers

1 **C.** You can only set Group Policies for password settings at the domain level. Some GPO settings only function properly when linked at the domain level. *See "Creating GPOs."*

2 **A.** The OU inherits the security settings. By default, Group Policy settings flow down through the Active Directory hierarchy via a process called inheritance. *Review "Managing GPO Inheritance."*

3 **B.** Disable or unlink the GPO. To reverse the effects of a Group Policy, you simply disable or unlink the GPO from the container. *See "Creating GPOs."*

4 **C.** Assign the administrator Read and Write permissions to the GPO. To delegate control over GPOs in Windows 2000, you can assign Read and Write permissions to the object to various staff members. *Review "Delegating Control Over GPOs."*

5 **B** and **C.** Place the Accounting Managers in a global security group. Remove the Read permission on the GPO for the Accounting Managers group. To filter Group Policy settings from affecting certain individuals, you should remove the Read permission for a security group. *Study "Filtering GPOs."*

6 **C.** Not Configured. The default state for a GPO setting is Not Configured. *See "Editing GPOs."*

7 **A.** Local, Site, Domain, Parent OU, Child OU. Windows 2000 processes Group Policy objects in a very specific order of precedence, starting with the Local GPO and continuing on to the Child OU GPOs. *Review "Managing GPO Inheritance."*

8 **D.** No Override. No Override ensures that a particular GPO's settings are applied to containers below in the AD hierarchy. No Override ignores any Block Policy Inheritance configurations. *Study "Overriding the default behavior."*

9 **C.** Active Directory Sites and Services. To link GPOs to site objects in Windows 2000, you use the Active Directory Sites and Service tool. *Review "Creating GPOs."*

10 **B, C,** and **D.** Here, the only incorrect statement is that you should use Block Policy Inheritance frequently. If possible, you should seldom use this setting. It makes troubleshooting difficult and adds unnecessary overhead in most situations. *Study "Overriding the default behavior."*

Implementing Group Policy

Chapter 8

Managing User Environments with Group Policy: Rule Your Domain

. . . .

Exam Objectives

▶ Controlling user environments by using administrative templates

▶ Managing network configuration by using Group Policy

▶ Assigning script policies to users and computers

. . . .

*O*ne of the wonders of Group Policy objects (GPOs) is that they help you to control user environments. For example, you could set restrictions so users cannot access the display settings via Control Panel, or you could force them to use certain color schemes or desktop configurations. You can even control how users access their personal data, making it available to them no matter how they access your corporate network.

For the exam, you should know about the methods of managing user environments that you implement using Group Policy objects. This chapter helps you prepare by reviewing the following topics:

    ✔ Using administrative templates

    ✔ Implementing folder redirection

    ✔ Configuring other critical network settings using Group Policy

    ✔ Securing the user environment

    ✔ Assigning scripts using Group Policy

Quick Assessment

Controlling
user
environments
by using
admin-
istrative
templates

1 Administrative templates modify the settings stored in two _____ sub-trees.

2 Administrative templates are available for both user and _____ accounts.

3 The _____ setting type enables you to manage Group Policy refresh intervals.

4 The _____ setting type enables you to control Web-based printing.

5 You use the _____ files setting to ensure that your users always have access to their important files.

Managing
network con-
figuration
by using
Group Policy

6 To ensure that users cannot manipulate their network settings, use the Network and _____ Connections node in Group Policy.

Assigning
script
policies to
users and
computers

7 You use the Computer Configuration node to assign Startup and _____ scripts.

8 You use the User Configuration node to assign Logon and _____ scripts.

9 The default timeout value for script processing is _____ minutes.

10 You can use various scripting languages thanks to the Windows Scripting _____.

Answers

1 *Registry.* See "Using Administrative Templates."

2 *Computer.* See "Using Administrative Templates."

3 *System.* See "Using Administrative Templates."

4 *Printers.* See "Using Administrative Templates."

5 *Offline.* Study "Managing the Network Configuration."

6 *Dial-up.* Review "Managing the Network Configuration."

7 *Shutdown.* Study "Using Script Policies."

8 *Logoff.* Study "Using Script Policies."

9 *Ten.* Study "Using Script Policies."

10 *Host.* Study "Using Script Policies."

Using Administrative Templates

The Administrative Templates section of the Group Policy snap-in offers one means for controlling user environments in a Windows 2000 network. You have Administrative Templates sections for both the User Configuration and the Computer Configuration, as shown in Figure 8-1. These sections contain all the Registry-based Group Policy settings, including Windows Components, System, Network, and Printers.

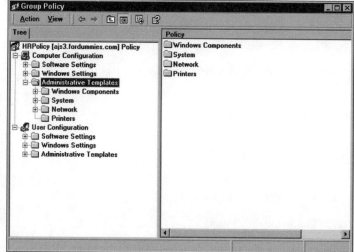

Figure 8-1:
The Administrative Templates section of the Computer Configuration node.

Windows 2000 stores User Configuration settings in the Registry's HKEY_CURRENT_USER section, while the Computer Configuration settings are stored in HKEY_LOCAL_MACHINE. Have fun exploring the many settings stored in the two Administrative Template sections within Group Policy. Windows 2000 has more than 450 different settings for configuring the user environment alone!

Because you are actually reconfiguring the Registry when you make changes using the Administrative Templates section of Group Policy, you should use caution. Many of these changes have dramatic effects on the system.

Table 8-1 details the types of settings that you find in the different sections of the Administrative Templates nodes.

Table 8-1	Types of Settings
With This Setting Type . . .	*You Can Control . . .*
Windows Components	The parts of Windows 2000 that a user can access
System	Many system settings, including Group Policy and disk quotas
Network	The properties of network and dial-up connections
Printers	Printer publishing in Active Directory and Web-based printing
Start Menu & Taskbar	The Start Menu and the taskbar
Desktop	Active Desktop
Control Panel	Important applications of Control Panel, including Add/Remove Programs, Display, and Printers

Understanding Folder Redirection

With Windows 2000's Active Directory, you can ensure that your users' data is always available to them, regardless of where they log on in your network. You accomplish this by redirecting folders that are normally part of a user's profile onto a central server in your network. Folder redirection is yet another configuration made possible through Group Policies, as shown in Figure 8-2.

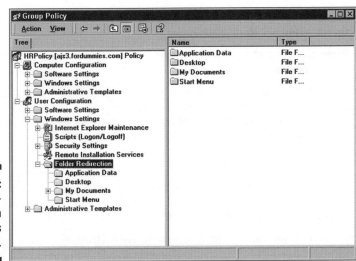

Figure 8-2:
Folder redirection in Windows 2000.

Unlike files that are part of a roaming user profile, files in redirected folders are not copied and saved to a system where the user logs on. In this way, folder redirection helps to protect confidential files and does not require storage space on a client system. Folder redirection also speeds up the logon and logoff processes for these roaming users. Thanks to the redirected folders, personal files are not transferred to the local system as part of the roaming user profile.

You can redirect the following folders:

✔ My Documents

✔ Start Menu

✔ Desktop

✔ Application Data

Lab 8-1 walks you through the steps necessary to redirect a folder using the Administrative Templates settings of Group Policy.

Lab 8-1   Redirecting a Folder

1. **Click Start⇨Programs⇨Administrative Tools⇨Active Directory Users and Computers.**

2. **Expand your domain in the console's left pane and then right-click the domain or OU that has a linked GPO for which you want to configure software settings.**

3. **Choose Properties from the shortcut menu and then click the Group Policy tab in the dialog box that's displayed.**

4. **Select the Group Policy object you want to configure and click the Edit button.**

5. **Expand the User Configuration node, the Windows Settings node, and then the Folder Redirection node.**

6. **Right-click the My Documents node and then choose Properties from the context menu.**

7. **In the Setting drop-down list, click Basic. Then, click Browse and then browse to the location where you want to redirect the folder. You should browse to a shared folder location using the My Network Places node so a universal naming convention (UNC) path is entered in the dialog box.**

If you want to have a subfolder for each user in the site, domain, or organizational unit, you can incorporate %username% into the UNC path — for example, \\Win2000profiles\docs\%username%. Including %username% in the path is recommended.

8. **In the Browse for Folder dialog box, click OK.**

9. **Click the Settings tab and then set each of the following options:**

   • **Grant the User Exclusive Rights to the Special Folder:** This setting is enabled by default. It grants the user and local system full rights to the folder. If this setting is disabled, no changes are made to the permissions on the folder. The permissions that apply by default remain in effect.

   • **Move the Contents of the User's Current Special Folder to the New Location:** This setting is enabled by default as well. It saves you the effort of moving the folder contents yourself initially.

   You should use the defaults in most cases.

10. **Choose one of the following two options that configure what is to happen if you remove the policy:**

    • Leave the Files in the New Location When Policy Is Removed.

    • Redirect the Folder Back to the Local User Profile Location When the Policy Is Removed.

11. **In the Special Folder Properties dialog box, click OK.**

You should always redirect the My Documents folder so your users always have access to their data. To make this data accessible to clients when they have no connection to the central server, you can use the Offline Files feature of the network share. The Offline Files feature enables the client to cache copies of the files from the network share on the local system, as shown in Figure 8-3. To make the network share available offline, right-click the shared folder and choose Properties from the shortcut menu. The Sharing tab has a Caching button that you can use to configure the offline file settings.

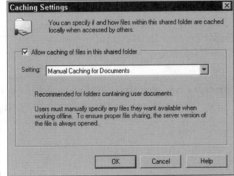

Figure 8-3:
Configuring
Offline Files.

The default cache size on the client is set to 10 percent of available disk space. You can change this setting by using the Default Cache Size Group Policy setting. You can also see how much space the cache is using by opening the Offline Files folder and choosing File⇨Properties.

Managing the Network Configuration

In addition to controlling the behavior of Offline Files using Group Policy, you can control your users' access and abilities regarding Network and Dial-up Connections. You configure these settings using the Network and Dial-up Connections node in Group Policy. This policy area is available under both Administrative Templates sections. Know the following settings for the exam:

- ✔ **Prohibit Deletions of RAS Connections:** This setting determines whether users can delete their private dial-up (RAS) connections. Private connections are those that are available only to one user. If you enable this policy, users (including administrators) cannot delete any RAS connections. This setting also disables the Delete option on the context menu for a RAS connection and on the File menu in Network and Dial-up Connections.

- ✔ **Prohibit Enabling/Disabling a RAS Connection:** This setting determines whether users can enable and disable local area connections. If you enable this policy, double-clicking the icon has no effect, and the Enable and Disable menu items are disabled. You should note that administrators can still enable and disable local area connections from Device Manager.

- ✔ **Prohibit Access to Properties of a LAN Connection:** Your users (even your users with administrative privileges) should not be nosing around in this Properties area because doing so just causes big-time trouble for you. This setting determines whether administrators can view and change the properties of a local area connection. If you enable this policy, the Properties menu items are disabled, and administrators cannot open the Local Area Connection Properties dialog box.

- ✔ **Prohibit Access to the Network Connection Wizard:** This setting determines whether users can use the Network Connection wizard, which creates new network connections. If you enable this policy, the Make New Connection icon does not appear in the Start menu or in the Network and Dial-up Connections folder. As a result, users cannot start the Network Connection wizard.

- ✔ **Prohibit TCP/IP Advanced Configuration:** This is another setting that typically saves you lots of time reconfiguring systems for your users. This setting locks them out of the Advanced TCP/IP settings area and thus saves you tons of trouble.

Securing the User Environment

Believe it or not, Group Policy also helps you to secure your Windows 2000 network. By importing security templates into Group Policy objects, you can easily standardize security settings across your entire network. To import a security template into a GPO, follow these steps:

1. **Access a template that contains the security settings you desire for your network, or create one.**

   For more information on creating and using security templates, see Chapter 15.

2. **In the Group Policy snap-in, expand the Computer Configuration and Windows Settings nodes, right-click the Security Settings node, and choose Import Policy, as shown in Figure 8-4.**

3. **In the Import Policy From dialog box, select the appropriate Security Template and click Open.**

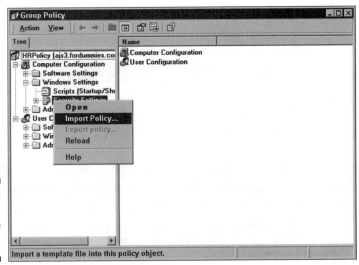

Figure 8-4:
Importing a
security
template.

Of course, you can also manually configure the security settings of the GPO. Simply double-click each security setting and select the state you want: Enabled, Disabled, or Not Configured.

Using Script Policies

You can use Group Policy objects to assign startup and shutdown scripts to computers, as well as logon and logoff scripts to users. As you might guess, you configure the startup and shutdown scripts in the Computer Configuration section of the Group Policy snap-in. You configure the logon and logoff scripts in the User Configuration section, as shown in Figure 8-5. You can assign multiple scripts for any of the startup/shutdown or logon/logoff events. The scripts are processed from top to bottom in each respective area.

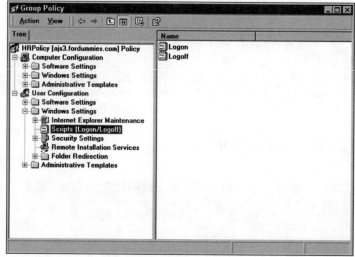

Figure 8-5:
Configuring
logon and
logoff
scripts.

Lab 8-2 walks you through the process of assigning logon scripts to users via
a Group Policy object.

Lab 8-2   Assigning a Logon Script

1. **Click Start⇨Programs⇨Administrative Tools⇨Active Directory Users
   and Computers.**

2. **Expand your domain in the console's left pane and then right-click the
   domain or OU that has a linked GPO for which you want to configure
   software settings.**

3. **Choose Properties from the shortcut menu and then click the Group
   Policy tab in the dialog box that's displayed.**

4. **Select the Group Policy object you want to configure and click the
   Edit button.**

5. **Expand the User Configuration node, the Windows Settings node, and
   then the Scripts node.**

6. **In the details pane, double-click the Logon icon.**

7. **In the Logon Properties dialog box, click Add.**

8. **In the Add a Script dialog box, set the options you want to use and
   then click OK:**

   • **Script Name:** Type the path to the script, or click Browse to search
   for the script file in the NETLOGON share of a domain controller.

- **Script Parameters:** Type any parameters you want to use, just as you would type them on the command line. For example, if your script included parameters called //logo (display banner) and //I (interactive mode), you would type the following:

```
//logo //I
```

9. **In the Logon Properties dialog box, specify any options you want to use:**

- **Logon Scripts for:** Lists all scripts currently assigned to the selected Group Policy object. If you assign multiple scripts, the scripts are processed according to the order you specify. To move a script up in the list, click it and then click Up; to move it down, click Down.

- **Add:** Opens the Add a Script dialog box, where you can specify any additional scripts to use.

- **Edit:** Opens the Edit Script dialog box, where you can modify script information such as name and parameters.

- **Remove:** Removes the selected script from the Logon Scripts list.

- **Show Files:** Enables you to view the script files stored in the selected Group Policy object.

10. **When you are finished configuring the Script dialog box, click OK.**

The default timeout value for script processing is ten minutes per script. You can change this configuration setting using Group Policy.

You have tremendous flexibility in the scripting language that you use with Windows 2000. Thanks in part to the default inclusion of the Windows Scripting Host, you may use VBScript, JScript, Perl, and MS-DOS batch files.

Prep Test

1 **How do you control the user environments in your Windows 2000 network? (Choose the best answer.)**

A ○ Imported Registry files

B ○ Administrative Templates of Group Policies

C ○ Computer Configuration of Group Policies

D ○ The Security Configuration and Analysis Tool

2 **Where do you configure the processing options of Group Policy for your Windows 2000 network?**

A ○ System

B ○ Network

C ○ Windows Components

D ○ Control Panel

3 **Your users complain that logging on to the network across WAN links takes a very long time. What should you do?**

A ○ Disable roaming user profiles.

B ○ Disable roaming user profiles across WAN links.

C ○ Disable Group Policy object processing.

D ○ Redirect the My Documents folder of the profile.

4 **What is the default cache size for Offline Files on a Windows 2000 client system?**

A ○ 10 percent of free disk space

B ○ 10 percent of total disk space

C ○ 5 percent of free disk space

D ○ 5 percent of total disk space

5 **How do you control the cache size for Offline Files on a Windows 2000 client system?**

A ○ Using an Administrative Templates setting

B ○ By configuring the properties of the network share

C ○ By modifying the Registry of the client

D ○ By installing the client using RIS

6 Brian wants medium security levels throughout his Windows 2000 network. What is the easiest way to ensure consistent security settings for the clients in his network?

A ○ Export a configured Registry and import it on the various systems.

B ○ Manually configure a Group Policy object for assignment to the systems.

C ○ Use SECEDIT to modify the settings on each system.

D ○ Import a security template into a GPO.

7 What is the default timeout period for script processing in Windows 2000?

A ○ 5 minutes

B ○ 10 minutes

C ○ 15 minutes

D ○ 20 minutes

8 You configure logon and logoff scripts as part of the _____ Configuration in a Group Policy object.

A ○ User

B ○ Computer

C ○ Network

D ○ System

9 Your users need to be able to access their working files even when they have no connection to the redirected My Documents location on the server. What should you do?

A ○ Enable roaming profiles.

B ○ Use disk-mirroring technology.

C ○ Enable Offline Files.

D ○ Configure the client systems with EFS.

10 Administrative Template GPO settings make changes to the Registries on local systems. The User Configuration section makes changes to which area of the Registry?

A ○ HKEY_LOCAL_MACHINE

B ○ HKEY_CURRENT_USER

C ○ HKEY_CURRENT_CONFIG

D ○ HKEY_USERS

Answers

1 **B.** Administrative Templates of Group Policies. Your primary mechanism for controlling and managing users' environments is the Administrative Templates section of Group Policy objects. *Review "Using Administrative Templates."*

2 **A.** System. You use the System node of Administrative Templates to control key Group Policy settings. *Study "Using Administrative Templates."*

3 **D.** Redirect the My Documents folder of the profile. You should always redirect the My Documents folder to ensure that users have their data available to them. By doing so, you can also dramatically improve the efficiency of roaming user profiles. *Review "Understanding Folder Redirection."*

4 **A.** 10 percent of free disk space. When you enable Offline Files behavior in your network, copies of network files are stored on the client in a cache. This cache size defaults to 10 percent of total free disk space. *See "Understanding Folder Redirection."*

5 **B.** By configuring the properties of the network share. To modify the caching behavior on clients, you can tweak the settings in the properties of the network share. *See "Understanding Folder Redirection."*

6 **D.** Import a security template into a GPO. You can use security templates to standardize the security settings of your Windows 2000 computers. You can easily import a security template into a Group Policy object. *See "Securing the User Environment."*

7 **B.** 10 minutes. You can configure logon, logoff, startup, and shutdown scripts in Windows 2000. For each of these areas, you can configure multiple scripts. The default script processing timeout value is 10 minutes. *Review "Using Script Policies."*

8 **A.** User. You configure logon and logoff scripts in the User Configuration section of a Group Policy object. *See "Using Script Policies."*

9 **C.** Enable Offline Files. When you enable Offline Files behavior in your network, copies of network files are stored on the client in a cache. This enables clients to access the files anytime. *See "Understanding Folder Redirection."*

10 **B.** HKEY_CURRENT_USER. Administrative Template settings of the User Configuration are stored in the HKEY_CURRENT_USER section of the Registry on the client. *Review "Using Administrative Templates."*

Chapter 9

Manage Software Using Group Policy: Now You See Word, Now You Don't

Exam Objectives

▶ Deploying software by using Group Policy

▶ Maintaining software by using Group Policy

▶ Configuring deployment options

▶ Troubleshooting common problems that occur during software deployment

*G*roup Policy objects (GPOs) provide an excellent means for distributing software in your Windows 2000 network. You can assign or publish applications to any of the Active Directory containers that Group Policy objects can be linked to: computers, domains, sites, or OUs. With GPOs, you can also maintain software applications and remove them if necessary. Once again, GPOs enable you to perform all these tasks from a central location!

For the exam, you must know how to deploy, maintain, and remove applications using Group Policy objects. This chapter completely prepares you by reviewing the following topics:

✔ Publishing or assigning software using GPOs

✔ Maintaining software using GPOs, including mandatory or optional upgrades or removals

✔ Configuring deployment options

✔ Troubleshooting deployments

Quick Assessment

Deploying
software by
using Group
Policy

Maintaining
software by
using Group
Policy

Configuring
deployment
options

Trouble-
shooting
common
problems
that occur
during
software
deployment

1 You want to have an application appear on the Start menu for a group of your users. You should _____ the application.

2 If you want to advertise an application in Control Panel's Add/Remove Programs applet, you should _____ the application.

3 Application maintenance includes _____ an application to the most current release.

4 When removing an application, you can choose to perform a(n) _____ removal or a(n) _____ removal.

5 You can create _____ for applications to organize their display in Add/Remove Programs.

6 Based on a file's _____, an appropriate application can be installed automatically when a user double-clicks that file.

7 You typically store the packages for software deployment in a software _____ point.

8 Software deployment using GPOs is made possible by the Windows _____ Service.

Answers

1 *Assign.* See "Deploying Software Using Group Policy."

2 *Publish.* Review "Deploying Software Using Group Policy."

3 *Upgrading.* Study "Maintaining Software Using Group Policy."

4 *Optional; Mandatory.* See "Maintaining Software Using Group Policy."

5 *Categories.* See "Reviewing Your Deployment Options."

6 *Extension.* See "Reviewing Your Deployment Options."

7 *Distribution.* See "Troubleshooting Common Deployment Problems."

8 *Installer.* See "Troubleshooting Common Deployment Problems."

Deploying Software Using Group Policy

You can deploy applications in your environment using *application assignment* or *application publishing*. When you assign applications, they automatically appear on the Start menu of a user's system. The installation occurs when the user selects the shortcut. Or, if you assigned the application using the Computer Configuration node, the application automatically installs upon the next reboot of the system.

When you publish applications, they appear in Control Panel's Add/Remove Programs applet, where they are available for installation by the user at any time.

With both the assignment and publishing methods, the application automatically installs if the user attempts to open a file associated with the application. You can change this default behavior, if necessary.

Do all these options seem a little confusing? Table 9-1 can help you keep all these deployment possibilities straight. By the way, you should memorize this table for the exam.

Table 9-1	Software Deployment Possibilities
Deployment Method	*Application Installed*
Publish	Via Add/Remove Programs
Assign (User Configuration)	From the Start menu
Assign (Computer Configuration)	Upon reboot

These features may seem truly remarkable, but it gets even better because all these options are completely configurable. You can easily create categories for the published applications in Add/Remove Programs, and you can easily configure which document types will launch the installation of the application. You can even customize the deployment of the application to specific areas of Active Directory to include specific settings. For example, custom dictionaries in a word processor could be deployed automatically to different areas of the world.

The Windows Installer Service enables you to deploy and manage software using Group Policy. This service contains two components: the Windows Installer service itself and a Windows Installer package. The Windows Installer service is a client-side service that automates the software installation service and maintains an existing installed application. A Windows

Installer package contains all the information needed to install or uninstall an application. This package consists of a Windows Installer file (.MSI) and any external source files needed to install or uninstall the application. Thanks to this Windows Installer technology, applications are resilient and can also be removed more cleanly than ever.

When I refer to *resilient applications,* I mean that the program you deploy actually can heal itself! If a critical file is deleted or is corrupt, the application automatically returns to the source files and replaces the missing or damaged file. Amazing!

Applications deployed using this technology can also be removed very *eloquently* — that is, they are uninstalled without leaving any files behind. These applications also uninstall without inadvertently breaking other applications.

Deploying software using Group Policy objects is a three-step process:

1. **Acquire or create a Windows Installer package file for the application.**

   Most applications designed for Windows 2000 come with multiple .MSI files designed for several different automated installation scenarios. If your application is pre-Windows 2000 or ships with no .MSI files, you can create your own using a third-party tool such as WinInstall Lite. You can find this tool in the Support directory on the Windows 2000 Server/ Advanced Server CD-ROM.

2. **Make available on your network the Windows Installer package file and any other files needed for installation.**

   You accomplish this task using a shared folder, of course. This shared folder is often referred to as your software distribution point.

3. **Create or configure a Group Policy object to deploy the application.**

   You can choose whether to assign or publish the application to either users or computers of a particular site, domain, or OU.

Reviewing Your Deployment Options

You can configure many options when you deploy software applications using Group Policy objects and Windows Installer packages. As I explain in the following section, you can configure some of these settings globally for all packages in a particular GPO by using the General tab in the Software Installation Properties dialog box, shown in Figure 9-1. You can also configure specific settings for individual packages using their respective package properties. (See "Automatic installation options," later in this chapter.)

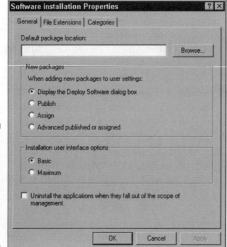

Figure 9-1:
The General
tab in the
Software
Installation
Properties
dialog box.

General settings

Lab 9-1 describes the steps for specifying certain defaults for all packages in
the GPO.

Lab 9-1	Specifying Software Installation Options

1. **Click Start⇨Programs⇨Administrative Tools⇨Active Directory Users
   and Computers.**

2. **Expand your domain in the left pane and then right-click the domain
   or OU that has a linked GPO for which you want to configure software
   settings.**

3. **Choose Properties from the shortcut menu and then click the Group
   Policy tab in the dialog box that's displayed.**

4. **Select the Group Policy object you want to configure and click the
   Edit button.**

5. **In the Group Policy snap-in, expand either the Computer or User
   Configuration node and double-click Software Settings to expand it.**

   This choice does have implications. For example, if you assign an application using the Computer Configuration node, the application is automatically installed the next time a system affected by the GPO is booted.
   You should also notice that you cannot publish applications using the
   Computer Configuration node.

6. **Right-click the Software Installation node and then choose Properties.**

7. **On the General tab in the Software Installation Properties dialog box (refer to Figure 9-1), type the full path to the default software distribution point for your Windows Installer package files in the Default Package Location field.**

Using this default location simplifies the process of configuring packages for deployment because Windows Installer knows just where to look for your package files each time you add a new package.

8. **Configure the remaining options on the General tab, as needed:**

   • **Display The Deploy Software Dialog Box:** With this option, you suppress the dialog box that displays each time you add a new package to the GPO. That dialog box asks if you want to publish or assign the application.

   • **Publish:** This option permits you to have packages published by default when you add them to the GPO. This option is not available when configuring defaults for the Computer Configuration node.

   • **Assign:** By choosing this option, you can have packages assigned by default when you add them to the GPO.

   • **Advanced Published Or Assigned:** This setting opens the Configure Package Properties dialog box, enabling you to configure additional settings.

   • **Basic:** This setting forces only a basic display of the application's installation process.

   • **Maximum:** With this setting, the user sees all messages and screens during the application's installation.

   • **Uninstall The Applications When They Fall Out Of The Scope Of Management:** This checkbox must have one of the longer titles in the history of Windows! This setting causes applications to automatically uninstall if the Group Policy object no longer applies to the user or computer. That's pretty nifty.

9. **Set options on the File Extensions and Categories tabs, as I explain in the following sections of this chapter.**

10. **Click OK to close the Software Installation Properties dialog box.**

Automatic installation options

You can have applications install automatically when a user double-clicks a file with a certain extension. By using the File Extensions tab in the Software Installation Properties dialog box, you can configure the extensions that trigger the installation and the priority of multiple file extensions, as shown in Figure 9-2.

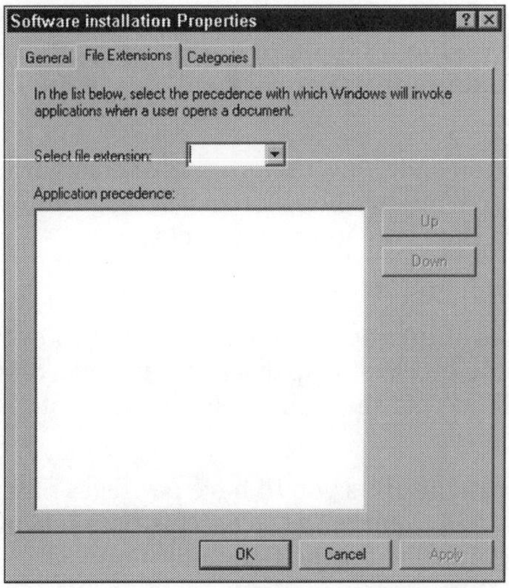

Software installation Properties ? X

General File Extensions Categories

In the list below, select the precedence with which Windows will invoke
applications when a user opens a document.

Select file extension: [▼]

Application precedence:

[   ]   [Up]
                           [Down]

[OK] [Cancel] [Apply]

Figure 9-2:
The File
Extensions
tab.

For example, Word and FrontPage both can edit .HTM files. If you create a
GPO for installing those applications, you need to decide which application
you want clients to install and use when they activate .HTM files. If you
decide on FrontPage for the client, you need to ensure that FrontPage is the
application of priority for .HTM files.

Application categories

You can help your users find published applications by creating categories in
which to display the applications in Control Panel's Add/Remove Programs
applet. By default, Windows 2000 does not provide any predefined software
categories. As you may have guessed, you configure these categories on the
Categories tab in the Software Installation Properties dialog box.

When you establish software categories in a Group Policy object, these settings take effect for the entire domain. Therefore, you need to define them
only once in your network.

Maintaining Software Using Group Policy

Your need to maintain software applications in your network may never
have been greater. Working in the IT industry means dealing with countless
patches, upgrades, and even the need for application removal. Fortunately,
Windows 2000's Group Policy features can simplify these software maintenance
tasks.

Upgrading applications

You can use your Group Policy objects to upgrade applications after you have deployed them using GPO technology. As Lab 9-2 demonstrates, upgrading applications with GPOs is simple to configure and saves you plenty of time and effort administering your Windows 2000 network.

Lab 9-2   Upgrading an Application

1. **Access the Group Policy snap-in that contains the application packages you have deployed in your network.**

2. **Select the Software Installation node.**

3. **In the right pane, right-click the Windows Installer package that is the upgrade package and choose Properties.**

   You are not selecting the package that is to be upgraded in this step.

4. **Select the Upgrades tab of the application's Properties dialog box and click Add.**

   In the resulting dialog box, you can add to the list of applications that are upgraded by this package.

5. **In the Add Upgrade Package dialog box, select either Current Group Policy Object or A Specific GPO, as shown in Figure 9-3. If you select the A Specific GPO option, click Browse and then select the GPO that contains the application to be upgraded.**

6. **After you select the correct GPO, select the package to upgrade.**

Figure 9-3:
The Add
Upgrade
Package
dialog box.

7. **Indicate how you want to handle the existing package and then click OK.**

   You have two options for dealing with the existing package:

   - Uninstall the Existing Package, Then Install the Upgrade Package

   - Package Can Upgrade Over the Existing Package

8. **On the Upgrades tab in the Properties dialog box, select the Required Upgrade For Existing Packages check box if you want to make the upgrade mandatory.**

9. **Click OK.**

Removing applications

Perhaps you decide that you no longer want to support a particular application in your network. Or perhaps clients in your network no longer use an application. In either case, the time has come to remove the application. Once again, GPOs to the rescue! Lab 9-3 shows how you remove applications.

Lab 9-3	Removing Applications

1. **Access the Group Policy snap-in for the GPO that contains the application package you want to uninstall.**

2. **Expand the Software Settings node and select the Software Installation node.**

3. **In the right pane, right-click the application you want to remove and choose All Tasks.**

4. **In the dialog box that's displayed, click Remove.**

   The Remove Software dialog box opens, as shown in Figure 9-4.

Figure 9-4:
Removing
an
application.

5. **Select one of the following removal options:**

   - **Immediately Uninstall The Software From Users And Computers:** Choosing this option ensures that the software is uninstalled immediately during the next reboot or logon.

- **Allow Users To Continue To Use The Software, But Prevent New Installations:** Choosing this option ensures that users can continue to use the application if they already have it installed. If they decide to remove the application, or if they have never installed it, no new installations of the package are permitted.

If you choose the Immediately Uninstall The Software From Users And Computers option, you are performing what is known as a *mandatory removal.* You perform an *optional removal* if you choose Allow Users To Continue To Use The Software, But Prevent New Installations.

6. **Click OK.**

Troubleshooting Common Deployment Problems

When troubleshooting application deployment or maintenance tasks, check Group Policy first. Verify that the underlying Group Policy configuration is correct and that a particular individual or computer experiences the desired results from the GPO that you have created. In many cases, a user or computer has not received the configuration you intended because the GPO does not actually affect the object. Remember the rules of inheritance and cumulative GPO effects when you are planning for application deployments in Active Directory.

With that said, you could go wrong in other areas with application deployment. Table 9-2 summarizes these other areas to assist you in your troubleshooting.

Table 9-2	Common Problems with Software Deployments and Maintenance
Symptom	*Solution*
Published applications do not appear in Control Panel	Ensure that your client is not a Terminal Services client.
Error message: `The feature you are trying to install cannot be found in the source directory`	Check your network for problems and ensure that the client has sufficient permissions on the application and the software distribution point.
After removal of an application, shortcuts still appear on desktop	Manually delete any shortcuts the user has created.

(continued)

Table 9-2 *(continued)*

Symptom	*Solution*
Error message: `Another Installation is Already in Progress`	Either an uninstall is processing in the background, or the user has attempted to launch two install processes simultaneously. Plan your deployments carefully so you never experience this error.
Launching a previously installed application starts the Windows Installer	This happens when the application is auto-repairing itself or adding new features. Do not stress out about this one — it is usually the desired behavior.
Error message: `Active Directory Will Not Allow this Package to be Deployed`	Check for a networking problem or a corrupt MSI package.

Prep Test

1 You want to install an application on a system in the Finance department the next time the system is rebooted. What should you do?

- **A** ○ Publish the application using the Computer Configuration.
- **B** ○ Assign the application using the Computer Configuration.
- **C** ○ Publish the application using the User Configuration.
- **D** ○ Assign the application using the User Configuration.

2 You want to install an application on systems in the Finance department if the users believe they need the application. What should you do?

- **A** ○ Publish the application using the Computer Configuration.
- **B** ○ Assign the application using the Computer Configuration.
- **C** ○ Publish the application using the User Configuration.
- **D** ○ Assign the application using the User Configuration.

3 You want an application to appear automatically on the Start menus of Accounting managers in your organization. What should you do?

- **A** ○ Publish the application using the Computer Configuration.
- **B** ○ Assign the application using the Computer Configuration.
- **C** ○ Publish the application using the User Configuration.
- **D** ○ Assign the application using the User Configuration.

4 What is the extension for a Windows Installer package in Windows 2000?

- **A** ○ MTI
- **B** ○ MSI
- **C** ○ EXE
- **D** ○ MEU

5 You want to create categories for your applications in Control Panel's Add/Remove Programs applet. How do you do this?

- **A** ○ Configure a GPO with the categories — one for the entire domain.
- **B** ○ Configure the categories in all GPOs in the network.
- **C** ○ You cannot configure categories.
- **D** ○ Configure the categories in the Add/Remove Programs application.

6 You need to remove an application from the Marketing department computers. You deployed the application using a Group Policy object. How should you remove the application?

A ○ Configure the GPO to remove the application.

B ○ Manually remove the application from the systems.

C ○ Export the appropriate Registry entries.

D ○ Use the Add/Remove Programs applet in Control Panel.

7 What is the first thing you should check if an application is not being deployed on a system as you had planned?

A ○ Ensure the application is being assigned.

B ○ Ensure the application is being published.

C ○ Ensure you have the correct permissions.

D ○ Ensure the GPO is being applied properly.

8 You want to upgrade an application that has been deployed in your network using a GPO. Before the installation of the upgrade, you want to uninstall the previous version. How should you do this?

A ○ Manually uninstall the previous version and then use the GPO to perform the upgrade.

B ○ Configure the GPO to uninstall the previous version and then install the new one.

C ○ Use the GPO to remove the previous version and manually install the upgrade.

D ○ Manually uninstall the previous version and manually install the upgrade.

9 How should you store your package files?

A ○ In a software distribution point

B ○ Locally on client systems

C ○ On the print server

D ○ In SYSVOL

10 You have removed an application from the systems in your Research department. You are dismayed to see shortcuts to the application on the desktops, however. What is the problem?

A ○ An uninstall using a GPO does not remove shortcuts.

B ○ Shortcuts created by users are not removed.

C ○ The application was not removed properly.

D ○ The GPO is not affecting the systems.

Answers

1 **B.** Assign the application using the Computer Configuration. Assigning the application using the Computer Configuration node causes the application to be installed upon the next reboot. *See "Reviewing Your Deployment Options."*

2 **C.** Publish the application using the User Configuration. Publishing the application will advertise it in Add/Remove Programs. You cannot publish applications using the Computer Configuration. Check out *"Reviewing Your Deployment Options."*

3 **D.** Assign the application using the User Configuration. Assigning the application makes it available on the Start menu. *See "Reviewing Your Deployment Options."*

4 **B.** MSI. The Windows Installer service in Windows 2000 uses the .MSI extension. You use these packages for software deployment using Group Policy objects. *See "Reviewing Your Deployment Options."*

5 **A.** Configure a GPO with the categories — one for the entire domain. You should configure categories for a single GPO only, because these settings are domainwide. *See "Application categories."*

6 **A.** Configure the GPO to remove the application. You can use Group Policy objects to remove applications that were deployed using the application deployment methods of Group Policy. *See "Removing applications."*

7 **D.** Ensure the GPO is being applied properly. When troubleshooting application deployments, first check whether a GPO is actually being applied to an entity. *Review "Troubleshooting Common Deployment Problems."*

8 **B.** Configure the GPO to uninstall the previous version and then install the new one. You can configure a GPO to perform upgrades of software packages. You can even have the GPO uninstall the previous version before installing the new version. *Study "Upgrading applications."*

9 **A.** In a software distribution point. You should create a software distribution point to store the package files used for automated deployments of software using Windows Installer service technology. *See "Reviewing Your Deployment Options."*

10 **B.** Shortcuts created by users are not removed. You can configure GPOs to remove software applications as well as install them. Keep in mind, however, that any shortcuts created by users will not be uninstalled. *Review "Troubleshooting Common Deployment Problems."*

Part V

Remote
Installation
Services

In this part . . .

Microsoft has taken great efforts to make deployment of Windows 2000 a simple matter for network administrators. In this part of the book, you take advantage of these efforts by reviewing a key new service in Windows 2000 called Remote Installation Services (RIS). RIS enables you to install Windows 2000 client systems from a central server. You can even accomplish this task without visiting the client system (provided you have the right hardware installed at the client).

In Chapter 10, you review the steps required to deploy client systems using RIS technology. In Chapter 11, you focus on securing your RIS environment to ensure that the convenience of this new service does not compromise the security of your network.

Chapter 10

Deploying Windows 2000 Using RIS: Presto!

Remote Installation Services (RIS) help you deploy Windows 2000 clients in your network. Thanks to RIS, you may not even have to visit the client system in order to carry out the installation! Simply connect the client system to the network, start the client system, and log on with a valid user account. After you accomplish these tasks, presto! Windows 2000 Professional installs using the configuration you desire.

For the exam, you need to know all about RIS. Most importantly, you need to fully understand the process of installing Windows 2000 Professional on client systems using the various options available to you with RIS. This chapter completely prepares you for this facet of the exam by covering the following topics:

✔ Understanding the RIS process

✔ Installing RIS images on clients

✔ Configuring the RIS server

✔ Managing your images

✔ Using RIS options

✔ Creating a RIS boot disk

✔ Troubleshooting RIS

Quick Assessment

Installing an image on a RIS client computer

1 If your client system does not have PXE technology installed, you should use a(n) _____ disk to start the RIS process.

2 The _____ imaging utility enables you to clone a sample client system.

Configuring remote installation options

3 You can configure how computer _____ and their names are generated during the RIS installation process.

4 You can have the client system account created in the same Active Directory location as the _____ account creating the system.

Managing images for performing remote installations

5 Part of managing your client images for RIS involves associating the appropriate _____ setup answer files.

6 You use the Add Installation _____ wizard to add a new client installation image.

Creating a RIS boot disk

7 Windows 2000 includes a boot disk creation utility called _____.

8 To use a boot disk, your computer must have a supported _____ adapter card installed.

Troubleshooting RIS problems

9 For multiple language installation image options, you need to replace the default WELCOME.OSC file with the _____ file.

10 Sometimes a backup of the RIS volume does not function properly when restored because of the _____ directory.

Answers

1   *Boot*. See "What Is RIS?"

2   *RIPrep*. Review "What Is RIS?"

3   *Accounts*. Study "Configuring RIS Options."

4   *User*. Study "Configuring RIS Options."

5   *Unattended*. Review "Managing Images."

6   *Image*. Study "Managing Images."

7   *RBFG.EXE*. See "Creating a RIS Boot Disk."

8   *Network*. Review "Creating a RIS Boot Disk."

9   *MULTILNG.OSC*. Study "Troubleshooting RIS."

10   *Single Instance Store (SIS)*. See "Troubleshooting RIS."

What Is RIS?

You may already know that Remote Installation Services enable you to easily install Windows 2000 client systems, but how does this technology actually work? And for that matter, exactly what can you do with it? This section answers those questions.

RIS relies upon Active Directory, DHCP, and DNS to provide the network infrastructure for its technology. Meanwhile, the client must support either Pre-Boot eXecution Environment (PXE) DHCP-based remote boot ROMs or a network card supported by a RIS boot disk. The client boots using one of these technologies and pulls the Windows 2000 installation from a RIS server. The client may pull either a standard CD-ROM type installation or an image of a preconfigured client desktop.

You can also use RIPrep to clone configured machines. By distributing a cloned image, you can distribute not only Windows 2000 Professional desktops, but also all the applications and configurations that a client might need. Talk about maximizing your weekend time!

Here's a quick rundown on how the RIS process works:

1. A RIS client boots up on the network and sends a request for DHCP and RIS services. A DHCP server responds with TCP/IP information for the client. Any available RIS server responds with its IP address and the name of the boot file needed by the client for use with that RIS server. The client is then prompted to press F12 to initiate service from the RIS computer.

2. The RIS server checks Active Directory for the existence of the client system requesting service. In this step, the RIS server is checking whether the system is prestaged. (A *prestaged* client is one that is prepared in advance for the RIS process.) This step adds security to the equation.

3. After the RIS server approves the client system, the Client Installation wizard is downloaded to the client computer. This wizard prompts the user to log on to the network.

4. RIS checks the user account used as logon against Active Directory. RIS uses the Group Policy settings that apply to the user to decide on the choice of images for installation and what other options the user might be able to use.

5. The user is presented with a list of the appropriate options and then asked to start the Remote OS Installation process.

If you plan to have your network users at the systems launching this installation, you can easily control all options in the Client Installation wizard that might get the users in trouble. In this way, you enable your users to help you implement the network!

Using RIS

Before you can take advantage of Remote Installation Services in your network, you must add and install RIS. Lab 10-1 describes the steps in this process.

Lab 10-1   Adding RIS

1. **Click Start⇨Settings⇨Control Panel.**

2. **Double-click the Add/Remove Programs icon to launch the applet shown in Figure 10-1.**

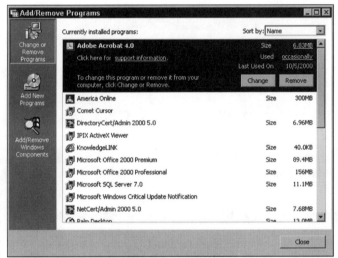

Figure 10-1:
The
Add/Remove
Programs
applet.

3. **Click the Add/Remove Windows Components button.**

4. **In the Windows Components Wizard dialog box, check the Remote Installation Services check box and click Next, as shown in Figure 10-2.**

5. **Insert the Windows 2000 Server CD-ROM when prompted so the wizard can load the necessary files.**

6. **On the Completing the Windows Components Wizard page, click Finish.**

7. **In the System Settings Change message box, click Yes to restart the server before completing the installation of RIS.**

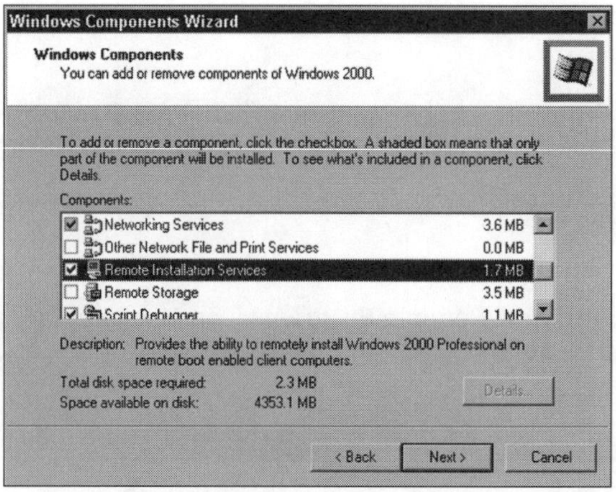

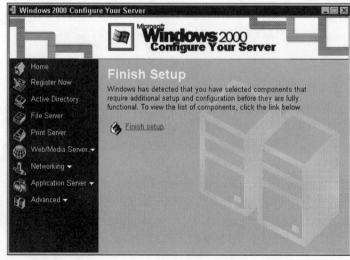

Figure 10-2:
The
Windows
Components
wizard.

After the system reboots, you can continue the installation and configuration of RIS in your Windows 2000 network, as I describe in Lab 10-2.

Lab 10-2   Configuring RIS

1. **Click Start➪Programs➪Administrative Tools➪Configure Your Server.**

2. **In the Configure Your Server dialog box, click Finish Setup, as shown in Figure 10-3.**

Figure 10-3:
Completing
the RIS
setup
process.

3. **In the Configure Remote Installation Services dialog box, click Configure to launch the Remote Installation Services Setup wizard.**

4. **In the Welcome to the Remote Installation Services Setup Wizard dialog box, click Next.**

5. **In the Remote Installation Services Setup wizard, complete the following information:**

   • **Remote Installation Folder Location:** Enter the drive and directory where you want to install Remote Installation Services, as shown in Figure 10-4. The drive should be dedicated to the RIS server and contain enough space to store as many client images as you plan to host with this server. At a minimum, you need a 4GB drive or partition.

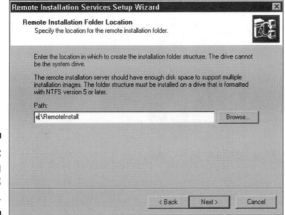

Figure 10-4:
Configuring
the RIS
drive.

   • **Windows 2000 Professional Source Path:** Enter the location of the Windows 2000 Professional files. This path can be the Windows 2000 Professional CD or the network share that contains the installation files.

   • **Friendly Description and Help Text:** Enter the friendly description for the client computer installation. This description will be displayed to users or clients of this server. Help text is used to describe the operating system installation choice to users or clients of Remote Installation Services.

6. **Click Finish to complete the wizard.**

After you complete this wizard, you can configure the available RIS options, as I describe in the following section. Then, you can begin deploying Windows 2000 Professional in your environment.

Configuring RIS Options

You should set the properties on your RIS servers so they respond to the requests of clients in the exact manner you want. Use the Active Directory Users and Computers console to access the properties of the RIS server, as shown in Figure 10-5.

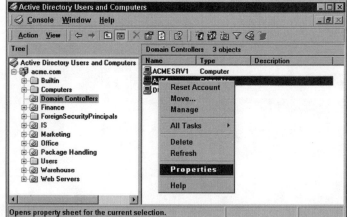

Figure 10-5: Accessing the properties for your RIS server.

In the RIS server's Properties dialog box, select the Remote Install tab, as shown in Figure 10-6. On this tab, you can set the following options, which you should know for the exam:

- ✔ **Respond To Client Computers Requesting Service:** By selecting this check box, you enable the RIS computer to respond to client requests.

- ✔ **Do Not Respond To Unknown Client Computers:** You use this check box to ensure that the RIS server responds only to client computers you have specified for use with RIS. Chapter 11 covers this option in greater detail.

By clicking the Advanced Settings button on the Remote Install tab, you access the following options, all of which may be fodder for exam questions:

- ✔ **Generate Client Computer Names Using:** This option enables you to specify the way in which RIS creates computer names for the newly installed systems.

- ✔ **Customize:** By clicking this button, you can create your own custom computer name creation procedure.

- ✔ **Client Account Location:** This setting enables you to specify exactly where in Active Directory the new computer account is created. As shown in Figure 10-7, you have the following options: Default Directory Service Location, Same Location As That Of The User Setting Up The Client Computer, and Use The Following Directory Service Location.

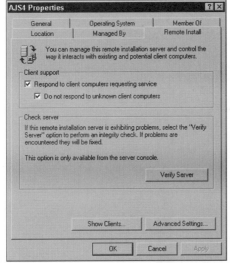

Figure 10-6:
The Remote
Install tab in
your
server's
Properties
dialog box.

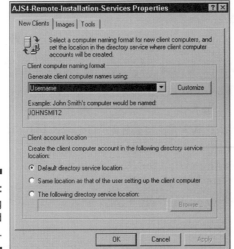

Figure 10-7:
Configuring
advanced
RIS options.

Managing Images

You create images using the RIPrep utility, which you find in the
RemoteInstall directory on the RIS server. You can create several images for
as many Windows 2000 Professional configurations as you need for your network. A single RIS server can host as many of these images as disk space
allows.

As shown in Figure 10-8, you use the Images tab in the Remote Installation Services Properties dialog box to add additional images to a particular server. Lab 10-3 walks you through the steps.

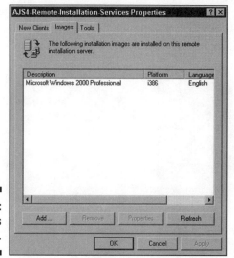

Figure 10-8:
The Images tab.

Lab 10-3   Adding a New Client Operating System Installation Image

1. **Click Start➪Programs➪Administrative Tools➪Active Directory Users and Computers.**

2. **In the console tree, right-click the applicable remote installation server.**

3. **Choose Properties and then click the Remote Install tab in the Properties dialog box that's displayed.**

4. **Click Advanced Settings and then click the Images tab.**

5. **Click Add to start the Add wizard.**

6. **Select Add a New Installation Image and then click Next to start the Remote Installation Setup wizard.**

7. **Click Next and then type the location of the Windows 2000 Professional installation files.**

   The location can be either a CD or network share.

8. **Enter the friendly description and help text and then click Next.**

9. **Review the installation summary and then click Finish.**

Creating a RIS Boot Disk

If your client computer does not contain a boot-enabled ROM, you can create a RIS boot disk to save the day. The boot disk uses the floppy disk drive to simulate the PXE boot process and pulls the client operating system from the remote installation server.

Figure 10-9 shows the Windows 2000 boot disk creation utility, named RBFG.EXE. You can find this program in *Server name**Share name*\ REMINST\Admin\I386\.

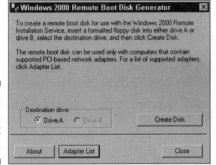

Figure 10-9:
Creating a
RIS boot
disk.

Lab 10-4 walks you through the steps for creating this disk.

Lab 10-4   Creating a RIS Boot Disk

1. **Click Start⇨Run.**

2. **Type the path of the RBFG.EXE utility (for example, *servername*\ REMINST\Admin\I386\RBFG.EXE) and then click OK.**

3. **Insert a formatted disk into the disk drive.**

4. **Click the Destination drive option and then click Create Disk.**

5. **Click Close when the disk is ready and then remove the disk from the drive.**

Troubleshooting RIS

Quite a bit could go wrong for you with Remote Installation Services. In this section, I cover some of the more common problems you could encounter.

Of course, you should be familiar with these problems and solutions for the exam:

- ✔ **You have command settings that are not being processed during an unattended installation.** Ensure that you are using the correct directory information if you are using the `OemPreinstall = yes` setting in a SIF file.

  These SIF (System Information) files store the configuration settings for the installation image. The information contained in the .SIF file is processed each time a client computer chooses the installation image using the Client Installation wizard. By modifying the .SIF file for the installation image, you can predetermine the configuration settings for each client installation image. For example, if all your client computers have the same type of display device, you can set the screen resolution prior to installation by modifying the [Display] information in the .SIF file.

- ✔ **Language choice options are not displayed during a client installation session.** For multiple language installations, you need to replace WELCOME.OSC with MULTILNG.OSC. Multiple language installations are often utilized in large multinational RIS implementations.

- ✔ **Following the restore of a RIS backup, RIS no longer works.** Ensure that your backup program restored the SIS (Single Instance Store) directory. Remote Installation Services cannot function properly without this directory. By providing a single location for storing files that RIS needs, the SIS directory saves space on the RIS server.

Prep Test

1 In order for RIS to function properly, you must have which of the following services configured correctly in your network? Choose all that apply.

  A ❑ DHCP

  B ❑ Active Directory

  C ❑ DNS

  D ❑ WINS

2 Your client systems do not support Pre-Boot eXecution Environment (PXE) DHCP-based remote boot ROMs. You still want to take advantage of RIS. What should you do?

  A ○ Replace all the client systems.

  B ○ Use a RIS boot disk.

  C ○ Use a DHCP solution.

  D ○ Use WINS.

3 You want to distribute Windows 2000 Professional systems throughout your network. In addition to Windows 2000 Professional, these systems should also have Microsoft Office and Adobe Photoshop installed on them. What should you do?

  A ○ Use RIS to deploy Windows 2000 Professional and then manually install the applications.

  B ○ Use RIS to deploy the applications and then manually install Windows 2000 Professional.

  C ○ Use RIS to deploy Windows 2000 Professional and use unattended installation scripts to install the applications.

  D ○ Use RIPrep to create an image of the desired client configuration and then deploy the image using RIS.

4 A RIS client in your Windows 2000 network obtains its TCP/IP configuration information from which type of server?

  A ○ DNS

  B ○ RIS

  C ○ DHCP

  D ○ DC

5 Your boss is concerned that using RIS in your network to deploy Windows 2000 Professional will dramatically jeopardize security. How should you respond?

A ○ Agree with your boss no matter what.

B ○ Indicate that you agree in most cases.

C ○ Indicate that this is correct but only in the default configuration.

D ○ Indicate that security can be maintained thanks to client system prestaging and user authorization.

6 During the installation of RIS, you should be prepared to ensure that you have enough disk space available for the RIS server. What is the recommendation from Microsoft?

A ○ At least 200MB of free space

B ○ At least a 4GB drive dedicated to RIS

C ○ At least 1GB of free space

D ○ At least 2GB of free space

7 You want to ensure that RIS does not respond to client systems that are not specified for Windows 2000 Professional installations in your network. What should you do?

A ○ Use a more secure alternative for client deployments.

B ○ Authorize the RIS server in Active Directory.

C ○ Authorize the clients in Active Directory.

D ○ Use the Do Not Respond To Unknown Client Computers option.

8 Allison wants to use a RIS boot disk to install Windows 2000 Professional on a client system in her network using RIS. Which statement is true?

A ○ The network card in the client must be supported by the boot disk utility.

B ○ She must have a Pre-Boot eXecution Environment (PXE) DHCP-based remote boot ROM.

C ○ The client system must be a BOOTP device.

D ○ She cannot install an image on the client, only a CD-ROM based installation.

9 You have restored RIS from a backup you had taken last week. You have restored this RIS backup and now you are dismayed to learn that RIS is no longer functioning properly. What is the most likely cause?

A ○ You did not restore the SIS directory properly.

B ○ You cannot restore a RIS installation from backup.

C ○ You did not use the Backup program found in Windows 2000 Server.

D ○ RIS was not functioning properly to begin with.

10 You want to deploy several different configurations of Windows 2000 Professional in your network. Each configuration will feature different installed applications. You are interested in using as little hardware for RIS as possible. What should you do?

A ○ Create a RIS server for each image you want to deploy.

B ○ Add these additional images to a single RIS server.

C ○ Use existing Windows 2000 Professional systems as alternate RIS servers.

D ○ Use a Windows 2000 Clustering solution.

Answers

1 **A, B,** and **C.** DHCP, Active Directory, DNS. RIS is not a very independent service at all. This service relies on DHCP, Active Directory, and DNS. All these additional services must be properly configured in order for RIS to function. *Review "What Is RIS?"*

2 **B.** Use a RIS boot disk. If your network card does not support Pre-Boot eXecution Environment (PXE) DHCP-based remote boot ROMs, you can boot the system to take advantage of RIS using a boot disk. RIS in Windows 2000 includes a boot disk-making utility. *See "Creating a RIS Boot Disk."*

3 **D.** Use RIPrep to create an image of the desired client configuration and then deploy the image using RIS. You should build a client system that has the proper configuration and required applications installed. You should then clone that system using RIPrep for deployment using RIS. *Study "Managing Images."*

4 **C.** DHCP. A client in the RIS process receives its TCP/IP configuration from a DHCP server. *See "What Is RIS?"*

5 **D.** Indicate that security can be maintained thanks to client system prestaging and user authorization. RIS has mechanisms built in to the process that provide for security. Systems can be prestaged in the process, and user credentials are checked for installations, making the process quite secure. *See "Configuring RIS Options."*

6 **B.** At least a 4GB drive dedicated to RIS. Microsoft recommends that you dedicate an entire hard drive for RIS. This drive should have at least 4GB of free space. *See "Using RIS."*

7 **D.** Use the Do Not Respond To Unknown Client Computers option. This check box ensures that RIS does not respond to clients that have not been prestaged in Active Directory. *See "Configuring RIS Options."*

8 **A.** The network card in the client must be supported by the boot disk utility. You have to make sure that your network card is one that is supported by the boot disk utility. See the Windows 2000 Help for a list of supported cards. *See "Creating a RIS Boot Disk."*

9 **A.** You did not restore the SIS directory properly. A frequent problem with the restoration of RIS backups is an improper restoral of the SIS directory, which renders RIS inoperative. *Review "Troubleshooting RIS."*

10 **B.** Add these additional images to a single RIS server. A single RIS server can host multiple images for client deployments. You add these images via the properties sheet for the RIS server. *Review "Managing Images."*

Chapter 11

Configuring RIS Security: Halt, Who Goes There?

. . . .

Exam Objectives

▶ Authorizing a RIS server

▶ Granting computer account creation rights

▶ Prestaging RIS client computers for added security and load balancing

. . . .

*S*ecurity is an important consideration in any network environment —
especially one that uses Remote Installation Services. You certainly do
not want users (or computer criminals) installing Windows 2000 Professional
systems as they see fit, or creating their own RIS servers in your network.
Fortunately, the RIS process includes built-in security mechanisms. You just
need to know how to configure them.

The exam strongly emphasizes the security components of Remote
Installation Services. This chapter helps you get ready for the exam by covering the following topics:

    ✔ Authorizing RIS servers

    ✔ Setting permissions on images

    ✔ Setting permissions for creating computer accounts

    ✔ Prestaging client systems

Quick Assessment

Authorizing a RIS server

1 An unauthorized RIS server is known as a(n) _____ server.

2 To authorize a RIS server, you use the _____ console.

Granting computer account creation rights

3 The _____ of Control wizard offers a simple means for granting users the ability to create computer accounts in Active Directory.

4 You can quickly refresh Group Policy by using the _____ utility.

Prestaging RIS client computers for added security and load balancing

5 When you prestage a client computer, you create a(n) _____ within Active Directory.

6 To prestage a computer, you need to know a unique identifier for that computer known as the _____.

Answers

1   *Rogue*. See "Authorizing a RIS Server."

2   *DHCP*. See "Authorizing a RIS Server."

3   *Delegation*. Review "Assigning Appropriate Rights and Permissions."

4   *SECEDIT*. Study "Assigning Appropriate Rights and Permissions."

5   *CAO*. Review "Prestaging Clients."

6   *GUID*. Review "Prestaging Clients."

Authorizing a RIS Server

You need to make sure that you set up the only RIS servers running in your network. You do not want unauthorized persons building their own Windows 2000 Professional systems without your knowledge. You will often hear these unauthorized RIS servers referred to as *rogue* servers.

Fortunately, Windows 2000 prevents the creation of rogue RIS servers. You (as a domain administrator) must authorize all RIS servers in the network. If an unauthorized RIS server attempts to start, Windows 2000 automatically shuts it down — a very cool feature, indeed.

As I explain in Lab 11-1, you perform RIS server authorization by using the DHCP server management console. You use this console to authorize both DHCP and RIS servers on your network.

Lab 11-1   Authorizing Your RIS Server

1. **Click Start⇨Programs⇨Administrative Tools⇨DHCP.**

2. **Right-click the DHCP node in the console's left pane and choose Manage Authorized Servers, as shown in Figure 11-1.**

3. **In the Manage Authorized Servers dialog box, shown in Figure 11-2, click Authorize.**

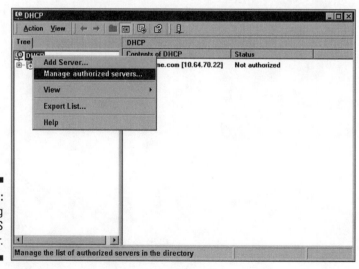

Figure 11-1: Authorizing a RIS server.

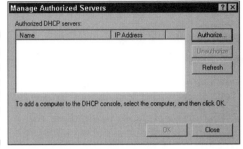

Figure 11-2:
The
Manage
Authorized
Servers
dialog box.

4. **In the Authorize DHCP Server dialog box, type the name or IP address of the RIS server you want to authorize and click OK.**

5. **In the DHCP message box, click Yes.**

6. **In the Manage Authorized Servers dialog box, select the RIS server and click OK.**

   Your RIS server is now authorized to respond to clients.

Assigning Appropriate Rights and Permissions

To enhance the security of your RIS environment, you must set the appropriate permissions and rights that relate to the RIS objects. For example, to ensure that your authorized personnel can add computers to your network, you must assign them the appropriate rights. This is one of several RIS security-related areas in which you must demonstrate proficiency for the exam. This section fully covers all these areas.

Setting permissions on your RIS images

You should definitely assign NTFS permission levels to the RIPrep images on your RIS server. By default, when you add a new image, it is available to all clients in the network — a less than secure situation. For greater control over the manner in which deployments get carried out, you set permissions to control access to your RIS images. For example, assume that you want to make the ITSalesAdministrators group responsible for the deployment of new Windows 2000 Professional Sales desktops. Only this group should have permissions for the applicable image on the RIS server. No other group in your network should use that RIS image.

Lab 11-2 describes the steps for setting permissions on RIS images.

Lab 11-2   Setting Permissions on RIS Images

1. **Click Start➪Programs➪Accessories➪Windows Explorer.**

2. **Right-click the \RemoteInstall\Setup*language*\Images\\
   image_name\i386\Templates folder and choose Properties.**

   This is the default installation location for RIS images. Your location may
   differ depending on the options you chose during installation.

3. **In the folder's Properties dialog box, click the Security tab, as shown
   in Figure 11-3.**

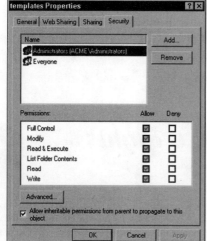

Figure 11-3:
Setting
security on
the
Templates
folder.

4. **Set the appropriate permissions for the group that needs to access the
   image and then click OK.**

By default, the Everyone group has Full Control permissions — certainly a
bad thing from a security perspective. You definitely want to remove this
group from the security list.

As is always the case when you set permissions in Windows 2000, you should
assign permissions to groups and not individual user accounts. Doing so
helps to reduce your administrative workload. As more users need the same
set of permissions, you can simply add their user accounts to the appropriate group.

Setting permissions for creating computer accounts

To install a client by using RIS, your users must have the appropriate rights and permissions assigned to their accounts so they can create a computer account in Active Directory. Lab 11-3 explains the steps for implementing this security measure.

Lab 11-3   Granting Users the Create Computer Rights

1. **Click Start➪Programs➪Administrative Tools➪Active Directory Users and Computers.**

2. **In the left pane of the AD Users and Computers console, right-click your domain and then choose Delegate Control.**

   This command launches the Delegation of Control wizard.

3. **Click Next in the Welcome to the Delegation of Control Wizard dialog box.**

   The Delegation of Control wizard simplifies the process of assigning rights to users or groups. You should use it whenever possible.

4. **In the wizard's Users Or Groups dialog box, click Add.**

5. **In the Select User, Computers, Or Groups dialog box, select the group for which you need to assign permissions and then click OK.**

6. **Click Next.**

7. **In the Tasks to Delegate dialog box, click Delegate The Following Common Tasks.**

8. **Select Join A Computer To The Domain and then click Next.**

   Figure 11-4 shows the Tasks to Delegate dialog box.

9. **Click Finish.**

Often, you want to assign these permissions on an OU-by-OU basis. To assign permissions in this way, you should rely on an old friend: Group Policy. Lab 11-4 reviews the steps for granting the Create Computer right to the members of an OU.

Lab 11-4   Granting Users the Create Computer Right for OUs

1. **Click Start➪Programs➪Administrative Tools➪Active Directory Users and Computers.**

2. **Right-click the applicable OU in the console's left pane and then choose Properties.**

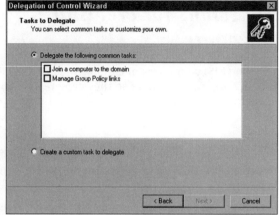

Figure 11-4:
Using the
Delegation
of Control
wizard.

3. **In the Properties dialog box, click the Group Policy tab.**

4. **Select the appropriate Group Policy object and click the Edit button.**

5. **In the Group Policy snap-in, expand Computer Configuration, Windows Settings, Security Settings, and Local Policies. Finally, click User Rights Assignment, as shown in Figure 11-5.**

6. **In the console's right-hand pane, double-click the Add Workstations To Domain policy.**

7. **In the Security Policy Setting dialog box, click Add.**

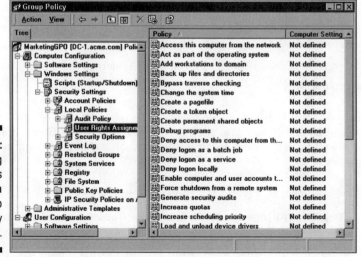

Figure 11-5:
Configuring
user rights
using a
Group
Policy
object.

8. **In the Add User Or Group dialog box, specify the users or group to which you need to assign the right and then click OK.**

9. **In the Security Policy Setting dialog box, click OK.**

10. **Close the Group Policy snap-in.**

In many cases, when you assign rights to users using the Group Policy method, you want the Group Policy settings to apply right away. Otherwise, you will have failed installation attempts on your hands. You can easily refresh Group Policy settings in your network by using the SECEDIT utility, as shown in Figure 11-6. At the command prompt, simply type the following command:

```
secedit /refreshpolicy machine_policy
```

Then, restart your computer.

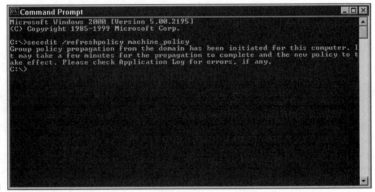

Figure 11-6:
Using
SECEDIT to
refresh
Group
Policy.

Prestaging Clients

To provide the highest degree of security possible with Remote Installation Services, you should prestage your client systems. When you prestage, you create a valid Computer Account Object (CAO) in Active Directory. When you configure your RIS server with Do Not Respond To Unknown Client Computers, RIS requires that this prestaging process has occurred. You must create the CAOs in order to permit RIS installations.

Prestaging enables you to define a computer name for the new installation, and you can specify which RIS server will service the client requests. By doing so, you can load-balance between RIS servers and control network traffic due to RIS.

If you plan to have users help you create these prestaged systems, you must provide them with the adequate permissions to do so. Lab 11-5 describes the necessary steps.

Lab 11-5   Setting Permissions for Prestaging

1. Click Start⇨Programs⇨Administrative Tools⇨Active Directory Users and Computers.

2. Choose View⇨Users, Groups, and Computers as Containers. Then, choose View⇨Advanced Features.

3. In the console's left pane, right-click the applicable computer account and choose Properties.

4. In the Properties dialog box, click the Security tab and then click Add.

5. Add the appropriate users or groups and click OK.

6. In the Properties dialog box, select the appropriate user or group.

7. In the Permissions area, select the Read, Write, Change Password, and Reset Password permissions and then click OK.

After you set the appropriate user permissions for creating prestaged systems, you can prestage your clients. Fortunately, the process is a simple one.

To prestage a computer, you define the computer in Active Directory using the Active Directory Users and Computers console. You must provide the Globally Unique Identifier (GUID) of the system. For most client computers that are PC98 or Net PC–compliant, you can find the GUID in the computer's system BIOS. You also may find the GUID on the outside of the computer case. If you cannot find the GUID of a client in these locations, you can use a packet sniffer such as Network Monitor to capture DHCP traffic and examine a DHCPDiscover packet sent by the client. You will find the GUID in the DHCPDiscover packet.

Lab 11-6 lists the steps for prestaging a client.

Lab 11-6   Prestaging a Client

1. Click Start⇨Programs⇨Administrative Tools⇨Active Directory Users and Computers.

2. In the console's left pane, right-click the OU for which you want to prestage a client and then choose New⇨Computer.

3. In the New Object - Computer dialog box, type the client computer name, select the user or group that is to join the computer to the domain, and then click Next, as shown in Figure 11-7.

The Allow Pre-Windows 2000 Computers To Use This Account check box is not a relevant setting for your RIS-based CAO. You would only use this option in a mixed network environment.

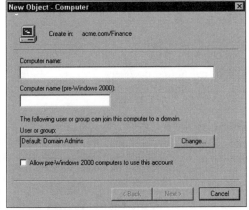

Figure 11-7:
Creating a
new CAO.

4. **In the Managed dialog box, select This Is A Managed Computer, type the GUID for the system in the Computers Unique ID field, and then click Next.**

5. **In the Host Server dialog box, select the Remote Installation server that you want to respond to the client and then click Next.**

6. **Click Finish.**

Prestaging is critical for maintaining security in your RIS environment, and you can plan on seeing related exam questions!

Prep Test

1 You want to ensure that users from the Sales department can only install their appropriate image file from the Remote Installation server. What should you do?

A ○ Prestage the client systems.

B ○ Create the appropriate RIS boot disks.

C ○ Set appropriate permissions on the image files.

D ○ Authorize the RIS server.

2 You are attempting to use RIS in your Windows 2000 network to install Windows 2000 client systems. You are booting the client systems using boot disks because these systems do not support PXE technologies. When you attempt the installation, the client systems cannot find the RIS server. You can see the RIS server on the network using My Network Places. What should you do?

A ○ Check the physical network connectivity between the clients and the RIS server.

B ○ Ensure that the RIS server has been authorized.

C ○ Install PXE-enabled network cards in the systems.

D ○ Reboot the RIS server.

3 How can you find the GUID of a client system? Choose all that apply.

A ❑ Analyze a DHCPDiscover packet from each client using Network Monitor.

B ❑ Check the properties of My Computer.

C ❑ Examine the system BIOS.

D ❑ Look in the Registry.

4 You want to ensure that your RIS server provides services only to prestaged systems. What should you do?

A ○ Authorize the RIS server.

B ○ Set permissions on the RIS server.

C ○ Only allow the RIS server to be accessed interactively.

D ○ Configure the RIS server with the Do Not Respond To Unknown Client Computers setting.

5 How can you easily permit several users in your network to create Windows 2000 Professional systems using RIS?

A ○ Use the Delegation of Control wizard to assign the appropriate permissions.

B ○ Add the users to the Power Users group.

C ○ Add the users to the Domain Admins group.

D ○ Add the users to the Enterprise Admin group.

6 You want to control the amount of traffic in your network due to Remote Installation Services. What should help you control traffic?

A ○ Authorizing your RIS servers

B ○ Using DHCP in your network

C ○ Prestaging client systems

D ○ Adding more powerful routers to your network

7 You want to ensure that client systems on the third floor of your office complex only request Remote Installation Services functions from a RIS server also located on the third floor. What should you do?

A ○ Define the RIS server in the appropriate subnet object.

B ○ Prestage the client systems.

C ○ Modify the Registries of the client systems.

D ○ Use boot disks to boot the clients.

8 You need to authorize your RIS server in Active Directory. Which administrative console should you use?

A ○ Configure Your Server

B ○ Active Directory Users and Computers

C ○ DNS

D ○ DHCP

9 Prestaging a client system involves which of the following tasks?

A ○ Creating a valid CAO in Active Directory

B ○ Authorizing the RIS server

C ○ Creating an organizational unit

D ○ Configuring permissions on the RIS server

10 You have permitted a group of users to create computer accounts in OUs using a Group Policy object. The users complain that they cannot use RIS to create the Windows 2000 Professional systems. You suspect that the problem involves the need to refresh Group Policy. Which utility can help you?

A ○ NTDSUTIL

B ○ GPRESULT

C ○ SECEDIT

D ○ REPLMON

Answers

1 **C.** Set appropriate permissions on the image files. You can control which users can install specific images by setting permissions on the image files. *Review "Assigning Appropriate Rights and Permissions."*

2 **B.** Ensure that the RIS server has been authorized. To prevent rogue RIS servers in your network, you must authorize your approved RIS systems in Active Directory. *Study "Authorizing a RIS Server."*

3 **A** and **C.** Analyze a DHCPDiscover packet from each client using Network Monitor; Examine the system BIOS. The GUID is sometimes printed on the machine case. If not, check the system BIOS or use a network "sniffer" to analyze DHCPDiscover packets. *See "Prestaging Clients."*

4 **D.** Configure the RIS server with the Do Not Respond To Unknown Client Computers setting. During the prestaging process, you must ensure that your system is configured to respond only to known clients. This is a simple check box setting in the system properties. *See "Prestaging Clients."*

5 **A.** Use the Delegation of Control wizard to assign the appropriate permissions. Whenever possible, you should use the Delegation of Control wizard for the assignment of permissions in Active Directory. *Review "Assigning Appropriate Rights and Permissions."*

6 **C.** Prestaging client systems. Prestaging systems helps with security and enables you to control which clients request services from specified RIS servers. *See "Prestaging Clients."*

7 **B.** Prestage the client systems. Thanks to prestaging, you can assign specific RIS clients to specific RIS servers. *See "Prestaging Clients."*

8 **D.** DHCP. You use the DHCP console to authorize DHCP servers as well as RIS servers. *See "Authorizing a RIS Server."*

9 **A.** Creating a valid CAO in Active Directory. The whole idea behind prestaging is creating a CAO in Active Directory. *See "Prestaging Clients."*

10 **C.** SECEDIT. You can use SECEDIT to refresh Group Policy objects in your Windows 2000 network. *Review "Assigning Appropriate Rights and Permissions."*

Part VI
Managing and Optimizing ADS

The 5th Wave   By Rich Tennant

"This part of the test tells us whether you're personally suited to the job of network administrator."

In this part . . .

*T*he chapters in this part of the book cover the tasks you must engage in to manage and optimize Active Directory Services. Here, you focus on managing the Active Directory objects, tuning ADS, and configuring replication of Active Directory information throughout your network. These tasks play important roles in the success of your Active Directory experience, and you will see plenty of exam questions on the topics that I cover in this part of the book.

In Chapter 12, you study the management tasks you typically perform with Active Directory objects, such as publishing and locating resources in Active Directory. In Chapter 13, you review steps for tuning ADS performance. In Chapter 14, you review all the aspects of replication in a Windows 2000 Active Directory setting.

Chapter 12

Managing Active Directory Objects

*M*aintaining an efficient, secure network that gives your users easy access to the tools and information they need poses a complex challenge. Fortunately, Windows 2000 and Active Directory simplify the management tasks that face network administrators. These tasks include moving Active Directory objects within a domain or between domains, searching for objects in Active Directory, and creating and managing user accounts.

You must know how to manage Active Directory objects for the exam. To help you prepare for exam questions involving management of Active Directory objects, this chapter reviews the following topics:

    ✔ Moving Active Directory objects within a domain and between domains

    ✔ Publishing file resources and printers in Active Directory

    ✔ Viewing published network services

    ✔ Locating objects in Active Directory

    ✔ Creating and managing user accounts

    ✔ Setting Active Directory permissions

    ✔ Delegating administrative control in Active Directory

Quick Assessment

1 You use the _____ command line utility to move Active Directory objects between domains in Windows 2000.

2 As you migrate users from one domain to another, the user accounts get new _____.

3 By assigning _____ to published resources, you help users find those resources.

4 The Find dialog box in Active Directory helps you create _____ queries.

5 You can create user accounts in Windows 2000 using JScript or _____.

6 You use the Active Directory _____ console to create new user accounts.

7 You use _____ groups to assign permissions in Windows 2000.

8 Use the _____ Features menu item to view security settings on Active Directory objects.

9 You should use the _____ wizard to assist in delegation.

10 Delegating control in your Active Directory network is key in a(n) _____ administrative model.

Answers

1 *MOVETREE*. Review "Moving Objects in Active Directory."

2 *SIDs*. See "Moving Objects in Active Directory."

3 *Keywords*. See "Publishing Resources."

4 *LDAP*. Study "Locating Resources."

5 *VBScript*. Review "Creating and Managing Accounts."

6 *Users and Computers*. Study "Creating and Managing Accounts."

7 *Security*. Review "Controlling Access to Resources."

8 *Advanced*. See "Controlling Access to Resources."

9 *Delegation of Control*. See "Delegating Administrative Control."

10 *Decentralized*. Review "Delegating Administrative Control."

Moving Objects in Active Directory

Moving objects around in Active Directory may involve moving objects from one location to another within a domain, or you might have to move objects from one domain to another. You need to know the details associated with either operation for the exam. Fortunately, you just need to remember some simple rules.

Moving objects within a domain

Moving objects within a domain is a simple process: Just right-click the object and choose Move, as shown in Figure 12-1. Windows 2000 displays a dialog box in which you simply choose the destination container object for the move. (In future versions of Windows 2000, you will be able to drag and drop Active Directory objects from one OU to another.)

A real-world example of moving an object within a domain involves moving a user account from one OU to another when the user transfers from one department to another in your organization. Moving the user's account enables the user to receive the benefits and restrictions you have defined for the new OU.

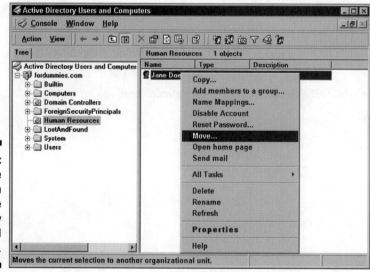

Figure 12-1:
The Move option in Active Directory Users and Computers.

What is not as straightforward (and what you need to know for the exam) is the effect that moving objects has on permissions. Here are the rules you must know:

✔ Permissions you assign directly to an Active Directory object remain with the object after you move the object.

✔ The object inherits the permissions assigned to the new OU and loses any previously inherited permissions.

You may have already figured this one out: An excellent strategy for administering Active Directory objects is to move objects that need similar permission settings into the same OU. By doing so, you can easily manage your network, assigning permissions and delegating authority effectively with just a few mouse clicks.

Moving objects between domains

In a multiple-domain Windows 2000 forest, you may need to move objects (users, organizational units, groups) between these multiple domains. You use the MOVETREE command line utility to perform many of these operations.

When you move users and groups to a new domain, they receive new security identifiers (SIDs). Fortunately, Windows 2000 running in native mode supports an attribute called SIDHistory. As you move a user from domain to domain, Windows 2000 populates SIDHistory so you do not have to reset permissions to objects each time you perform the move operation.

MOVETREE assists you with most move operations between domains. And in those cases for which MOVETREE cannot do the job, you can turn to another utility called NETDOM. MOVETREE can

✔ Move most Active Directory objects (including nonempty containers) from one domain to another in the same forest.

✔ Move domain local and global groups between domains. These groups cannot contain members, however. The domains must exist within the same forest.

✔ Move universal groups and their members between domains of the same forest.

MOVETREE can move *most* Active Directory objects. Those that it cannot move when you try to relocate groups of objects become *orphaned.* Windows 2000 places these orphaned objects in a special container called LostAndFound. You can view this container by using the Advanced View feature of Active Directory Users and Computers. (You can review the Advanced View feature of Active Directory Users and Computers in Chapter 10.)

You must have the appropriate administrative permissions to use MOVETREE from the command prompt. This command uses the following syntax:

```
MOVETREE {/start | /startnocheck | /continue | /check} /s
        SrcDSA /d DstDSA /sdn SrcDN /ddn DstDN [/u
        [Domain\]Username /p Password] [/verbose] [{/? |
        /help}]
```

The italicized entries in this syntax represent information you must provide. Table 12-1 describes the switches you can use with the MOVETREE command.

Table 12-1	MOVETREE Command Switches
Switch	**What It Does**
/start	Initiates the move operation
/startnocheck	Starts a MOVETREE operation with no /check
/continue	Continues the execution of a previously paused or failed MOVETREE operation
/check	Performs a test run of the MOVETREE operation
/s *SrcDSA*	Specifies the source server's fully qualified domain name (FQDN)
/d *DstDSA*	Specifies the destination server's FQDN
/sdn *SrcDN*	Specifies the distinguished name of the object you are moving from the source
/ddn *DstDN*	Specifies the distinguished name of the object you are moving to the destination
/u	Runs MOVETREE under the credentials of the username and password provided
/verbose	Causes MOVETREE to display more details as it runs
/?	Displays help about MOVETREE

MOVETREE creates log files when operations are performed. You can check these log files for information regarding the success or failure of MOVETREE events:

✔ **MOVETREE.ERR:** Lists any errors encountered.

✔ **MOVETREE.LOG:** Lists statistical results of the operation.

✔ **MOVETREE.CHK:** Lists any errors detected from MOVETREE being executed in check mode.

MOVETREE moves computer objects from one domain to another for you, but it cannot disjoin the computer from the source domain and join it to the target domain. This limitation makes NETDOM a much better utility for moving computers between domains in a Windows 2000 Active Directory setting.

NETDOM uses the following syntax to move computer accounts:

```
MOVETREE {/NETDOM move /D:domain [/OU:ou_path] [/Ud:User
            /Pd:{Password|*}] [/Uo:User /Po:{Password|*}]
            [/Reboot:[time_in_seconds]]
```

Table 12-2 describes the switches you use with the NETDOM command.

Table 12-2	NETDOM Command Switches
Switch	*What It Does*
/domain	Identifies the target domain
/OU:*ou_path*	Specifies the target OU
/Ud:*User*	Indicates the user account used to make the connection with the target domain
Pd:{*Password*|*}	Enters the password for the user account used to connect to the destination domain; if you use *, NETDOM prompts for the password
/Uo:*User*	Identifies the user account used to make the connection to the source domain
/Po:{*Password*|*}	Enters the password for the user account used to connect to the original domain; if you use *, NETDOM prompts for the password
/Reboot:[*time_in_seconds*]	Specifies that the computer being moved should shut down and reboot automatically in the given number of seconds after the move operation

Publishing Resources

By publishing resources in Active Directory, you advertise their availability to groups of users on the network. Thanks to this resource publication, users can easily find network resources that they need to access. This is a much-needed enhancement to the old browser services of previous NT versions. You can even use descriptions and keywords when publishing resources, making them even easier to find.

Publishing shared folders

If you have a shared folder that many users need to access, you should publish the shared folder in Active Directory. You complete this simple process using the Active Directory Users and Computers console, as Lab 12-1 demonstrates.

Lab 12-1	Publishing a Shared Folder

1. **Click Start➪Programs➪Administrative Tools➪Active Directory Users and Computers.**

2. **Expand your domain in the console's left pane.**

3. **Right-click the organizational unit in which you want to publish the shared folder and then choose New➪Shared Folder.**

   As shown in Figure 12-2, the AD Users and Computers snap-in displays the New Object - Shared Folder dialog box.

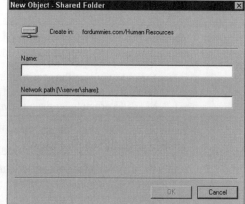

Figure 12-2:
Creating a
shared
folder object
in Active
Directory.

4. **Enter a name for the published share.**

5. **Type the UNC path to the shared folder in the Network Path field and then click OK.**

Publishing shared printers

When you create and share a printer on a Windows 2000 Server participating in a Windows 2000 Active Directory domain, the printer is automatically published in Active Directory. You can control this default behavior using the List In The Directory check box, which you find on the Sharing tab in the printer's

Properties dialog box, as shown in Figure 12-3. By default, the check box is selected, which causes the automatic publishing behavior. If you do not want a specific printer published, simply uncheck this box.

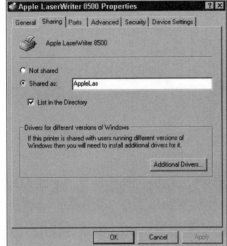

Figure 12-3:
Controlling
the publish-
ing of a
shared
printer.

However, the publishing of printers shared on previous Windows NT systems requires more involvement on your part. These printers are not automatically published in Active Directory. Fortunately, publishing these shared printers in Active Directory is just as easy as publishing folder shares. Lab 12-2 describes the process.

Lab 12-2   Publishing a Pre-Windows 2000 Shared Printer

1. **Click Start➪Programs➪Administrative Tools➪Active Directory Users and Computers.**

2. **Expand your domain in the console's left pane.**

3. **Right-click the OU in which you want to publish the shared printer and then choose New➪Printer.**

4. **In the New Object - Printer dialog box, type the printer share's network path and click OK.**

To view published printers in Active Directory, you must modify the default view in the Active Directory Users and Computers console. By choosing View➪Users, Groups, and Computers as Containers, you can view your Active Directory printer objects, as shown in Figure 12-4. Note that you only have to do this to view your Windows 2000 printer shares. You can see any printers shared via early Windows versions without making the change to the Active Directory Users and Computers console view.

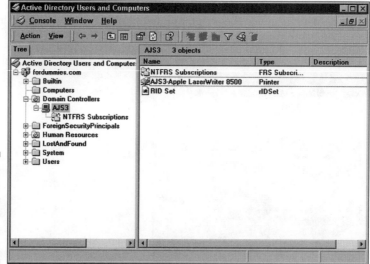

Figure 12-4:
Viewing a
printer
object in
Active
Directory.

Viewing published network services

Network-enabled services (for example, certificate services) are also automatically published in your Active Directory forest. These services are published in the directory so other administrators can find them using Active
Directory Sites and Services. Because the services are published in this way,
administrators can focus on managing a service regardless of which computer provides the service or where the computer is physically located in the
network.

Service information that is published in Active Directory should be useful to
many clients throughout your network and should not change frequently.
Microsoft takes care of this for you with most services.

Lab 12-3 describes the steps for viewing published network services.

Lab 12-3	Viewing Published Network Services

1. **Click Start➪Programs➪Administrative Tools➪Active Directory Sites
   and Services.**

2. **In the console's left pane, select Active Directory Sites and Services.**

3. **Choose View➪Show Service Node.**

4. **Expand the Services node now visible in the Active Directory Sites
   and Services console.**

5. **Expand the Public Key Services node to view the published network
   services of this category, as shown in Figure 12-5.**

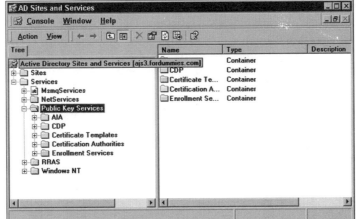

Figure 12-5:
Viewing the
published
services in
Active
Directory.

Locating Resources

You (and your users) can easily and efficiently find resources in Active
Directory by using the very handy Find dialog box shown in Figure 12-6. This
nifty Windows 2000 interface component generates Lightweight Directory
Access Protocol (LDAP) queries for you and poses them to the global catalog
server(s) in your network. The global catalog is a partial replica of the key
Active Directory objects for which users frequently search. Lab 12-4 reviews
the steps for using the Find dialog box.

Figure 12-6:
The Find
dialog box in
Active
Directory.

Lab 12-4	Finding Objects in Active Directory

1. **Click Start➪Programs➪Administrative Tools➪Active Directory Users
   and Computers.**

2. **Right-click your domain in the console's left-hand pane and choose
   Find.**

3. **Specify what you want to find, using the various options available in the Find dialog box:**

   - **Find:** Provides a list of objects for which you can search, including users, computers, printers, and shared folders. The Find criteria change based upon the object for which you are searching. For example, if you are searching for Users, Contacts, and Groups, you can search on Name and Description criteria. If you are searching for Printers, you can search on Name, Location, or Model, to name a few.

   - **In:** Enables you to specify where you want to search. You can search the entire Active Directory, a specific domain, or an OU.

   - **Advanced:** Enables you to define a wide variety of search criteria to help you find objects. The contents of this tab change depending on the object for which you are searching.

By choosing View➪Filter Options, you can tell the Active Directory Users and Computers console to display only certain types of objects. This command becomes increasingly useful as the number of Active Directory objects in your forest continues to grow.

Creating and Managing Accounts

Windows 2000 Active Directory certainly shines in the area of user account management, greatly simplifying the processes of creating and managing accounts.

Creating accounts

You can create user accounts in Windows 2000 Active Directory by using a simple wizard in the Active Directory Users and Computers console, or you can use more automated methods. These automated methods include VBScripts or JScripts executed against the Windows Scripting Host. Also, Windows 2000 includes two utilities — LDIFDE and CSVDE — that permit the importing of accounts in LDAP or comma-separated file formats. For more information on using scripts to create user accounts, visit http://msdn.microsoft.com. For more information on LDIFDE or CSVDE, use the Windows 2000 help system.

Lab 12-5 describes the wizard-based procedure for creating a user account.

Lab 12-5   Creating a User Account

1. **Click Start⇨Programs⇨Administrative Tools⇨Active Directory Users and Computers.**

2. **Expand your domain in the console's left-hand pane.**

3. **Right-click the organizational unit in which you want to create a user account and choose New⇨User.**

   Windows 2000 opens the New Object - User dialog box, as shown in Figure 12-7.

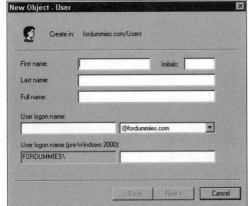

Figure 12-7:
Creating a
new user
account.

4. **Type the user's first name.**

5. **Type the user's initials.**

6. **Type the user's last name.**

7. **Modify the full name, as desired.**

8. **In the User Logon Name field, type the name you want the user to log on with and, from the drop-down list, click the User Principle Name (UPN) suffix that must be appended to the user logon name (following the @ symbol).**

9. **If the user is to log on with a different name from computers running Windows NT or Windows 9x, enter that user logon name in the User Logon Name (Pre-Windows 2000) field.**

10. **Click Next.**

11. **In the Password and Confirm password fields, type the user's password.**

12. **Select the appropriate password options and then click Next.**

13. **After reviewing the options you configured in the wizard, click Finish.**

Configuring the new user account

To configure additional properties of a user account, right-click the account and choose Properties from the shortcut menu. You can also copy an account to save time when creating additional accounts that share similar properties.

Each Active Directory user account has various security-related options that you should understand for the certification exam. These options determine how Windows 2000 authenticates someone who is logging on to the network. Figure 12-8 shows several reasonably self-explanatory options that are specific to passwords:

- ✔ User Must Change Password At Next Logon
- ✔ User Cannot Change Password
- ✔ Password Never Expires
- ✔ Store Passwords Using Reversible Encryption

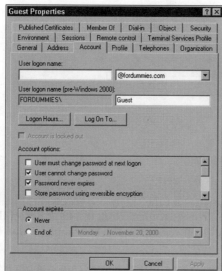

Figure 12-8:
Some user account options.

Use the Store Passwords Using Reversible Encryption option if you have users logging on to your Windows 2000 network from Apple Macintosh computers.

The Account Disabled option prevents users from logging on with the selected account. Use disabled accounts as templates for common user accounts that you create using the copy command, as I describe earlier in this section.

You can use the remaining options to configure security-specific information for Active Directory user accounts:

- Smart Card Required For Interactive Logon
- Account Is Trusted For Delegation
- Account Is Sensitive And Cannot Be Delegated
- Use DES Encryption Types For This Account
- Don't Require Kerberos Preauthentication

Use the Smart Card Required For Interactive Logon option to securely store public and private keys, passwords, and other types of personal information for the user account. To use this option, you must have a smart-card reader attached to the user's computer, and the user must have a personal identification number (PIN) to log on to your network.

By using the Account Is Trusted For Delegation option, you enable a user to assign responsibility for management and administration of a portion of the domain namespace to another user, group, or organization.

Use the Account Is Sensitive And Cannot Be Delegated option if you do not want the account delegated for management to another account.

Select the Don't Require Kerberos Preauthentication option if the account uses another implementation of the Kerberos protocol.

Finally, select the Use DES Encryption Types For This Account option if you need the Data Encryption Standard (DES). DES supports multiple levels of encryption, including MPPE Standard (40-bit), MPPE Standard (56-bit), MPPE Strong (128-bit), IPSec DES (40-bit), IPSec 56-bit DES, and IPSec Triple DES (3DES).

Managing accounts with groups

Instead of assigning permissions to individual user accounts, you can increase your efficiency by using Windows 2000 security groups to assign rights and permissions to user accounts.

Active Directory has three types of groups: domain local, global, and universal. Universal groups are available only in native mode, however.

Use the following strategy for assigning permissions to resources in Windows 2000:

1. **Group your users into global groups.**

   Typically, you group users according to job function. For example, create an AccountingManagers group to gather your accounting managers.

2. **If you have multiple domains, with similar global groups in more than one domain, gather multiple global groups and place them into a universal group.**

   For example, if you have accounting managers in each of several domains, gather those multiple global groups and place them into a universal group.

3. **Create a domain local group in the domain that has the resource for which you need to assign permissions.**

4. **Grant the appropriate permissions to the domain local group. Place global groups or universal groups inside the domain local group, as necessary.**

In a native-mode domain, you can also take advantage of group nesting. Group nesting enables you to place global groups inside other global groups, or domain local groups inside other domain local groups. Use nesting sparingly, however, because it can make your network much more complex than it needs to be. Microsoft recommends only one level of nesting.

Windows 2000 provides you with built-in groups. Use these built-in groups whenever possible in Windows 2000 Active Directory. For the exam, you should know the built-in domain local groups and their capabilities, as I describe in Table 12-3.

Table 12-3	Built-In Domain Local Groups
Group	*What Members Can Do*
Account Operators	Create, delete, and modify users and groups
Administrators	Perform all administrative tasks on the domain
Backup Operators	Back up and restore all servers using Windows Backup
Guests	Perform only tasks for which you have granted rights
Pre-Windows 2000 Compatible Access	Access NT 4 Remote Access Services (RAS) servers (provided for backward compatibility in mixed-mode environments)

Group	What Members Can Do
Print Operators	Set up and manage network printers
Replicator	Support Active Directory replication functions
Server Operators	Share disk resources and back up and restore files
Users	Perform only tasks for which you have granted rights

A user that belongs to multiple groups (global groups, of course) experiences the cumulative effect of all the permissions received from the various group memberships. Take the following example:

Group Memberships and Permissions for John Doe	
Global Group Name	*Permissions Resulting from Group Membership*
SalesManagers	Full Control
SalesAdvisors	Read
Managers	Change

Thanks to the cumulative permissions, John Doe enjoys Full Control over the resource. Take John Doe out of the Managers group, and he still gets Full Control because he still gets the cumulative effect from his membership in the SalesManagers and SalesAdvisors groups.

In an interesting exception to this rule, if John Doe belongs to a global group that has been explicitly denied access to the resource, John Doe gets no access, regardless of the permissions for any other groups to which he belongs!

Controlling Access to Resources

For controlling access to Windows 2000 Active Directory objects, rather than reinvent the wheel, Microsoft simply developed a system almost identical to the NTFS (New Technology File System) method for protecting files and folders.

The term *granular* is an important one for describing the control you have over access to Windows 2000 Active Directory objects. You have a high level of control over exactly what gets permissions and you can assign a wide variety of permissions.

You can assign permissions to an OU, a hierarchy of OUs, or a single object. Permission types vary appropriately based on the type of object you are securing. For example, you can grant the Reset Password permission to one of your assistants for all the users in a OU. On the other hand, of course, you will find no such thing as a Reset Password permission for a Printer object.

You assign standard and special permissions to Active Directory objects. Table 12-4 describes the standard permissions.

Table 12-4	Standard Object Permissions
Permission	*Permits the User to . . .*
Full Control	Use all standard permissions, change permissions, and take ownership of objects
Read	View objects and their attributes, including permissions
Write	Change object attributes
Create All Child Objects	Add any type of child object to an OU
Delete All Child Objects	Remove any type of object from an OU

Special permissions include the standard set and a whole host of additional settings, as you can see in Figure 12-9. These special permissions give you more granular control over object access. These special permissions include

✔ List Contents

✔ Delete Subtree

✔ Read Permissions

✔ Modify Permissions

✔ Modify Owner

✔ Create User Objects

✔ Delete User Objects

And this is just to name a few! For the exam, realize that you should strive to use the standard permissions whenever possible because doing so simplifies administration.

As Lab 12-6 shows, you can easily set permissions by using the Active Directory Users and Computers console. As you review in the next section of this chapter, however, the Delegation of Control wizard offers the simplest means for making these assignments. (See "Delegating Administrative Control," later in this chapter.) Use it whenever possible.

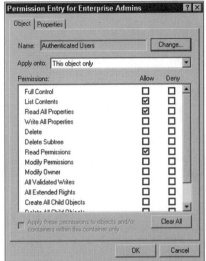

Figure 12-9:
Special per-
missions in
Active
Directory.

Lab 12-6   Assigning Permissions for an Active Directory Object

1. **Click Start⇨Programs⇨Administrative Tools⇨Active Directory Users and Computers.**

2. **Open the console's View menu and ensure that Advanced Features is selected.**

3. **Right-click an object and choose Properties.**

4. **Use the settings on the Security tab in the Properties dialog box to add groups and allow or deny permissions.**

5. **To view and select special permissions, click the Advanced button on this tab.**

6. **Click OK twice to close the Access Control Settings and Properties dialog boxes.**

Like Group Policy objects in Active Directory, permissions set on Active Directory containers (OUs, for example) automatically flow down to child objects through a process known as *inheritance*. If necessary, you prevent inheritance of permissions by turning off the Allow Inheritable Permissions From Parent To Propagate To This Object option. You control this setting with a check box on the Security tab in the object's Properties dialog box, as shown in Figure 12-10. If you prevent inheritance, Windows 2000 gives you the choice of keeping any previously inherited permissions or pitching them. Once again, nice flexibility.

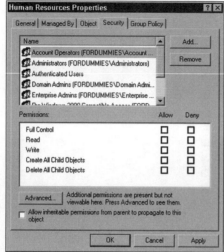

Figure 12-10:
Blocking
permission
inheritance.

For the exam, and in "real life," you should use the blocking of policy inheritance only sparingly. Design your Active Directory structure so you do not have to block policy inheritance frequently. Overuse of this feature can slow down your Windows 2000 network and make troubleshooting permissions issues a real pain.

Each object in Active Directory has an owner. By default, any user that creates an object in Active Directory is the owner of that object. That user has full control over the object and can also control the permissions assigned to the object.

Domain administrators have a unique capability in Windows 2000: As a domain administrator, you can take ownership of any object in the Active Directory. You click the Advanced button on the Security tab to open the Access Control Settings dialog box. This dialog box enables you to take ownership of an object. Although you can take ownership of any object in Active Directory, you cannot transfer ownership. Also realize that Windows 2000 tracks these ownership changes. An Owner field associated with the object stores the SID of the object's owner.

Delegating Administrative Control

You certainly have enough to do as a Windows 2000 administrator, and you may need to have staff members assist you in managing the network. On the other hand, you certainly do not want to give them full-blown administrative privileges, especially if some of these "assistants" are non-IT personnel.

Windows 2000 ADS provides a solution to this dilemma with the Delegation of Control wizard. This wizard magically sets permissions for you on Active Directory objects. Using the Delegation of Control wizard, you can delegate the following tasks to a user:

- ✔ Changing properties of OUs
- ✔ Creating, modifying, or deleting objects of a particular type in a specific OU
- ✔ Modifying select properties on particular objects in a specific OU

Lab 12-7 spells out the steps for delegating administrative control.

Lab 12-7	Delegating Administrative Control

1. **Click Start⇨Programs⇨Administrative Tools⇨Active Directory Users and Computers.**

2. **Right-click a container object in the console's left pane and choose Delegate Control.**

3. **In the Delegation of Control wizard, click Next.**

4. **In the wizard's Users and Computers dialog box, use the Add button to select users, groups, or computers to which you want to delegate control. Click Next.**

5. **In the Tasks to Delegate dialog box, select the tasks you want to delegate, or create your own custom tasks.**

   As shown in Figure 12-11, the common tasks are

   - **Create, delete, and manage user accounts:** Allows for creation and deletion of accounts, as well as the modification of account properties.

   - **Reset passwords on user accounts:** Enables the user to reset passwords for all user accounts located in a particular OU.

   - **Read all user information:** Enables the user to read all attributes of objects in a particular OU.

   - **Create, delete, and manage groups:** Enables the user to create, delete, and modify the attributes of groups located in a particular OU.

   - **Modify the membership of a group:** Enables the user to change the membership of groups in a particular OU.

   - **Manage Group Policy links:** Enables the user to add, delete, or modify the Group Policy links of a particular OU.

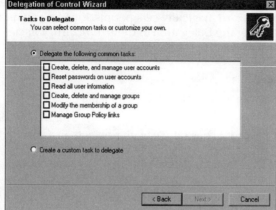

Figure 12-11:
Using the
Delegation
of Control
wizard.

6. **Click Next.**

7. **Click Finish to complete the wizard.**

Of course, you should delegate authority with care. If possible, delegate at the OU level, and document everything you do. Remember, you're the one responsible for how all this delegation ultimately works out! You should also delegate permissions to groups whenever possible. By doing so, you can dramatically ease your administrative burden.

Prep Test

1 You have moved a printer object from one OU to another in your Active Directory implementation. What happens to the permissions that you assigned for this object?

A ○ They are removed.

B ○ They are retained.

C ○ They revert to Full Control for the owner of the destination OU.

D ○ They revert to Full Control for the owner of the source OU.

2 You have moved a printer object from one OU to another in your Active Directory implementation. What happens to the permissions for the object? Choose two.

A ❑ The permissions you set on the printer object are retained.

B ❑ The permissions you set on the printer object are removed.

C ❑ The printer inherits new permissions from the destination OU.

D ❑ The printer retains permissions inherited from the source OU.

3 You need to move a computer from one domain to another in your Active Directory forest. You want to accomplish this task with the least administrative work possible. What should you do?

A ○ Use the NETDOM utility.

B ○ Use the MOVETREE utility.

C ○ Use the NTDSUTIL utility.

D ○ Recreate the user account in the new domain.

4 What objects in Active Directory can you move from one domain to another with the MOVETREE utility? Choose all that apply.

A ❑ Universal groups and their members

B ❑ Computer accounts

C ❑ Domain local groups and their members

D ❑ Global groups and their members

5 You have installed a printer on Windows 2000 Server in your Active Directory domain. You want to publish this printer in Active Directory. What should you do?

A ○ Create a Printer object for the printer using the Active Directory Users and Computers console.

B ○ Create a Printer object for the printer using the Active Directory Sites and Services console.

C ○ Create a Printer object for the printer using the NTDSUTIL utility.

D ○ Do nothing.

6 You do not want a specific printer published in Active Directory. The printer is attached to a Windows 2000 Server in the domain. What should you do?

A ○ Do nothing.

B ○ Clear the List In The Directory checkbox to eliminate the printer publishing.

C ○ Do nothing. Printers are forced to be published in this scenario and cannot be removed.

D ○ Remove the printer using the Active Directory Users and Computers console.

7 You need to prevent a specific user from having access to a resource in your network. You remove the user from the Managers group. This group has Full Control permission on the resource. Much to your surprise, the user still has access. What is the most likely problem?

A ○ The user is a member of the Administrators group.

B ○ The user is a member of another group that has permissions on the resource.

C ○ The user created the resource.

D ○ The use is the manager of the resource.

8 You need to give a user access to a particular resource in your Windows 2000 Active Directory domain. You have placed the user account in the Managers group. This group has Full Control for the resource. Oddly enough, the user cannot access the resource. What is the problem?

A ○ The user is not a member of the Administrators group.

B ○ The user has a corrupt profile.

C ○ The user is a member of a group that has been explicitly denied access to the resource.

D ○ The user account has an old access token.

9 You want to have one of your peers assist you in managing your Windows 2000 domain. Specifically, you want this individual to be able to create user accounts for you in the Accounting OU. What should you do?

A ○ Place the user in the Domain Admins group.

B ○ Place the user in the Power Users group.

C ○ Use the Active Directory Users and Computers console to manually assign the appropriate permissions.

D ○ Use the Delegation of Control wizard to assign the permissions.

10 A user has left your company but your server still has a folder that only the former employee has permissions to view. What should you do as the administrator of the domain?

A ○ Delete the folder.

B ○ Take ownership of the folder and change the permissions.

C ○ Use the EFS system to read the folder's contents.

D ○ Remove the Read Only attribute from the folder.

Answers

1 **B.** They are retained. Permissions that you specifically assign to an Active Directory object are retained when you move the object in Active Directory. *Study "Moving Objects in Active Directory."*

2 **A and C.** The permissions you set on the printer object are retained, The printer inherits new permissions from the destination OU. You can move an object in Active Directory, and the object retains the permissions that you specifically assigned. Note that the object does inherit the new permissions assigned to the parent container. *Study "Moving Objects in Active Directory."*

3 **A.** Use the NETDOM utility. Both NETDOM and MOVETREE can move computers from one domain to another. You should use NETDOM, however, because it can have the system actually join the new domain. *Review "Moving Objects in Active Directory."*

4 **A and B.** Universal groups and their members, Computer accounts. MOVETREE can move most Active Directory Objects (including nonempty containers) from one domain to another in the same forest. It can also move domain local and global groups between domains, and universal groups and their members between domains of the same forest. *Review "Moving Objects in Active Directory."*

5 **D.** Do nothing. Windows 2000 print shares are automatically published in Active Directory. *See "Publishing Resources."*

6 **B.** Clear the List In The Directory checkbox to eliminate the printer publishing. To avoid having a Windows 2000 shared printer published in Active Directory, you can use the List In The Directory checkbox in the shared printer's properties. *See "Publishing Resources."*

7 **B.** The user is a member of another group that has permissions on the resource. Remember that permissions are cumulative for users that belong to multiple Windows 2000 security groups. *Review "Creating and Managing Accounts."*

8 **C.** The user is a member of a group that has been explicitly denied access to the resource. If a user account is a member of a group that has been explicitly denied access to a particular resource, the user does not get access to the resource regardless of other group memberships. This is an important exception to the cumulative permissions rule. *Review "Managing accounts with groups."*

9 **D.** Use the Delegation of Control wizard to assign the permissions. You should use the Delegation of Control wizard to assign permissions at the OU level whenever possible in your network. Be sure to document your changes carefully. *See "Delegating Administrative Control."*

10 **B.** Take ownership of the folder and change the permissions. As an administrator, you can always take ownership of a resource in Windows 2000. *Review "Controlling Access to Resources."*

Managing Active Directory Objects

Chapter 13

Managing Active Directory Performance: Time to Tune the Server

Exam Objectives

▶ Monitoring, maintaining, and troubleshooting domain controller performance

▶ Monitoring, maintaining, and troubleshooting Active Directory components

*Y*ou should be very attentive to the performance of the domain controllers in your network. Fortunately, Windows 2000 provides many built-in tools to ensure that you can successfully monitor and maintain your systems. In addition to monitoring your domain controllers, you should monitor and maintain the Active Directory database itself. Again, Windows 2000 provides many tools to help you with this task. This chapter covers the methods and tools you use to monitor both the server and the database components.

For the exam, you need to know all about monitoring and maintaining the server and the Active Directory database. This chapter reviews all you need to know, including

✔ Using Performance Monitor

✔ Using System Monitor and Event Viewer

✔ Moving the Active Directory database

✔ Defragmenting the Active Directory database

Quick Assessment

Monitoring, maintaining, and trouble-shooting domain controller performance

1 The _____ log contains errors, warnings, or information generated by applications.

2 The _____ performance object contains many counters that report on Active Directory performance.

3 You use the _____ Monitor to view graphs regarding Active Directory's performance.

4 You can create _____ to notify you of potential Active Directory performance issues that are developing.

Monitoring, maintaining, and trouble-shooting Active Directory components

5 The _____ file stores all the Active Directory database objects on the domain controller.

6 _____ are markers that indicate an object has been deleted.

7 You use the _____ utility to move the Active Directory database.

8 You use the _____ utility to defragment the Active Directory database.

Answers

1   *Application*. See "The Event Viewer console."

2   *NTDS*. Review "System Monitor."

3   *System*. Study "System Monitor."

4   *Alerts*. Study "Performance logs and alerts."

5   *NTDS.DIT*. Review "Modifying Active Directory."

6   *Tombstones*. See "Garbage collection."

7   *NTDSUTIL*. Review "Moving the Active Directory database."

8   *NTDSUTIL*. See "Defragmenting the Active Directory database."

Controlling Domain Controller Performance

You want to keep your domain controllers performing as efficiently as possible. The performance of your domain controllers has a noticeable effect on your overall network performance, and your users will certainly give you high marks if they can log on quickly and find resources easily.

The Event Viewer console

To monitor events that occur on your Windows 2000 domain controllers, you use the Event Viewer — a near-perfect tool for this task. Figure 13-1 shows the Event Viewer.

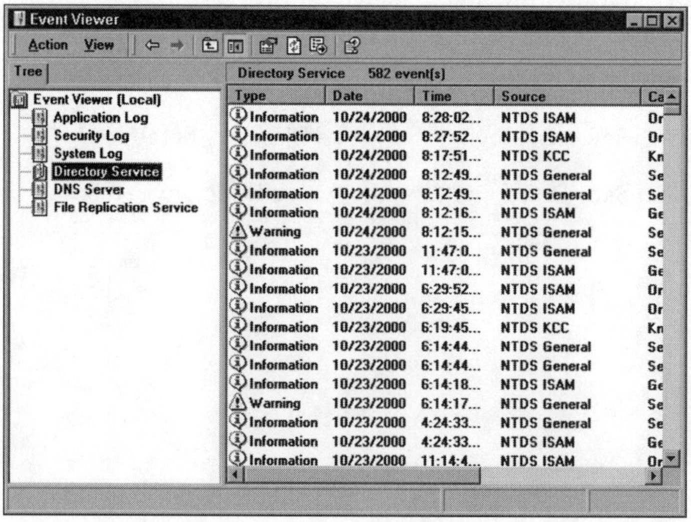

Figure 13-1:
The Windows 2000 Event Viewer.

Event Viewer can report events concerning applications, the system, security, or the directory service. The Event Viewer is critical for obtaining information after problems occur. For example, if a service on your domain controller fails, you need to check Event Viewer for valuable clues about the reasons for the failure. In many cases, you check Event Viewer messages against Microsoft's support Web site to troubleshoot your Windows 2000 server.

The Event Viewer contains logs that are specific to various areas of management. Table 13-1 describes the different logs that are available.

Table 13-1	The Event Logs
Log	*What It Contains*
Application	Errors, warnings, or information generated by applications
Directory Service	Errors, warnings, or information generated by Active Directory services
Security	Information about the success or failure of audited events
File Replication Service	Errors, warnings, and information that the File Replication service generates
System	Errors, warnings, and information generated by Windows 2000

By default, all users can view the logs, with the exception of the security log. Only you and other system administrators can view the security log.

Some additional services that you install cause Windows 2000 Server to create additional logs. For example, if you install DNS, a DNS log is installed in Event Viewer.

Using the Event Viewer is simple: Just click Start⇔Programs⇔Administrative Tools⇔Event Viewer.

Event Viewer is one of those nifty Windows 2000 tools that you can use to monitor remote systems, not just the system at which you logged on. Lab 13-1 reviews the steps for monitoring a remote system with Event Viewer.

Lab 13-1   Viewing the Event Log of a Remote System

1. Click Start⇔Programs⇔Administrative Tools⇔Event Viewer.

2. Right-click the Event Viewer (Local) node in the console's left pane and choose Connect to Another Computer.

3. In the Select Computer dialog box, shown in Figure 13-2, click Another Computer and type the network name, IP address, or DNS address for the name of the computer that you want to monitor. You can also browse for the computer.

4. Click OK.

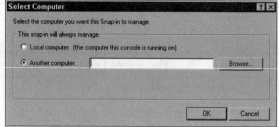

Figure 13-2:
You can
monitor
another
system with
Event
Viewer.

By choosing View➪Find in Event Viewer, you can search for specific events. Choose View➪Filter to restrict Event Viewer's display to only certain events.

The Performance console

Windows 2000's Performance console enables you to monitor local and remote systems in your Windows 2000 network, as well as summarize performance data. With this information, you can take a more proactive approach to systems administration.

The Performance console has two components: the System Monitor and performance logs and alerts. The combination of these tools enables you to create baselines, diagnose historical performance issues, and send alerts regarding resource issues.

System Monitor

System Monitor, shown in Figure 13-3, enables you to measure the performance of your domain controller and Active Directory services. The tool provides an incredible degree of flexibility, enabling you to define the type and source of data to monitor, as well as the sampling parameters for data collection. For example, you can have System Monitor capture a specific memory statistic for your domain controller at fixed intervals, such as every five minutes for a period of several hours. You also have great control over how System Monitory displays the data. Possible displays include charts, histograms, and report views. You have full control over all formatting options, including font, colors, and other characteristics.

Before you can actually monitor the health of your domain controller with System Monitor, you need to specify the performance objects and performance counters that you want to monitor. A *performance object* provides counters for measuring the performance of a certain system component.

Windows 2000 has many performance objects and numerous counters associated with each of these objects, giving you have an incredible number of statistics you can choose to monitor. Table 13-2 lists several performance objects and counters you should know for the exam, along with guidelines for using them.

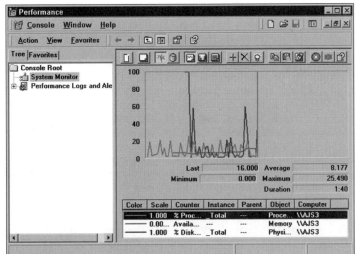

Figure 13-3:
System
Monitor.

Table 13-2   Important Performance Objects and Counters

Resource	Object\Counter	Suggested Threshold
Disk	Physical Disk\% Disk Time	90%
Memory	Memory\Available Bytes	Less than 4MB
Network	Network Segment\ % Net Utilization	Depends on network medium
Processor	Processor\% Processor Time	85%
Server	Server\Pool Paged Peak	Amount of physical RAM

As you might guess, you also need to monitor specific counters regarding Active Directory Services. The NTDS performance object provides these counters. You can access this object after you install ADS. Some important counters to measure for this object are

> ✓ **DRA Inbound Object Updates Remaining in Packet:** This counter provides the number of object updates received in the current directory replication update packet that have not yet been applied to the local server. This number tells you whether the domain controller you are monitoring is receiving the changes, but taking a long time applying them to the Active Directory database.

✔ **DRA Pending Replication Synchronizations:** The counter gives you the number of directory synchronizations queued for the domain controller but not yet processed. This counter helps to determine whether you have a replication backlog involving the domain controller: The larger the number, the larger the backlog.

✔ **LDAP Client Sessions:** This counter reports on the number of connected LDAP client sessions, giving you an excellent indication of how often the domain controller services Active Directory-related requests from clients in your network.

✔ **LDAP Bind Time:** This counter identifies the time, in milliseconds, taken for the last successful LDAP binding. This counter helps you identify how efficiently your domain controller is servicing query requests from clients in your network. The lower number, the better.

Lab 13-2 reviews the procedure for using the System Monitor to collect statistical information about the performance of your server.

Lab 13-2	Monitoring Domain Controller Performance

1. **Click Start➪Programs➪Administrative Tools➪Performance.**

2. **Right-click System Monitor in the console's right-hand pane and choose Add Counters.**

3. **In the Add Counters dialog box, select Use Local Computer Counters as shown in Figure 13-4.**

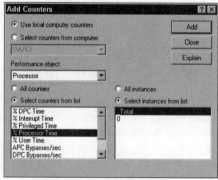

Figure 13-4:
The Add Counters dialog box.

4. **In the Performance Object list, choose Memory.**

5. **In the Select Counters From List area, select Available Bytes and then click the Add button to add this counter.**

You can easily add other counters to this same console using the steps I describe here. Be careful, however. Adding too many counters to a console at one time can hinder the performance of your server, or even the network. Also, using too many counters may hinder your ability to interpret the data.

6. **Click Close to begin analyzing data regarding available bytes of memory on your domain controller.**

I cannot emphasize this point too strongly: Carefully plan what you want to monitor and why, because monitoring an excessive number of counters at once can actually inhibit the server's performance. You may want to set up a remote system specifically for the purpose of system monitoring. Doing so may give you a more accurate set of data because the result set is not skewed by the monitoring process.

Performance logs and alerts

Windows 2000's performance logs and alerts enable you to create counter logs, trace logs, and system alerts. Counter logs enable you to collect performance data in a log file format. Later, you can import this data into a database or spreadsheet application for analysis, or you can simply use the built-in System Monitor application to view the data.

Remember that physical disk counters are enabled by default in Windows 2000, but you have to execute **diskperf -yv** at the command prompt in order to enable logical drive and volume counters.

You use trace logs to record data when certain activities such as disk I/O operations or page faults occur. Trace logs differ from counter logs, which do not wait for an event to occur, but simply sample data at a prescribed interval.

For both counter and trace logs, you define the start and stop times, filenames, file types, file sizes, and other needed parameters. Typically, you need administrator permissions to configure these options and create a counter or trace log.

An alert works with the performance objects and counters you use for monitoring information regarding the performance of the system. Using this data, you create an alert for a selected counter. If the selected counter's value exceeds or falls below a specified setting, the alert gets triggered. If the alert gets triggered, you can have it write an event to the application log, send a network message to a computer, start a performance log, or run a program that you specify. Lab 13-3 reviews the steps for creating an alert.

Lab 13-3   Creating an Alert

1. **Click Start⇨Programs⇨Administrative Tools⇨Performance.**

2. **Double-click Performance Logs and Alerts and then click Alerts.**

3. **Right-click a blank area in the right pane and choose New Alert Settings.**

4. **In the New Alert Settings dialog box, type the name of the alert and click OK.**

5. In the Comment box (see Figure 13-5), type a comment that describes the alert and then click Add.

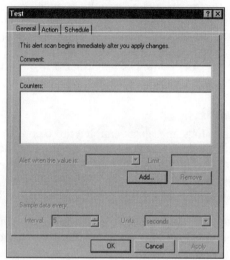

Figure 13-5:
Creating a
new alert.

6. In the Select Counters dialog box, select the computer for which you want to create an alert.

7. In the Performance Object list, select an object to monitor.

8. Select the counters you want to monitor and click Add.

9. Click Close when you are finished.

   The Select Counters dialog box closes, and you can configure the alert criteria.

10. In the Alert When The Value Is list, specify Under or Over. In the Limit box, specify the value that triggers the alert.

11. In the Sample Data Every section, select the amount and measurement characteristic for the update interval.

12. On the Action tab in the alert's dialog box, select the action that occurs when the alert is triggered.

13. On the Schedule tab in the alert's dialog box, configure the schedule used for the alert.

14. Click OK when finished.

Of course, this alerts feature is quite useful for monitoring the health of your domain controllers. Just imagine the flexibility you gain by configuring the server to notify you if it thinks it might be getting sick!

Controlling ADS Performance

To improve the performance of Active Directory, you may need to move or defragment the database. You also need to understand the various tools that Windows 2000 includes to help maintain this all-important database. This section reviews all you need to know regarding this topic for the exam.

Modifying Active Directory

For the exam, you must realize that Windows 2000 treats each request to add to or modify Active Directory in any way as a *transaction*. Treating these changes as transactions ensures that they complete in their entirety, or are rolled back. In this way, Windows 2000 helps to ensure consistency in the Active Directory database and helps you to rely on Active Directory in your Windows 2000 network.

The Active Directory database actually has its own database engine called the Extensible Storage Engine (ESE). This engine uses the following files to ensure database consistency and health:

- ✔ **NTDS.DIT:** This is the file that actually holds the Active Directory database objects. The DIT extension stands for directory information tree. By default, this file is located in the *systemroot*\NTDS folder.

- ✔ **EDB*.LOG:** These are transaction log files for the database system. Each of these files can grow to 10MB. Each log filename includes an incremented number — that is, EDB1.LOG, EDB2.LOG, and so on.

- ✔ **EDB.CHK:** The database engine uses this checkpoint file to track the data not yet written to the database file.

- ✔ **RES1.LOG and RES2.LOG:** These are reserved transaction log files. They ensure sufficient free disk space for transaction logging.

When you modify the Active Directory database, the following process occurs:

1. The Extensible Storage Engine loads the information to be modified into memory.

2. ESE then records an entry in the transaction log file.

3. ESE writes the changes stored in memory to the database file, NTDS.DIT.

4. The checkpoint file, EDB.CHK, is updated to indicate that the logged change has actually been committed to the database.

Garbage collection

After every 12 hours of continuous operation, your domain controller scans the database for tombstones, deletes them, and defragments the database. This process is affectionately referred to by Microsoft as the *garbage collection* process. The 12-hour period is called the *garbage collection interval. Tombstones* are objects that have been marked for deletion in Active Directory. Typically, you mark an object for deletion by right-clicking the object in one of the consoles and then choosing Delete. Windows 2000 takes these objects you delete and moves them to a Deleted Objects folder. All this seemingly extra work helps to ensure that these deletions are properly replicated to all the other domain controllers in your network.

The time period between marking the object for deletion and actually deleting it is known as the *tombstone lifetime.* This time period is configurable and defaults to 60 days.

To configure the garbage collection interval and tombstone lifetime, use the ADSI Edit console to connect to the Configuration container on the domain controller. In the configuration partition, open the properties of Configuration/Services/Windows NT/Directory Service. In the Select Which Properties To View field, select the garbageCollPeriod and tombstoneLifetime attributes and edit their values.

During the garbage collection process, your domain controller defragments the Active Directory database. This process rearranges the data that is written in the database and can also compact the database. This process is known as an *online defragmentation* of the database. Later in this chapter, you review the other method of defragmentation (see "Defragmenting the Active Directory database"). You should be familiar with both methodologies for the exam.

Moving the Active Directory database

For the exam, you need to know how to move the Active Directory database using the NTDSUTIL command. This command not only moves the database from one location to another, but it also updates the appropriate Registry keys so Active Directory can still function. Lab 13-4 reviews the procedure for moving the Active Directory database.

Lab 13-4	Moving the Active Directory Database

1. **Before you do anything else, back up the Active Directory database. (See Chapter 4 if you need to review the backup procedure.)**

2. **Restart the domain controller and press F8 to display the Windows 2000 Advanced Options menu.**

3. **Choose Directory Services Restore Mode and press Enter.**

4. **Log on using a local administrator account and password.**

5. **At the command prompt, type** NTDSUTIL **and press Enter.**

6. **Type** files **and press Enter.**

7. **Type the following command:**

   ```
   move DB to drive: | directory
   ```

   where *drive* and *directory* represent the location where you want to move the database.

8. **Type** quit **and press Enter.**

9. **Type** quit **and press Enter again.**

10. **Restart the domain controller normally.**

You can also move the transaction logs files to another location. Use the following NTDSUTIL command to accomplish this task:

```
move logs to drive: | directory
```

Defragmenting the Active Directory database

As more and more Active Directory database changes occur in your implementation, your database may become fragmented. This causes increased delays in your network as Windows 2000 searches the fragmented database. To overcome this problem, you defragment the database. This process rewrites the records in the database, writing them into contiguous sectors on disk and thus enhancing performance.

As I explain in the section "Garbage collection," earlier in this chapter, defragmentation can occur online. This process happens at 12-hour intervals as part of the garbage collection process. Online defragmentation rearranges pages in the database, but does not reduce the size of the database. It merely optimizes data storage in the database and optimizes available space for new objects.

This section focuses on *offline defragmentation*. Offline defragmentation rearranges pages within the database, and creates a new, compacted version of the database file. Depending on the amount of fragmentation, this new file may be considerably smaller than the original.

During this defragmentation process, your domain controller is literally offline. This is not something you want to do during production time in your company.

Lab 13-5 describes the steps for performing an offline defragmentation of the Active Directory database.

Lab 13-5	Defragmenting the Active Directory Database

1. **Before you do anything else, back up the Active Directory database. (See Chapter 4 if you need to review the backup process.)**

2. **Restart the domain controller and press F8 to display the Windows 2000 Advanced Options menu.**

3. **Choose Directory Services Restore Mode and press Enter.**

4. **Log on using a local administrator account and password.**

5. **At the command prompt, type NTDSUTIL and press Enter.**

6. **Type** files **and press Enter.**

7. **Type the following command:**

```
compact to drive: | directory
```

   Choose a directory location that you can easily remember here and that has sufficient space to hold a copy of the Active Directory database file.

8. **Type** quit **and press Enter.**

9. **Type** quit **and press Enter again.**

10. **Copy the new NTDS.DIT file over the old NTDS.DIT on your drive system.**

11. **Restart the domain controller as you normally would.**

Active Directory support tools

Windows 2000 includes many Active Directory-related tools that you need to know for the exam. For each of these tools, you should have a general understanding of what it does and how it can help you manage Active Directory. Here is a quick summary of these tools to ensure that you are ready.

LDP.EXE: Active Directory Administration Tool

LDP.EXE enables you to perform LDAP operations against the Active Directory database. These operations include searches, modifications, and deletions. You can use this tool in troubleshooting, viewing objects stored in Active Directory and their metadata, including security and replication information.

REPLMON.EXE: Active Directory Replication Monitor

The Active Directory Replication Monitor is an incredibly powerful tool that you use to assist in replication management in Windows 2000. You can view detailed status information, force synchronization between domain controllers, view the topology in a graphical format, and monitor your domain controllers.

REPADMIN.EXE: Replication Diagnostics Tool

REPADMIN.EXE is a command-line tool for diagnosing replication problems that may be occurring between your Windows 2000 domain controllers. With this tool, you can see the replication topology as it would appear from your domain controller's perspective. You can also use this tool to create your own replication topology.

DSASTAT.EXE: Active Directory Diagnostic Tool

DSASTAT.EXE is a command-line tool for comparing and detecting differences between naming contexts on different domain controllers. By using this tool, you can easily determine whether two of your domain controllers are completely up to date with each other.

SDCHECK.EXE: Security Descriptor Check Utility

SDCHECK.EXE is a command-line tool that displays the security descriptor for any object stored in Active Directory. You can view the Access Control Lists (ACLs) that define which users have which permissions on the object.

SDCHECK.EXE also displays any permissions that an object inherits from a parent object.

NLTEST.EXE

The NLTEST.EXE command-line tool helps you perform numerous administrative tasks, including

- Testing trust relationships
- Forcing shutdowns
- Finding a PDC (primary domain controller)
- Forcing Active Directory to synchronize with down-level NT 4 domain controllers

ACLDIAG.EXE: ACL Diagnostics

The ACLDIAG.EXE command-line tool helps you diagnose and troubleshoot problems with permissions on Active Directory objects. This utility does a great job reading these permissions settings and outputting the information to a file for reporting purposes.

DSACLS.EXE

By using the DSACLS.EXE utility, you can easily manipulate ACLs set on directory service objects. You can make these changes very efficiently from a command-line environment with this tool.

Prep Test

1 The DHCP service running on your domain controller has stopped functioning. You want some information regarding the crash so you can troubleshoot it. Specifically, you want to make sure it does not happen to other Windows 2000 DHCP servers running in your network. Which tool should you use to get information about why the DHCP service failed?

A ○ System Monitor

B ○ Network Monitor

C ○ Replication Monitor

D ○ Event Viewer

2 You are interested in viewing any information or errors generated by Active Directory Services. Which Event Viewer log should you check?

A ○ System

B ○ Security

C ○ Directory Service

D ○ File Replication Service

3 Which System Monitor performance object provides counters for monitoring Active Directory?

A ○ ADO

B ○ NTDS

C ○ DirectServ

D ○ LDAP

4 Which counter in System Monitor permits you to view the number of directory synchronizations queued for the domain controller but not yet processed?

A ○ DRA Pending Replication Synchronizations

B ○ LDAP Client Sessions

C ○ LDAP Bind Time

D ○ DRA Inbound Object Updates Remaining in Packet

5 Which type of log in performance logs and alerts gets triggered by some system activity?

A ○ Alert

B ○ Trace

C ○ Counter

D ○ Profiler

6 Which file is used to record checkpoints in the transactional logging process for Active Directory changes?

A ○ RES1.LOG
B ○ NTDS.DIT
C ○ EDB.CHK
D ○ EDB*.LOG

7 Which of the following choices represents a valid step in the process you use to move the Active Directory database?

A ○ Restart the system in Directory Services Restore Mode.
B ○ Use the Replication Monitor to stop replication from the domain controller.
C ○ Use the RELOCATE DB command with NTDSUTIL.
D ○ Restart the system in Safe Mode with Networking Support.

8 Which NTDSUTIL command do you use to move the Active Directory database?

A ○ move database
B ○ move DB
C ○ transfer DB
D ○ compact DB

9 Which NTDSUTIL command do you use to defragment the Active Directory database?

A ○ compact DB
B ○ compact to
C ○ jetpack to
D ○ jetpack DB

10 You need to force replication in your Windows 2000 Active Directory environment. Which tool should you use?

A ○ NTDSUTIL
B ○ DSACLS
C ○ NLTEST
D ○ REPLMON

Answers

1 **D.** Event Viewer. The Event Viewer is a near-perfect tool for viewing information regarding service failures. *See "The Event Viewer console."*

2 **C.** Directory Service. The Directory Service log displays information and error messages from Active Directory Services. *Study "The Event Viewer console."*

3 **B.** NTDS. The NTDS performance object contains many useful counters for gathering information about Active Directory Services. *See "System Monitor."*

4 **A.** DRA Pending Replication Synchronizations. This counter provides the number of directory synchronizations queued for the domain controller but not yet processed. This counter helps you determine whether you have a replication backlog involving the domain controller — the larger the number, the larger the backlog. *See "System Monitor."*

5 **B.** Trace. A trace log is activated by some type of system event. Contrast this to a counter log, which is utilized at fixed intervals. *Review "Performance logs and alerts."*

6 **C.** EDB.CHK. Active Directory Services uses this file in the transactional logging process for modifying the Active Directory database. *Study "Modifying Active Directory."*

7 **A.** Restart the system in Directory Services Restore Mode. Before using NTDSUTIL to move the Active Directory database or defragment it, you must restart the system in Directory Services Restore Mode. *Review "Moving the Active Directory database."*

8 **B.** move DB. You use the move DB command with NTDSUTIL in order to move the Active Directory database. *See "Moving the Active Directory database."*

9 **B.** compact to. You can use compact to with NTDSUTIL to defragment the Active Directory database. This process is known as offline defragmentation. *See "Defragmenting the Active Directory database."*

10 **D.** REPLMON. The Active Directory Replication Monitor can assist you in many ways when managing Active Directory. For example, it can force replication in your Active Directory environment. *Review "Active Directory support tools."*

Chapter 14

Managing Active Directory Replication

....

Exam Objectives

▶ Managing intrasite replication
▶ Managing intersite replication

....

C ompared to NT 4, the Windows 2000 directory services offer tremendous advances in the handling of replication. Windows 2000 ADS gives
you tremendous control over exactly how the system performs replication.
ADS also does away with many inefficiencies that plague previous replication
strategies, handling numerous details with no administrator intervention
whatsoever. More great news about Active Directory replication: It simply
works, and administrators do not need to configure much at all. Of course,
you need to know everything in this chapter for the exam!

You need to know all the details of Active Directory replication, including
replication between Active Directory sites and within Active Directory sites.
To help you prepare for the exam, this chapter reviews the following topics:

  ✔ Understanding the Active Directory replication process

  ✔ Resolving replication conflicts

  ✔ Using connection objects

  ✔ Using sites and site links to control replication

  ✔ Troubleshooting replication

  ✔ Implementing successful replication strategies

Quick Assessment

Managing
intrasite
replication

1 Replication within Active Directory sites is designed to work with _____, reliable connections.

2 An update at a domain controller that did not perform the update is called a(n) _____ update.

3 Replication _____ is the time needed for a change on one domain controller to replicate to another domain controller.

4 Creating the replication topology between domain controllers is the job of the _____.

Managing
intersite
replication

5 A site _____ connects two Active Directory sites.

6 Replication traffic between sites is compressed to _____ percent of its original size before it is transmitted.

7 The default cost of a site link is _____.

8 A site link _____ consists of two or more site links.

Answers

1 *Fast.* See "Understanding How Active Directory Replication Works."

2 *Replicated.* Review "Understanding How Active Directory Replication Works."

3 *Latency.* Study "Understanding How Active Directory Replication Works."

4 *Knowledge Consistency Checker.* Study "Reviewing Replication Topologies."

5 *Link.* See "Optimizing Active Directory Replication."

6 *10 to 15%.* Review "Optimizing Active Directory Replication."

7 *100.* Review "Optimizing Active Directory Replication."

8 *Bridge.* See "Optimizing Active Directory Replication."

Understanding How Active Directory Replication Works

Windows 2000 Active Directory features a multimaster replication model. Consequently, you and your peer administrators can make changes at any domain controller in your forest, and these changes get updated at each and every domain controller. This process is known as *replication.* The term *replication latency* refers to the amount of time these changes take to reach a domain controller from another domain controller.

Although replication does give you more to worry about as an administrator, and it causes additional network traffic, this multimaster replication model does have its advantages. With the exceptions of the Flexible Single-Master Operations roles that I describe in Chapter 3, the replication model that Active Directory uses is not susceptible to the failure of a single server in the network. Remember, in a Windows NT network, the failure of the primary domain controller means no more updates to the directory service.

As I explain in Chapter 3, Active Directory uses sites to group well-connected computers in your network, as shown in Figure 14-1. Replication within these sites assumes fast, reliable network connections. You refer to this type of replication as *intrasite replication.*

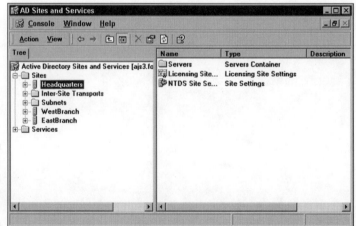

Figure 14-1:
Active
Directory
sites.

Refer to replication between sites as *intersite replication.* It functions differently from intrasite replication because network connectivity between Active Directory sites is neither as fast, nor as reliable as connectivity within a site.

The following types of activities initiate replication:

✔ Adding objects to Active Directory

✔ Modifying properties of existing objects

✔ Moving objects

✔ Deleting objects

When you or another administrator make any of these changes at a specific domain controller, they are known as *originating updates.* An originating update triggers what are known as *replicated updates* to all other domain controllers in the forest.

How does Windows 2000 trigger the replication of these updates? Windows 2000 triggers replication through a process known as *change notification.* When you make a change, the Active Directory engine waits five minutes by default and then sends a message to the first replication partner. This system waits for 30 seconds by default and then notifies its direct replication partner — and so on and so on. By default, if no changes occur in one hour, Windows 2000 triggers replication.

Windows 2000 considers some Active Directory changes as urgent. These changes involve security-sensitive actions — for example, password changes and account lockout events. Active Directory calls these changes *urgent replication activities,* and they have no waiting period for change notification. In fact, these changes are immediately sent to one machine — the PDC emulator — to ensure that they are rapidly honored within the network. This feature should cut down on help desk calls in your network from users who cannot log on properly because of replication latency.

Reviewing Replication Topologies

For the exam, you need to understand how the replication topology is generated in your Windows 2000 network. Replication topology dictates which domain controllers replicate with which in your network. In pure Active Directory terms, the replication topology is the layout of connection objects between domain controllers in your forest. *Connection objects* are one-way replication paths between domain controllers. These connection objects form a network of direct and transitive replication partners that encompass all the domain controllers in your network. As I explain in the section "Monitoring Replication Traffic," later in this chapter, you can actually view these objects using the Active Directory Replication Monitor.

Here's the great news regarding the replication topology in Active Directory: The Knowledge Consistency Checker (KCC) runs on every domain controller in the forest and creates the topology for you. This process faithfully does its job at periodic intervals, always monitoring the network for new domain controllers and network communication difficulties. As magical as this sounds, understand that the KCC does have help in generating this topology. It uses the sites and subnets you have created in your network, following the guidelines I describe in Chapter 3.

In addition to the connection objects that the Knowledge Consistency Checker creates, you need to know how to create connection objects yourself. Although you seldom need to do so, you better know how for the exam! Lab 14-1 describes the steps in this process.

Lab 14-1   Creating a Connection Object

1. **Click Start⇨Programs⇨Administrative Tools⇨Active Directory Sites and Services.**

2. **In the console's left pane, click the domain controller for which you want to manually add or configure a connection.**

3. **Right-click NTDS Settings and choose New Active Directory Connection.**

4. **In the Find Domain Controllers dialog box, shown in Figure 14-2, select the domain controller that you want to include in the connection object and then click OK.**

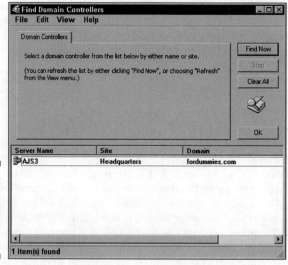

Figure 14-2:
The Find
Domain
Controllers
dialog box.

5. **In the New Object - Connection dialog box, enter a name for the new Connection object and then click OK.**

You can also force the Knowledge Consistency Checker to check the replication topology whenever *you* are ready. This check

 ✔ Runs a process that considers the cost of intersite connections.

 ✔ Checks whether any previously available domain controllers are no longer available.

 ✔ Checks whether new domain controllers have been added.

 ✔ Uses this information to add or remove connection objects to create a more efficient replication topology.

Lab 14-2 reviews the process you use for checking the replication topology.

Lab 14-2   Checking the Topology

1. **Click Start⇨Programs⇨Administrative Tools⇨Active Directory Sites and Services.**

2. **In the console's left pane, double-click the server that you want to use to check the replication topology.**

3. **Right-click NTDS Settings and choose All Tasks⇨Check Replication Topology, as shown in Figure 14-3.**

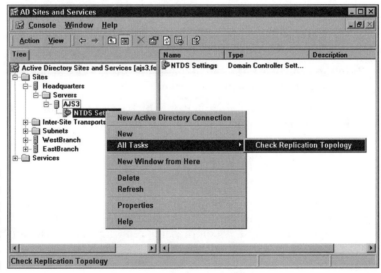

Figure 14-3:
Checking the replication topology.

Optimizing Active Directory Replication

Although the KCC takes care of the topology for you, optimizing replication in Active Directory is definitely up to you, and you need to know all about it for the exam. To optimize Active Directory replication, you must carefully create the objects that control replication in Active Directory: subnets, sites, site links, and site link bridges. Chapter 3 describes the steps for creating these objects.

The sites you create in your network enable you to control more than just replication traffic; these sites also help to control logon traffic. When a user logs on, Windows 2000 directs the logon request to a domain controller within the same site as the user. By doing so, Windows 2000 helps to minimize logon times because of the fast connections between systems within the same site.

Typically, you do not need to do much in the way of configuration for your intrasite replication traffic. As I explain in the section "Understanding How Active Directory Replication Works," earlier in this chapter, the change notification process triggers intrasite replication. Windows 2000 does not bother to compress this replication traffic because, after all, you should have adequate bandwidth within your sites, by definition.

You can force replication within a site by using the Active Directory Replication Monitor, as you review in the section "Monitoring Replication Traffic," later in this chapter. As Lab 14-3 demonstrates, Windows 2000 has another method for forcing intrasite replication built right in to the Active Directory Sites and Services console. Make sure you know about both methods for the exam.

Lab 14-3   Forcing Replication

1. **Click Start➪Programs➪Administrative Tools➪Active Directory Sites and Services.**

2. **In the console's left pane, expand the Sites node, expand one of your sites, and then expand the Servers node.**

3. **Select the domain controller on which an update was made and then select NTDS Settings.**

4. **Right-click the connection object for the replicating partner, choose Replicate Now, and then click OK.**

Unlike intrasite replication, replication between sites requires much more configuration on your part. By definition, bandwidth between sites is neither as fast nor as reliable as bandwidth within a site. Windows 2000 helps to overcome this limitation by compressing replication traffic to approximately 10 to 15 percent of its original size before sending it between sites. Although this compression helps to preserve bandwidth between sites, it does nothing to increase efficiency. In fact, the compression taxes the processors of the domain controllers involved.

Be sure to review the information in Chapter 3 of this book so you know how to create site links and site link bridges. These objects are critical for scheduling replication between sites. You should configure replication between sites so that it occurs during periods of low bandwidth usage on the links.

Fortunately, you define site links using several configuration components that give you to have a high degree of control over exactly how replication occurs. Be sure you understand these components for the exam. Chapter 3 of this book details exactly where you can access these settings:

- ✔ **Transport:** The transport defines the networking protocol used to transfer the replication information between sites. You have two choices: Remote Procedure Calls (RPC) or Simple Mail Transfer Protocol (SMTP). RPC is the default; in fact, you must use it for your intrasite replication. It is also an excellent choice for the intersite replication transport. SMTP is another option for intersite replication, but it is asynchronous, which means it ignores any schedules you have configured for intersite replication. Also, SMTP is limited for use between different domains located in different sites.

- ✔ **Member sites:** You can define exactly which sites are connected by a particular site link. Of course, you typically configure a site link to connect two sites in your network because the site link represents a physical WAN connection.

- ✔ **Cost:** Cost is a critical configuration component of a site link, especially if you implement multiple site links between two sites because you have multiple WAN connections between the sites. Cost enables you to give priority to one site link over another. Windows 2000 always attempts to use the site link with the lowest assigned cost. The default site link cost is 100, but you can assign any cost, as appropriate, from 1 to 32,767. Typically, you assign a low cost to a reliable, higher speed WAN connection and assign a higher cost to a slower, less reliable connection.

- ✔ **Schedule:** Using the schedule component of a site link, you can define the exact times that replication can occur. This component enables you to schedule intersite replication for off-peak times. You can schedule right down to the hour interval.

- ✔ **Replication interval:** The replication interval component defines how often replication can occur in a given schedule window. This interval can range from 15 to 10,080 minutes.

Managing Site Licensing

The exam has been known to slip in questions regarding the new site licensing feature found in Windows 2000 Active Directory. As an administrator, you can use this tool to ensure that your organization complies with the Microsoft software licensing agreements. This tool enables you to monitor license purchases, deletions, and usage in your Active Directory environment.

The site licensing function relies on the License Logging service that runs on each server in a site. These servers replicate licensing information to a centralized database on a server you designate within a site, enabling you to monitor all licensing information for your site from a central location. This server is known as the *site license server* for your site. You access this licensing information from the Licensing utility located in the Administrative Tools group.

Windows 2000 picks a default site license server for you: the first domain controller created in a site. You can move this server role to any server in the site, as I explain in Lab 14-4.

Lab 14-4   Selecting a Site License Server

1. **Click Start➪Programs➪Administrative Tools➪Active Directory Sites and Services.**

2. **Select the site where you want to assign a site license server.**

3. **In the console's right-hand pane, right-click Licensing Site Settings and then choose Properties.**

4. **In the Licensing Site Settings Properties dialog box, shown in Figure 14-4, click Change.**

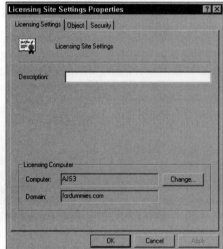

Figure 14-4: The Licensing Site Settings Properties dialog box.

5. **In the Select Computer dialog box, select the computer you want to designate as the site license server and then click OK.**

6. **In the Licensing Site Settings Properties dialog box, click OK.**

Monitoring Replication Traffic

As I explain in previous sections of this chapter, you have many ways to control replication traffic in your Windows 2000 network. For the exam, you also need to know how to monitor this replication traffic so you can adjust your replication controls as necessary.

Active Directory Replication Monitor, shown in Figure 14-5, is your main tool for this purpose. In addition to displaying a cool graphical representation of your replication topology, this utility performs many other tasks, including

- ✔ Enabling you to view the results of the Knowledge Consistency Checker.
- ✔ Forcing the Knowledge Consistency Checker to recalculate a replication topology.
- ✔ Forcing synchronization between two domain controllers.
- ✔ Permitting you to view objects that have not yet replicated from one domain controller to another.
- ✔ Collecting statistical information regarding the impact replication has on your network.
- ✔ Tracking failed replication attempts, including statistics regarding these failures.
- ✔ Tracking direct versus transitive replication between domain controllers.

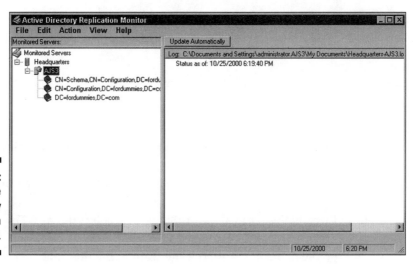

Figure 14-5:
The Active
Directory
Replication
Monitor.

The Active Directory Replication Monitor is not installed in Windows 2000 Server by default. You find it in the Support directory of your CD-ROM, among the Windows 2000 Support Tools. After you install it, you can start monitoring replication in your network, as I describe in Lab 14-5. In order to install the Active Directory Replication Monitor, navigate to the Support\Tools directory on the Server CD-ROM and run SETUP.EXE.

Lab 14-5 Monitoring Replication

1. **Click Start⇨Programs⇨Windows 2000 Support Tools⇨Tools⇨Active Directory Replication Monitor.**

2. **Choose View⇨Options to open the Active Directory Replication Monitor Options dialog box, as shown in Figure 14-6.**

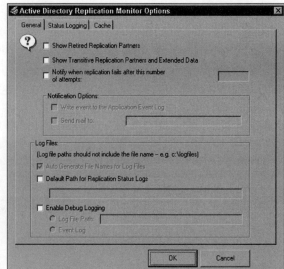

Figure 14-6: The Active Directory Replication Monitor Options dialog box.

3. **Click the Status Logging tab.**

4. **Select the Display Changed Attributes When Replication Occurs option and then click OK.**

5. **Right-click the Monitored Server node and choose Add Monitored Server.**

6. **In the Add Server to Monitor dialog box, select the Add The Server Explicitly By Name option and then click Next.**

7. **Type the name of the server you want to monitor and click Finish. (Sadly enough, the interface does not include a Browse button, so you must know the name.)**

The Active Directory Replication Monitor also has a command-line component named REPADMIN. REPADMIN performs many of the same functions as its GUI partner does and gives you the convenience of the command-line interface. Here are the options you should know for the exam:

- ✔ **/sync:** Starts a replication event for the specified naming context between the source and destination domain controllers.

- ✔ **/showreps:** Displays the replication partners for each naming context that is held on the specified domain controller. The output also indicates whether the domain controller is also a global catalog server.

- ✔ **/showvector:** Displays the up-to-datedness information for a specified naming context. This vector indicates whether a replica is up to date with its replication partners.

- ✔ **/showmeta:** Displays the replication metadata for any object stored in Active Directory, such as attribute ID, version number, originating and local Update Sequence Number (USN), and the originating DSA's GUID and date/time stamp.

- ✔ **/showtime:** With no arguments, displays the current system time in both the directory service format and string format. The string format displays both the local and UTC time zones. Alternatively, `showtime` accepts a directory service time value and converts it to string format for both the local and the UTC time zones.

Troubleshooting Replication

Hopefully, the replication processes in your Windows 2000 network will go very smoothly, but you may need to resolve some common issues. For the exam, you should know how to resolve the following issues:

- ✔ **Replication fails to complete.** Make sure you have configured your sites and site links properly. If you forget a site link between two of your sites, replication will definitely fail.

- ✔ **Replication is too slow.** Typically, this problem means you need to work on the scheduling of replication. A common problem involves two sites that cannot replicate with each other during a certain period of time each week. Develop the schedule in such a way that systems do not have to replicate via other sites because you were too restrictive with your scheduling between two sites.

- ✔ **Replication increases your network traffic dramatically.** You should not encounter this problem if you have scheduled your replication to occur during non-peak times in your network. If you have been careful with scheduling replication and you are still having the problem, you may need to consider upgrading your networking technologies to provide higher bandwidth.

✔ **Clients are experiencing slow logons or global catalog query responses.** Ensure that these clients have the necessary servers in sites near them and they have adequate bandwidth to communicate with these servers. The last thing you want in your network is hundreds of clients attempting to log on via one of your very slow site links. In this case, you may need to add domain controllers or WAN links to your link network design.

✔ **You see an error in the Directory Service log of Event Viewer indicating that the** KCC was unable to complete the topology for the distinguished name of the site. This message identifies an exception error with the KCC service. In this case, you should run REPADMIN /kcc in order to reset a particular Registry entry.

Replication Musts

For the exam, you need to know several approaches to managing replication that Microsoft considers critical. These "must-know" methods are as follows:

✔ **Place at least one domain controller in every site.** This recommendation can drastically reduce client logon times in your network. You do not want clients logging on using domain controllers located in far-off sites in your network. This logon traffic also helps to saturate your WAN links if you permit it to occur. Locating at least one domain controller in each site helps to eliminate this problem.

✔ **Place at least one global catalog server in each site.** Of course, this recommendation is similar to the preceding point about domain controllers. Your clients need access to a global catalog server in order to query Active Directory so they can find objects. They also need access to one of these servers because global catalog servers store critical universal group membership information for clients in your forest. Placing a global catalog server in each site eliminates the need for traffic across slower WAN links.

✔ **Place at least one DNS server in each site.** Well, this is getting to be a pattern isn't it? Remember, DNS is the location service for Active Directory clients. Consequently, they need access to a DNS server in order to find all the other servers they need. Once again, speed things up and preserve your WAN bandwidth by placing these servers in high bandwidth sites with your clients.

✔ **Schedule replication across site links during off-peak hours.** By using the scheduling components of site links, you can easily ensure that replication occurs when traffic across your WAN links is low.

Prep Test

1 Which phrase refers to replication between Active Directory sites?

   A ◯ Intrasite replication

   B ◯ Intersite replication

   C ◯ Multimaster replication

   D ◯ Master replication

2 You have just changed several passwords for user accounts in your Windows 2000 Active Directory network. When will these changes replicate to all domain controllers?

   A ◯ Immediately

   B ◯ Within a five-minute interval

   C ◯ Within a fifteen-minute interval

   D ◯ As soon as network utilization dips below 20 percent

3 What tool do you use to manually create a connection object in your replication topology?

   A ◯ Active Directory Users and Computers

   B ◯ Active Directory Domains and Trusts

   C ◯ Active Directory Sites and Services

   D ◯ Schema Manager

4 Which site link configuration component is most useful to you when you are configuring several site links between sites and you need to create a backup path for replication traffic?

   A ◯ Transport

   B ◯ Cost

   C ◯ Member sites

   D ◯ Bridges

5 You have a fractional T1 line and a 56K dial-up connection connecting two sites in your Windows 2000 network. You have left the site link assigned to the T1 line with the default cost of 100. What cost should you assign to the 56K dial-up connection?

   A ◯ 50

   B ◯ 75

   C ◯ 100

   D ◯ 200

6 Users are complaining that the network responds very slowly when they try to log on and find resources that are advertised in Active Directory. Which server(s) should you ensure are located in the same site with these users? Choose all that apply.

A ❑ DNS

B ❑ Global catalog

C ❑ WINS server

D ❑ Domain controller

7 You have multiple Windows 2000 domains set up in your company's Active Directory forest. You also have multiple sites configured. Which of the following statements are true? Choose all that apply.

A ❑ You may use the SMTP protocol.

B ❑ You may use the RPC protocol.

C ❑ Data replicated between sites is compressed.

D ❑ Data replicated within sites is compressed.

8 You have made numerous Active Directory changes and you are concerned that these changes have not replicated throughout your Active Directory infrastructure. What should you do?

A ○ Force replication using the Active Directory Users and Computers console.

B ○ Force replication using the Active Directory Replication Monitor.

C ○ Force replication by using the Windows Registry.

D ○ Force replication using a Group Policy.

9 You want to force replication in your network using the command prompt. What tool should you use?

A ○ REPADMIN

B ○ NTDSUTIL

C ○ DSACLS

D ○ REPMON

10 Which of the following choices is the replication transport protocol used for intrasite replication?

A ○ SMTP

B ○ RPC

C ○ IPX

D ○ AppleTalk

Answers

1 **B.** Intersite replication. You should refer to replication between Active Directory sites as intersite replication. *See "Understanding How Active Directory Replication Works."*

2 **A.** Immediately. Security-related changes to Active Directory are considered urgent. As such, they immediately trigger Active Directory replication as part of a process called urgent replication. *See "Understanding How Active Directory Replication Works."*

3 **C.** Active Directory Sites and Services. Although you seldom have to do so, you manually create connection objects in the replication topology by using the Active Directory Sites and Services tool. *See "Reviewing Replication Topologies."*

4 **B.** Cost. Site link costs are used to prioritize usage between multiple site links. *See "Optimizing Active Directory Replication."*

5 **D.** 200. You typically assign higher costs for slower or less reliable WAN connections. Windows 2000 uses these links less frequently than it uses other, lower-cost links. *Review "Optimizing Active Directory Replication."*

6 **A, B,** and **D.** DNS, global catalog, and domain controller. Clients need quick connections to DNS, global catalog, and domain controllers in order to find servers, locate Active Directory objects, and log on. *Study "Replication Musts."*

7 **A, B,** and **C.** You may use the SMTP protocol. You may use the RPC protocol. Data replicated between sites is compressed. Because this network has multiple sites and multiple domains, SMTP as a transport protocol may be a possibility. RPC is always a possibility for a transport protocol. Remember, data replicated between Active Directory sites is compressed. *See "Understanding How Active Directory Replication Works."*

8 **B.** Force replication using the Active Directory Replication Monitor. You can force replication using the Active Directory Replication Monitor utility. *Review "Monitoring Replication Traffic"*

Managing AD Replication

9 **A.** REPADMIN. You use the REPADMIN utility from the command prompt in order to accomplish many advanced tasks regarding Active Directory replication. *See "Monitoring Replication Traffic."*

10 **B.** RPC. The RPC transport protocol is your only option for an intrasite replication transport protocol. *Review "Optimizing Active Directory Replication."*

Part VII

Active Directory
Security Solutions

The 5th Wave   By Rich Tennant

"As a candidate for network administrator, how well-versed are
you in remote connectivity protocols?"

In this part . . .

*L*ately, security seems more important than ever, with diverse organizations suffering expensive, highly disruptive security breaches every day! Because of these concerns, Microsoft has invested heavily in the security mechanisms included within Windows 2000's Active Directory. Some of these security features are brand new to the Windows 2000 operating system, while others are tried-and-true components of Windows NT 4 and previous versions. As a Windows 2000 certification candidate, you must know all about these security measures in Windows 2000's directory services. This part of the book focuses on these security mechanisms.

In Chapter 15, you examine the use of security group policies in Active Directory, and you review the use of the brand-new Security Configuration and Analysis tool. In Chapter 16, you review the use of auditing in Windows 2000.

Chapter 15

Security Policies: Raise the Drawbridge

- -

Exam Objectives

▶ Applying security policies by using Group Policy

▶ Creating, analyzing, and modifying security configurations by using Security Configuration and Analysis and security templates

- -

1 n Windows 2000, you make many important security settings using Group Policy objects (GPOs). This chapter focuses strictly on the security settings possible with these objects. (You can review GPOs in Chapters 7, 8, and 9.) This chapter also introduces two new tools in Windows 2000: the Security Configuration and Analysis tool and security templates. These tools offer tremendous assistance for securing your network.

For the exam, you need to know how to set security using Group Policy. You also need to know all the nuances of Security Configuration and Analysis and security templates. To help you get ready for the exam, this chapter covers the following topics:

- ✔ Assigning user and logon rights
- ✔ Assigning user privileges
- ✔ Using IPSEC
- ✔ Using security templates
- ✔ Using the Security Configuration and Analysis tool
- ✔ Troubleshooting a security configuration

Quick Assessment

Applying security policies by using Group Policy

1 You should always assign user rights to _____ accounts, not user accounts.

2 The _____ account always retains the right to log on as a service.

3 _____ grant users the ability to perform special actions on the network.

4 Some privileges can actually override _____ set on an object.

Creating, analyzing, and modifying security configurations by using Security Configuration and Analysis and security templates

5 The Security Configuration and Analysis console uses a(n) _____ to store the information it needs to function properly.

6 You can import a security _____ into the Security Configuration and Analysis tool.

7 Security templates have a(n) _____ extension.

8 Windows 2000 provides you with a set of _____ security templates, easing your workload when it comes to setting security in your network.

Answers

1   *Group*. See "Assigning user rights."

2   *LocalSystem*. Review "Logon rights."

3   *Privileges*. Study "Privileges."

4   *Permissions*. Study "Privileges."

5   *Database*. See "Using Security Configuration and Analysis."

6   *Template*. Review "Using Security Configuration and Analysis."

7   *.INF*. See "Working with security templates."

8   *Predefined*. Review "Working with security templates."

Applying Security Policies Using Group Policy

Just when you thought Group Policy objects could do no more for you in your Windows 2000 network, you discover that they also handle many important security settings. By using GPOs to set key security settings, you can apply consistent security settings to multiple users and computers in one simple step. This chapter details the security settings you need to know for the exam.

Assigning user rights

User rights in Windows 2000 consist of privileges and logon rights, as shown in Figure 15-1. Do not confuse user rights with the permissions you set on resources in your network. In many cases, these privileges and logon rights actually transcend the permissions set on resources in the network. Because user rights are so powerful, you must understand them and know the specific capabilities of some of them.

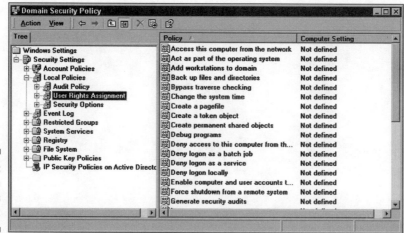

Figure 15-1: Privileges in Windows 2000.

Similar to the manner in which you assign resource permissions, you should always apply user rights to group accounts as opposed to individual user accounts. Doing so cuts down dramatically on your administrative workload and makes tracking of rights so much easier for you. You have enough to do without trying to figure out the special user rights needed by everyone in your network and then attempting to assign them all on a user-by-user basis.

Just like with resource permissions, when you assign user rights to a security group, all members of the group inherit the rights. If a user belongs to multiple groups, that user gains the cumulative effect of all the user rights assigned to those groups. Also, you can easily remove user rights for a particular user: Simply remove the user from the appropriate group. Lab 15-1 lists the steps for assigning user rights.

Lab 15-1   Assigning User Rights

1. **Use the Active Directory Users and Computers console to access the GPO you want to use for setting user rights.**

   See Chapter 7 if you need to review procedures for editing GPOs.

2. **In the left pane of the Group Policy snap-in, click Computer Configuration.**

3. **Double-click Windows Settings and then double-click Security Settings.**

4. **Double-click Local Policies and then double-click User Rights Assignment.**

5. **In the console's right-hand pane, right-click the user right you want to assign and then choose Security.**

6. **In the Security Policy Setting dialog box, click the Define These Policy Settings check box, as shown in Figure 15-2.**

Figure 15-2:
Assigning
user rights.

7. **Click the Add button and then add the appropriate user or group.**

8. **Click OK three times to close all dialog boxes and finish the configuration.**

In the following sections, you can review the two types of user rights: privileges and logon rights.

Privileges

As their name implies, privileges enable you to grant users the ability to perform specific actions in the network. Remember that many of these privileges can override resource permissions set in your network. For example, users with the Backup Files and Directories privilege can back up files for which they have been explicitly denied access. This is powerful stuff, indeed!

Table 15-1 describes the privileges that you should know for the exam. Notice how many of these privileges already are assigned to the built-in groups of Active Directory!

Table 15-1	Windows 2000 Privileges
Privilege	*What It Does*
Act As Part of the Operating System	Permits the user account to act as a low-level service on a system. It is typically reserved for special accounts that are needed by applications such as Microsoft Message Queue Server. Be careful with this one!
Add Workstations to a Domain	Enables the user to add computer accounts to a specific domain. Keep in mind that you can also use the Delegation of Control wizard to assign this permission.
Back Up Files and Directories	Enables users to back up for you on the network. Remember that this privilege applies, regardless of resource permissions the users may have.
Change the System Time	Enables the user to set the time on a system. Duh!
Create a Pagefile	Not only enables the user to create a pagefile, but also permits the user to change the sizes of existing pagefiles.
Debug Programs	Enables a user to attach a debugger to any process. Be careful with this one, too! This privilege permits access to critical and sometimes highly sensitive operating system component information.
Load and Unload Device Drivers	Enables a user to install and uninstall device drivers. Another one to be careful with.
Manage Auditing and Log	Enables users to help you manage auditing in Security Windows 2000, including viewing and clearing the security log in Event Viewer. (See Chapter 16 for more about auditing.)
Profile System Performance	Permits a user to use Windows NT and 2000 performance monitoring tools against the system.

Privilege	What It Does
Restore Files and netDirectories	Enables a user to restore backed up files on the work for you. Notice that this privilege is separate from Back up Files and Directories.
Shut Down the System	Enables the user to gracefully shut down the local computer. In this context, *gracefully* refers to using the Start menu as opposed to having the user physically pull the plug.
Synchronize Directory Data	Enables you to have users assist with directory Service synchronization tasks. Administrators have this one by default, of course.
Take Ownership of Files Objects	Permits the user to take ownership of objects. Other Administrators also have this one by default.

Logon rights

You use logon rights in your network to specify how a user account can log on to a system. Table 15-2 details the logon rights you should know for the exam. You also need to realize that the special LocalSystem account in Windows 2000 has almost all the logon rights assigned to it, which makes it a very special account. Windows 2000 uses this account to run many processes that need a robust set of user rights in order to function.

Table 15-2	Windows 2000 Logon Rights
Logon Right	**What It Does**
Access this Computer from the Network	Permits users to access the computer from across the network. Contrast this to the user being able to log on interactively to the system. (*Logging on interactively* means physically logging on to the system from the key-board.) By default, Administrators, Everyone, and Power Users have this right.
Deny Access to this Computer from the Network	Prevents users from accessing the computer from across the network. This logon right (or lack thereof) comes in very handy for securing a system.
Log on Locally	Permits a user to belly up to the keyboard and log on locally. By default, only Administrators, Account Operators, Backup Operators, Print Operators, and Server Operators have this right on all systems.
Deny Log on Locally	Prevents users from logging on locally. Again, very useful in securing a system.

Assigning IPSec policies

Microsoft is very proud of the fact that Windows 2000 supports IPSec (TCP/IP Security). Therefore, you better know it for the exam.

IPSec protects the TCP/IP communications protocol used by Windows 2000. This protection is essential if you often have sensitive information transferring throughout your network. In fact, that characteristic forms the basis for your first decision regarding IPSec: whether or not you need to use it. If you determine that your security needs are minimal, you leave TCP/IP in the default configuration, which has IPSec disabled.

For a medium- to high-risk network, Windows 2000 provides predefined IPSec policies that are perfectly appropriate for your needs. Here are the predefined policies of IPSec:

- **Client (Respond Only):** You use this setting for computers that usually do not need secure communications. For example, use this setting for a computer that only needs to use IPSec when requested by another system in your network.

- **Server (Request Security):** You use this setting for systems that should use IPSec most of the time. With this policy, the computer accepts unsecured traffic, but always attempts to secure additional communications by requesting security from the original sender. This policy enables the entire communication to be unsecured if the other computer is not IPSec-enabled.

- **Secure Server (Require Security):** Use this setting for computers that should always use secure TCP/IP communications. This policy rejects unsecured incoming communications, and outgoing traffic is always secured. Unsecured communications are not permitted, even if a peer system is not IPSec-enabled.

You assign IPSec policies using Group Policy. Of course, you then link this Group Policy object to a computer account, site, domain, or organizational unit. By assigning IPSec to a container object such as a domain or an OU, you can easily implement the IPSec policy against multiple systems simultaneously.

For the exam, you need to remember the following points, however:

- IPSec policies that you apply to a domain override local, active IPSec policy if that computer is a member of the domain.

- IPSec policies that you assign to organizational units override domain-level policy for any members of that OU. Also, the lowest-level OU IPSec policy overrides IPSec policy for higher-level OUs for any members of that organizational unit.

✔ You should definitely assign policies at the highest possible level to provide the greatest effect with the least amount of administrative effort.

✔ IPSec policy remains active even after you delete the Group Policy object you used for assigning it. You must unassign the IPSec policy before you delete the policy object.

Lab 15-2 describes the steps for assigning an IPSec policy.

Lab 15-2   Assigning an IPSec Policy

1. **Use the Active Directory Users and Computers console to access the GPO you want to use for setting user rights.**

   See Chapter 7 if you need to review the steps for editing GPOs.

2. **In the left pane of the Group Policy snap-in, click Computer Configuration.**

3. **Double-click Windows Settings and then double-click Security Settings.**

4. **Click the IP Security Policies folder, as shown in Figure 15-3.**

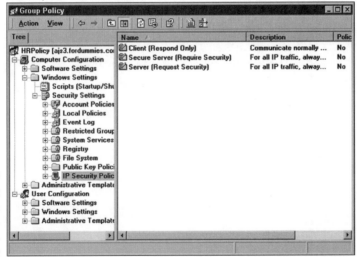

Figure 15-3: Setting an IPSec policy.

5. **In the console's right-hand pane, right-click the policy you want to assign and then choose Assign.**

Watch out if you are configuring IPSec remotely from a client system that does not support IPSec. After you turn on this powerful feature, you cannot communicate with the IPSec network.

Using Security Templates and Security Configuration and Analysis

Microsoft has certainly added some exciting new security-related features to Windows 2000 — for example, security templates and the Security Configuration and Analysis console. With security templates, you can easily centralize your method of defining security in your network, and the Security Configuration and Analysis console helps you enforce these security settings.

Working with security templates

A security template conveniently stores a group of Windows 2000 security settings for you in a simple text file with an INF extension. Figure 15-4 shows an example of a security template. As I explain in this section, this file makes setting consistent security settings a snap. By using security templates, you can set all Group Policy security configurations with the exception of IPSec and Public Key policies.

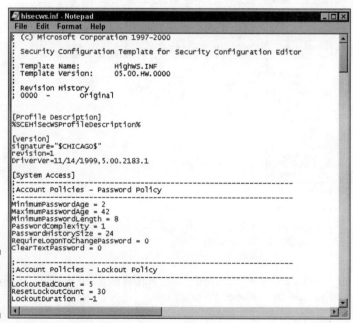

```
hisecws.inf - Notepad                                         _ □ X
File  Edit  Format  Help
; (c) Microsoft Corporation 1997-2000

; Security Configuration Template for Security Configuration Editor

; Template Name:        HighWS.INF
; Template Version:     05.00.HW.0000

; Revision History
; 0000    -       Original


[Profile Description]
%SCEHiSecWSProfileDescription%

[version]
signature="$CHICAGO$"
revision=1
DriverVer=11/14/1999,5.00.2183.1

[System Access]
;------------------------------------------------------------
;Account Policies - Password Policy
;------------------------------------------------------------
MinimumPasswordAge = 2
MaximumPasswordAge = 42
MinimumPasswordLength = 8
PasswordComplexity = 1
PasswordHistorySize = 24
RequireLogonToChangePassword = 0
ClearTextPassword = 0

;------------------------------------------------------------
;Account Policies - Lockout Policy
;------------------------------------------------------------
LockoutBadCount = 5
ResetLockoutCount = 30
LockoutDuration = -1
```

Figure 15-4: A security template.

You use a security template by importing it into a Group Policy object. What a quick and easy way to configure that GPO! You then assign the GPO to your Active Directory container or computer object.

To make your life as an administrator even easier, Microsoft provides a large set of predefined security templates. You can find these security templates in the *systemroot*\Security\Templates folder, as shown in Figure 15-5. The templates are designed for a wide variety of security needs and system roles. You can use these templates as they are, modify them, or use them to create your own new and improved templates. Table 15-3 describes the predefined templates provided in Windows 2000.

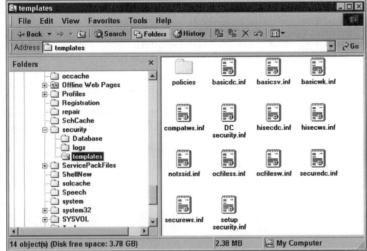

Figure 15-5:
The predefined security templates.

Table 15-3 **The Windows 2000 Predefined Templates**

Template Name	Description
BASICDC.INF	Default domain controller security settings
BASICSV.INF	Default server security settings
BASICWK.INF	Default workstation security settings
COMPATWS.INF	Compatible workstation or server security settings
DC SECURITY.INF	Default security settings updated for domain controllers
HISECDC.INF	Highly secure domain controller security settings
HISECWS.INF	Highly secure workstation or server security settings
NOTSSID.INF	Removes the Terminal Server User SID from Windows 2000 Server
OCFILESS.INF	Optional Component File Security for server

(continued)

Table 15-3 *(continued)*

Template Name	Description
OCFILESW.INF	Optional Component File Security for workstation
SECUREDC.INF	Secure domain controller security settings
SECUREWS.INF	Secure server or workstation security settings
SETUP SECURITY.INF	Out-of-the-box, default security settings

Notice that most of these security templates follow a very distinct naming convention. This is no coincidence.

- ✔ BASIC*.INF files return security settings to their default values.

- ✔ COMPAT*.INF templates allow for the largest number of applications to run successfully in Windows 2000 given the security settings.

- ✔ SECURE*.INF templates provide recommended security settings for medium-security environments.

- ✔ HISEC*.INF files provide security settings commonly found in a high-security environment. In fact, these security settings are so strict that Windows 2000 systems using them cannot communicate with previous Windows versions.

The easiest way for you to manage security templates is using the Security Templates console. Interestingly enough, the Security Templates console does not get installed in your Administrative Tools area by default. You have to build the console from scratch, as I explain in Lab 15-3.

Lab 15-3   Accessing the Security Templates Console

1. **Click Start⇨Run.**

2. **In the Run dialog box, type** mmc **and click OK.**

3. **Choose Console⇨Add/Remove Snap-In and then click Add in the dialog box that's displayed.**

4. **In the Add Standalone Snap-In dialog box, shown in Figure 15-6, select Security Templates and click the Add button.**

5. **Click Close and then click OK.**

6. **Choose Console⇨Save.**

7. **Enter the name you want to assign to this console and click the Save button.**

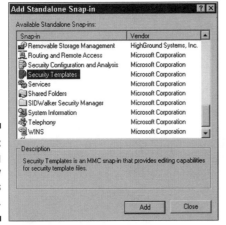

Figure 15-6:
Accessing
the Security
Templates
console.

Your Security Templates console now appears on the Administrative Tools menu. Using this Security Templates console, you can easily customize your predefined templates and create new ones from scratch.

For the exam, you also need to know how to import a security template into a Group Policy object. After all, that's how you actually put these files into use! Lab 15-4 reviews the steps in this process.

Lab 15-4   Importing a Security Template into a GPO

1. **Use the Active Directory Users and Computers console to access the GPO you want to use for setting user rights.**

   See Chapter 7 if you need to review the steps for editing GPOs.

2. **In the console's left pane, right-click Security Settings and choose Import Policy, as shown in Figure 15-7.**

3. **In the Import Policy From dialog box, select the security template you want to import and click Open.**

4. **Initiate the security settings you have just imported by performing one of the following actions:**

   • **Type** secedit /refreshpolicy machine_policy **at the command prompt.**

   • **Restart your computer.**

   • **Sit back and wait. As you know, Group Policy refreshes periodically.**

You can also export security policies from a GPO to create your own template. This capability is very useful if you want to return to particular security settings you have configured in Windows 2000. Just import your template back in, and the settings are restored!

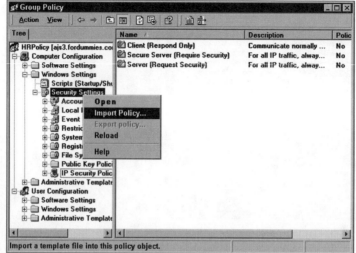

Figure 15-7:
Importing a
security
template.

Using Security Configuration and Analysis

Figure 15-8 shows the Security Configuration and Analysis console — a very cool utility for analyzing the security settings in your network, viewing the results, and reconfiguring the security settings to meet your goals. Typically, you would have to purchase a third-party add-on if you wanted this type of utility for Windows. However, this fairly sophisticated tool comes built into the operating system.

The console uses a database underlying the Microsoft Management Console (MMC) interface to perform the security analysis. Speaking of the MMC, you need to build one to access the console, just like you do for the Security Templates console. (See the preceding section in this chapter.)

Why do you need a tool like the Security Configuration and Analysis console? Because Administrators, Power Users, and the like constantly make slight changes to security settings so they can accommodate new scenarios that pop up in the network from time to time. Increasingly, these changes to the security configuration do not get reversed, and before you know it, you have security holes that you could drive a truck through.

With the Security Configuration and Analysis console, you can easily analyze the security settings in your network and get recommendations about how you can quickly get your Windows 2000 implementation back into shape. Sure enough, the Security Configuration and Analysis console performs these tasks using the security templates and its database engine.

Fortunately, for the exam, you do not need to know all the implementation details. Just understand the following steps for successfully using the Security Configuration and Analysis tool:

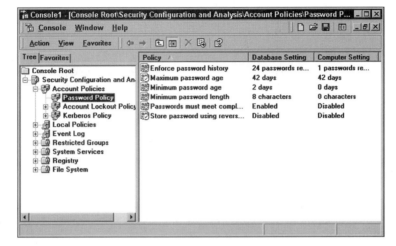

Figure 15-8:
The Security
Configura-
tion and
Analysis
console.

1. **Access the Security Configuration and Analysis tool by building a Microsoft Management Console.**

2. **Set a working security database in the Security Configuration and Analysis console.**

3. **Import the appropriate security template into the console.**

4. **Analyze the security settings against the template and view the results.**

5. **Configure the appropriate security settings based on these results and remember, the tool does this for you automatically, as shown in Figure 15-9.**

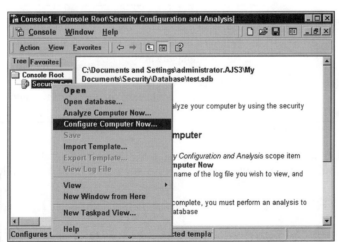

Figure 15-9:
Configuring
security.

Using SECEDIT

Another security-related addition to Windows 2000 that you need to know for the exam is SECEDIT. In Chapter 7, I explain how you use SECEDIT to force Group Policy refreshes in your Windows 2000 network. This section takes a closer look at SECEDIT.

SECEDIT is a command-line tool. Here's the really nifty thing about it: When you call it from a batch file or task scheduler, it can automatically create and apply templates and analyze system security. Of course, you can also run it dynamically from the command prompt.

This tool is useful if you have multiple computers that you need to analyze and reconfigure with security settings, and you want to perform these tasks off-hours.

The switches you use with SECEDIT are pretty straightforward indeed, and should not be too hard for you to remember for the exam, especially considering what you know about the Security Configuration and Analysis console. (See the preceding section in this chapter.) Table 15-4 describes the SECEDIT commands you should know for the exam.

Table 15-4	SECEDIT Commands
Command	*What It Does*
/analyze	Causes SECEDIT to analyze your security configuration
/configure	Configures security settings on systems by applying a stored security template
/refreshpolicy	Forces Group Policy to refresh in your network
/export	Exports a stored template from a security database to a security template file
/validate	Validates the syntax of a security template you want to import into a database for analysis or application to a system

Of course, all these commands require additional configuration specs. Fortunately, however, you do not need to know that level of detail for the exam!

Troubleshooting a Security Configuration

Well, with all this fancy security technology, there are bound to be areas where you can get into a bit of trouble. For the exam, you should be familiar with these possible occurrences and their fixes:

- ✓ **Error message in Event Viewer from scecli - ID 1202.** This error often results from failing to refresh Group Policy after changes have been made. Use SECEDIT to refresh Group Policy.

- ✓ **Error message:** `Failed to Open the Group Policy Object.` Typically, this message involves a network-related error. In fact, it usually involves a problem with the DNS configuration. Ensure that you have a proper DNS configuration implemented.

- ✓ **Your security settings are not taking effect.** First, ensure that you have refreshed Group Policy. Also, verify that another GPO is not overriding your security configuration. If necessary, review the precedence of Group Policy objects I describe in Chapter 7 and this chapter.

- ✓ **Policies from your Windows NT domain do not migrate to Windows 2000.** Well, you cannot do anything about this problem. Group Policies have changed completely from NT 4 to Windows 2000. Currently, you have no way to use your NT 4 policies in an Active Directory domain.

Prep Test

1 You need to grant the Profile System Performance privilege to several interns in your organization. How should you do this?

   A ○ Grant the privilege to the user accounts using Group Policy.

   B ○ Grant the privilege to the appropriate global group that contains the interns.

   C ○ Place the interns in the Domain Admins group.

   D ○ Place the interns in the Power Users group.

2 You have hired an assistant right out of college to assist you with some network administration tasks. The assistant just called to inform you that he cannot log on to one of the domain controllers in the West branch. You ensure that intern is pressing Ctrl+Alt+Del properly at the machine. What is the most likely problem?

   A ○ The user is not a member of the Domain Admins.

   B ○ The user is not a member of the Enterprise Admins.

   C ○ The user does not have the Access this Computer from the Network logon right.

   D ○ The user does not have the Log on Locally user right.

3 You want to ensure that a system in your Accounting department responds to requests for IPSec communications when requested. You do not care if the system uses IPSec any other time. What policy should you set?

   A ○ Client (Respond Only)

   B ○ Server (Request Security)

   C ○ Secure Server (Require Security)

   D ○ Optional (Require Security)

4 You want to ensure that a system in your Finance department uses IPSec at all times during network communications. What policy should you set?

   A ○ Client (Respond Only)

   B ○ Server (Request Security)

   C ○ Secure Server (Require Security)

   D ○ Optional (Require Security)

5 You want to increase security for a system in the Marketing department. You want the system to attempt IPSec communications whenever possible, but you still want it to communicate with other machines if they do not support IPSec. What policy should you set?

A ○ Client (Respond Only)

B ○ Server (Request Security)

C ○ Secure Server (Require Security)

D ○ Optional (Require Security)

6 **You want to assign an IPSec policy in your Windows 2000 network. At what level should you set this policy?**

A ○ At the highest container level possible

B ○ At the lowest container level possible

C ○ Always at the site level

D ○ Anywhere but the domain level

7 **You want to ensure that your Windows 2000 security settings do not cause applications to stop running at any point. Which security template should you use for this purpose?**

A ○ BASICWK.INF

B ○ COMPATWS.INF

C ○ DC SECURITY.INF

D ○ HISECDC.INF

8 **Which SECEDIT switch do you use to analyze the security configuration of a particular system?**

A ○ /configure

B ○ /refreshpolicy

C ○ /analyze

D ○ /compare

9 **Which functions can the Security Configuration and Analysis console perform? Choose all that apply.**

A ❏ Provide suggestions for securing a system to a specified level.

B ❏ Enforce a particular configuration.

C ❏ Allow for importing of specific security templates.

D ❏ Enforce IPSec policies.

10 **You want to automate the tasks that you routinely perform with the Security Configuration and Analysis console. What utility should you use to do this?**

A ○ NTDSUTIL

B ○ SECEDIT

C ○ SECCONFIG

D ○ REPLMON

Answers

1 **B.** Grant the privilege to the appropriate global group that contains the interns. You should always attempt to assign user rights to groups as opposed to individual user accounts. Doing so eases the administrative workload. *See "Assigning user rights."*

2 **D.** The user does not have the Log on Locally user right. Because the user is trying to log on interactively at the system, the user needs the Log on Locally user right. *Review "Logon rights."*

3 **A.** Client (Respond Only). With the Client IPSec policy selected, the system only uses IPSec when a peer system asks it to do so. *See "Assigning IPSec policies."*

4 **C.** Secure Server (Require Security). Your system better be able to use IPSec to communicate with a server using this policy, or tough luck. This is the strongest policy setting you can have. *See "Assigning IPSec policies."*

5 **B.** Server (Request Security). In this case, the system tries to communicate using IPSec whenever possible. It will still talk to another system if that system does not support IPSec, however. *See "Assigning IPSec policies."*

6 **A.** At the highest container level possible. To ease your administrative workload, set your IPSec policy at the highest container level possible. With this configuration, you can easily assign the policy to many systems in one step. *See "Assigning IPSec policies."*

7 **B.** COMPATWS.INF. This security template ensures that your security settings are compatible with the greatest number of applications. *Review "Working with security templates."*

8 **C.** /analyze. Believe it or not, it is that simple. You use the /analyze switch to analyze security settings with SECEDIT. *See "Using SECEDIT."*

9 **A, B,** and **C.** Provide suggestions for securing a system to a specified level. Enforce a particular configuration. Allow for importing of specific security templates. Security templates cannot enforce IPSec policies, and the Security Configuration and Analysis tool is based on security templates. *See "Working with security templates."*

10 **B.** SECEDIT. SECEDIT is the command-line utility for analyzing and enforcing security policies in Windows 2000. *Review "Using SECEDIT."*

Chapter 16

Auditing: Know Every Move Your Users Make

● ●

Exam Objectives

▶ Monitoring access to shared folders

▶ Implementing an audit policy

▶ Monitoring and analyzing security events

● ●

*T*o be really confident in the security of your network, you must constantly monitor critical resources. In this way, you can quickly catch attempted security breaches and close the doors that have been discovered into your network. Fortunately, Windows 2000 has built-in tools to assist you in these endeavors. You can easily monitor access to shared folders and you can audit access to just about anything!

For the exam, you need to master all these monitoring and auditing tasks. To help you prepare, this chapter covers the following topics:

> ✔ Monitoring shared resources
>
> ✔ Setting an audit policy
>
> ✔ Auditing files and folders
>
> ✔ Auditing Active Directory objects
>
> ✔ Implementing essential auditing practices

Quick Assessment

Monitoring
access to
shared
folders

1 To monitor the shared folders on your server, use the _____ node in the Shared Folders snap-in.

2 You can easily monitor shares and open files by using the _____ console.

3 To update the list of shared folders in your console display, use the _____ command.

4 You can easily disconnect a user from an open _____.

Implementing
an audit
policy

5 To audit access in your Windows 2000 network, you must configure an audit _____

6 To audit access to printers, you must enable auditing of _____ access.

7 To guard against a random password attack, you should configure a(n) _____ audit for logon/logoff.

Monitoring
and
analyzing
security
events

8 You view audit results in the Event Viewer's _____ log.

Answers

1 *Shares*. See "Monitoring Access to Shared Folders."

2 *Computer Management*. Review "Monitoring Access to Shared Folders."

3 *Refresh*. See "Monitoring Access to Shared Folders."

4 *File*. See "Monitoring Access to Shared Folders."

5 *Policy*. Review "Creating an Audit Policy."

6 *Object*. Review "Implementing Auditing."

7 *Failure*. See "Implementing Auditing."

8 *Security*. Study "Implementing Auditing."

Monitoring Access to Shared Folders

Figure 16-1 shows the Computer Management console — your ticket to monitoring shared folders on a server. In fact, you can easily monitor user sessions and files that users open by accessing the server remotely. To access the Computer Management console, simply right-click the My Computer icon on your server's desktop and choose Manage. You can also access the Computer Management console by clicking Start⇨Programs⇨Administrative Tools⇨Computer Management.

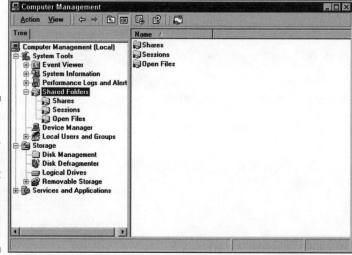

Figure 16-1:
The Computer Management console and the Shared Folders snap-in.

You use the Shares node of the Shared Folders snap-in to view the shared folders on your server. As shown in Figure 16-2, you can then view the following information:

- ✔ **Shared Folder:** The name of the shared folder on the server
- ✔ **Shared Path:** The path to the shared folder
- ✔ **Type:** The operating system that must be used to access the shared folder
- ✔ **# Client Redirections:** The number of clients with remote connections to the share
- ✔ **Comment:** The comment you added to the share when you created it

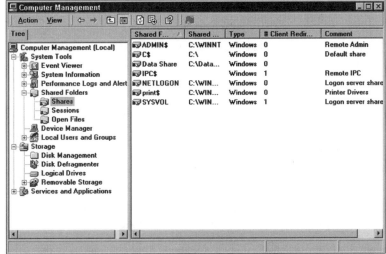

Figure 16-2:
The Shares
node.

To manage shares while you monitor them, simply right-click the share in the
right-hand pane of the Computer Management snap-in and choose Properties
from the shortcut menu. Using the share's Properties dialog box, shown in
Figure 16-3, you can easily change specific settings on the share. For example,
if users can no longer connect to the share, perhaps the maximum number of
connections permissible has been reached. You can easily increase that maximum number using the settings in the share's Properties dialog box.
Remember, however, that you must have the correct number of Client Access
Licenses (CALs) for the server.

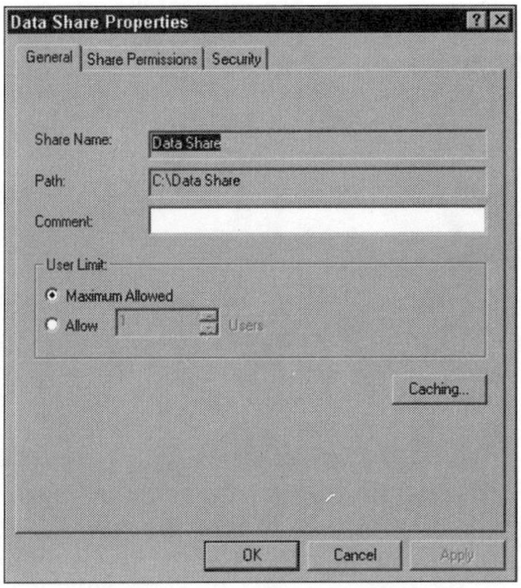

Figure 16-3:
Accessing
share
properties.

You can also monitor open files on the server with the Open Files node. For example, you can disconnect users from these files, or notify them to close the files themselves. Typically, you make this notification because you are shutting down the server. The Open Files node details the following information:

- ✔ **Open File:** The name of the open files on the computer

- ✔ **Accessed By:** The user that has the file open

- ✔ **Type:** The operating system running on the computer where the user is logged on

- ✔ **# locks:** The number of locks on the file; these are typically requested by programs that need exclusive access to the file

- ✔ **Open Mode:** The type of access the user's application requested when it opened the file — Read or Write, for example

You also can easily disconnect users from one open file or all open files on the server. To disconnect all users from all open files, simply right-click the Open Files node and choose Disconnect All Open Files, as shown in Figure 16-4. To disconnect all users from one open file, select the open file from the right-hand pane, right-click the file, and choose Close Open File.

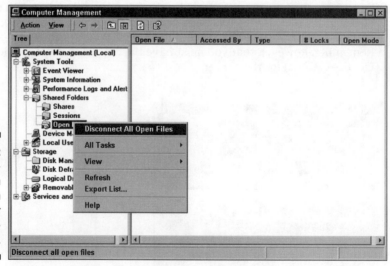

Figure 16-4: Disconnecting all open files in Computer Management.

Now, you certainly don't want to rudely disconnect your users from their open files. Doing so could cause corruption with the file, not to mention nasty phone calls. You should definitely send them a message before you rudely disconnect them! As you might guess, sending them a message is simple: Right-click the Shared Folders snap-in and choose Send Console Message from the shortcut menu.

Creating an Audit Policy

Auditing is a very powerful way for you to monitor security in your Windows 2000 network. With auditing, you can monitor your users as they access files, folders, Active Directory objects, printers, and much more in your network. You track these activities with events that the system records in the Event Viewer's security log. The log reports the action that was performed, the user that did it, the success or failure of the event, when the event occurred, and even the system where the user was located when the incident occurred.

Before you can configure auditing in your Windows 2000 network, you must create an audit policy. The audit policy defines exactly which types of events you want to track on the Windows 2000 systems. Table 16-1 describes the types of events you can audit — know them for the exam!

Table 16-1	Types of Auditing Events
Event Category	*What It Audits*
Account logon	Logon requests to domain controllers
Account management	Changes made to user accounts, including creations and deletions
Directory service access	Access to Active Directory objects (after you configure the specific Active Directory objects you want to audit)
Logon events	Users logging on and off, including network connections to systems
Object access	Access to such resources as files, folders, or printers (after you configure the resources that you want to audit)
Policy change	Changes made to user security options, user rights, or audit policies
Privilege use	The use of privileges that you may have assigned to groups of users (not including logging on, which is covered by another audit policy setting)
Process tracking	Actions that programs perform
System events	Security-related events, including computer shutdowns and restarts

In Lab 16-1, you review the procedure for setting the audit policy for your network. In the following section, you take a look at actually designating auditing on resources.

Lab 16-1   Setting an Audit Policy

1. **Click Start⇨Programs⇨Administrative Tools⇨Active Directory Users and Computers.**

2. **In the console's left pane, right-click Domain Controllers and then choose Properties.**

3. **On the Group Policy tab in the Properties dialog box that's displayed, click the policy in which you want to set your audit policy and choose Edit.**

4. **In the left pane of the Group Policy snap-in, click the Computer Configuration node.**

5. **Double-click Windows Settings, double-click Security Settings , and then double-click Local Policies.**

6. **Finally, double-click Audit Policy.**

7. **In the console's right-hand pane, right-click the event category you want to audit and choose Security.**

8. **In the Security Policy Setting dialog box, shown in Figure 16-5, click Define These Policy Settings and then select one or both of the following options:**

   • **Success:** Audit success events for the category.

   • **Failure:** Audit failure events for the category.

9. **Click OK.**

10. **Refresh Group Policy so these changes take effect quickly. You can easily refresh Group Policy by using SECEDIT at the command prompt. Type the following command:**

```
SECEDIT /refreshpolicy
```

Figure 16-5:
Configuring
an audit
policy.

Implementing Auditing

After you set an audit policy and select Object Access and Directory Service Access as event categories that you want to audit, you need to configure auditing on the resources, as I explain in Lab 16-2.

Lab 16-2   Auditing Folder or File Resources

1. **Click Start⇨Programs⇨Accessories⇨Windows Explorer.**

2. **Right-click the file or folder that you want to audit and choose Properties.**

3. **In the Properties dialog box, click the Security tab.**

4. **On the Security tab, click the Advanced button.**

5. **On the Auditing tab in the Access Control Settings For dialog box for the selected file or folder, click the Add button to add the users or groups for which you want to audit access and then click OK when you are finished.**

6. **In the Auditing Entry For dialog box, shown in Figure 16-6, select the Successful or Failed check boxes or both for the specific events you want to audit and then click OK.**

7. **In the Apply Onto list (available only for folders), specify where objects are audited. Click OK.**

8. **To prevent changes that are made to parent OUs from applying to this very important OU you just configured, clear the Allow Inheritable Auditing Entries From Parent To Propagate To Third Object check box.**

9. **Click OK.**

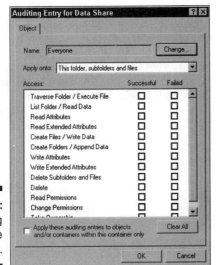

Figure 16-6:
Auditing
resource
access.

Auditing of Active Directory objects is just like auditing for file and folder access. First, you set up the appropriate audit policy. Then, you specify which objects should be audited, who you want to audit, and what types of access you want to track. Simply use the Active Directory Users and Computer console and the Properties pages of objects to set up the auditing specifics.

Auditing printer access is just as simple. Use a printer's Properties dialog box to access the Security tab and the auditing feature. Remember, you must have an auditing policy created for Object Access.

Analyzing Security Events

To view the results of auditing, use the Event Viewer's security log. Lab 16-3 details the steps for analyzing these security events.

Lab 16-3 Analyzing Security Events

1. **Click Start⇨Programs⇨Administrative Tools⇨Event Viewer.**

2. **In the left pane, click the Security Log node.**

   If auditing is properly configured, security events appear in the right-hand pane. Failure events appear with a lock symbol, while success audits appear with a key symbol.

3. **To analyze the details of a particular security event, simply double-click the event in the right-hand pane.**

The EventLog service is responsible for creating these logs. This service starts automatically when you start your Windows 2000 Servers. By default, only administrators can gain access to security logs.

To further ensure that you catch security breaches and other security-related events, you can enforce that all auditable activities are logged by halting the computer when the security log is full. To make this configuration change, set the security log to either Overwrite Events Older Than *n* Days or Do Not Overwrite Events (Clear Log Manually). Then use the Registry Editor (REGEDT32) to create or assign the following registry key value:

- **Hive:** HKEY_LOCAL_MACHINE\SYSTEM
- **Key:** \CurrentControlSet\Control\Lsa
- **Name:** CrashOnAuditFail
- **Type:** REG_DWORD
- **Value:** 1

This change takes effect the next time the computer is started.

Auditing Musts

You must follow some very specific rules and guidelines when you configure auditing in your network. As you might expect, you should know these rules and guidelines for the exam:

- ✔ **Determine whether you need to track trends in system usage.** If so, plan to use the Event Viewer's archive feature to prevent logs from becoming too large or filling completely. Rather than use auditing for this purpose, I recommend that you turn to some third-party tool for monitoring your system usage trends.

- ✔ **Review security logs frequently.** Auditing really does no good if you do not review the results that you achieve from auditing. Check the security log frequently so you can actually catch security breaches.

- ✔ **Define a useful, manageable audit policy.** Don't go wild, auditing anything and everything in your network. You end up with so much data that it tells you practically nothing. You could also dramatically slow down your network. Just stick to auditing sensitive and confidential data at first and then move on from there.

- ✔ **Audit resource access for the Everyone group instead of the Users group.** This approach helps you to catch external hackers that may be on your network. These folks do not show up in the Users group.

- ✔ **Audit all administrative tasks by the administrators group.** This is an excellent practice if you have lots of "junior admins" that could get you into trouble with their actions. And remember, thanks to the Delegation of Control capabilities in Active Directory, you really should not have that many Admins anyway.

Table 16-2 offers several useful guidelines for handling auditing for specific problems.

Table 16-2	Auditing Guidelines
Threat	*Audit Event*
Random password attack	Failure audit for logon/logoff
Stolen password break-in	Success audit for logon/logoff
Misuse of privileges	Success audit for privilege use
Improper access to files	Success and failure audits for object access
Improper access to printers	Success and failure audits for printer usages
Virus outbreaks	Success and failure audits for process tracking

Prep Test

1 You want to monitor shared folder access on your Windows 2000 server. Which tool should you use?

A ○ Computer Management

B ○ Active Directory Users and Computers

C ○ Active Directory Sites and Services

D ○ Active Directory Domains and Trusts

2 You are viewing the results in the Shared Folders area. Which statistic tells you how many users are connected to the Shared Folder?

A ○ # Users

B ○ Users

C ○ # Client Redirections

D ○ # Connections

3 You are monitoring the number of connections to a shared folder on your server. You know more users are currently connecting to the resource, but the number of users displayed is not increasing. What is the most likely problem?

A ○ The Shared Folder node is not functioning properly.

B ○ Active Directory is not installed properly.

C ○ You do not have the appropriate privileges.

D ○ You are not refreshing the display.

4 You are attempting to configure auditing on a resource in your Windows 2000 domain. The option you want to configure is unavailable, however. What is the most likely reason?

A ○ You have not configured an appropriate audit policy.

B ○ Active Directory is not installed properly.

C ○ You do not have the appropriate privileges.

D ○ Auditing is broken.

5 You want to audit for possible virus attacks in your network. For which event should you audit?

A ○ Object access

B ○ Process tracking

C ○ Directory object access

D ○ Account administration

6 **Where do you configure auditing on folders or files in Windows 2000?**

A ○ Active Directory Users and Computers

B ○ Active Directory Sites and Services

C ○ Active Directory Domains and Trusts

D ○ The Windows Explorer

7 **Where do you view the results of auditing?**

A ○ Active Directory Users and Computers

B ○ The Windows Explorer

C ○ The Event Viewer

D ○ The Performance Console

8 **Which command can you use to notify users that you are about to disconnect them from a resource?**

A ○ Send Console Message

B ○ Send Message

C ○ Report to User

D ○ Disconnect Message

9 **Which auditing event category do you use to track security-related events?**

A ○ Process tracking

B ○ Object access

C ○ System events

D ○ Directory object access

10 **Which auditing event category do you use to track resource access?**

A ○ Process tracking

B ○ Object access

C ○ System events

D ○ Directory object access

Answers

1 **A.** Computer Management. The Computer Management console is a simple way to monitor access to shared folders. *See "Monitoring Access to Shared Folders."*

2 **C.** # Client Redirections. The # of Client Redirections area displays the number of users connected to the shared folder. *See "Monitoring Access to Shared Folders."*

3 **D.** You are not refreshing the display. The display of Shared Folders does not refresh automatically. *See "Monitoring Access to Shared Folders."*

4 **A.** You have not configured an appropriate audit policy. Before you can audit for specific events, you must configure an audit policy in your network. *Review "Creating an Audit Policy."*

5 **B.** Process tracking. Process tracking auditing is an excellent way to monitor your network for virus activity. *See "Creating an Audit Policy."*

6 **D.** The Windows Explorer. You can use the Windows Explorer to configure auditing on specific resources. *Review "Implementing Auditing."*

7 **C.** The Event Viewer. You use the Event Viewer's security log to view the results of auditing. *Study "Implementing Auditing."*

8 **A.** Send Console Message. Use the Send Console Message command to send messages to users regarding disconnects. *See "Monitoring Access to Shared Folders."*

9 **C.** System events. For security-related events, create an audit policy that tracks system events. *Study "Creating an Audit Policy."*

10 **B.** Object access. To audit files, folders, or printers, use the object access category. *See "Creating an Audit Policy."*

Part VIII
The Part of Tens

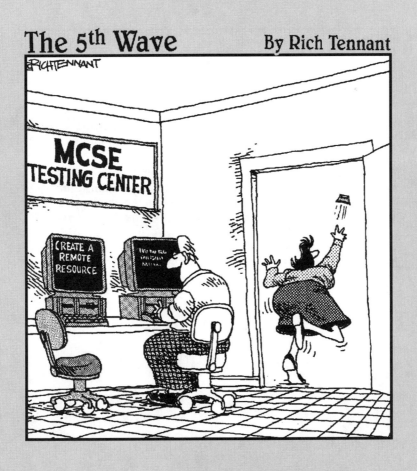

The 5th Wave — By Rich Tennant

MCSE TESTING CENTER

CREATE A REMOTE RESOURCE

In the part . . .

*H*ere it is: The Part of Tens. This part of the book provides handy information to help you on exam day.
With the tips and hints I offer in this part of the book, you
can look forward to your exam session and not fear it!

In Chapter 17, I cover some tips that help you on exam
day. In Chapter 18, I answer the common questions that
everyone seems to have about the exam. Again, the goal is
for you to look forward to this event — after all, you're
paying for it!

Chapter 17

Ten Great Tips for Taking the Real Thing

In This Chapter

▶ Scheduling the test wisely

▶ Reading carefully

▶ Watching the clock

▶ Remembering to use your scratch paper

▶ Avoiding cheating

▶ Using more great test-taking strategies

*I*n previous chapters, I give you all the information you need to know for the exam. Here, I cover some classic exam-day tips that help you really go over the top. These tried-and-true tips have helped me and many others succeed on exam day. Enjoy!

Schedule Wisely

Typically, you can schedule an exam on the same day that you take it. Take advantage of this scheduling freedom! I am always amazed when I talk to MCSE candidates who schedule the exam for a month or more down the road and then start studying. Sure enough, test time comes, and they are not ready because of all the things that came up during the month. They take the test at the scheduled time and fail because they were not ready. Don't let this happen to you.

If your favorite test center is so very busy that you must schedule weeks in advance, call and reschedule if you are not ready. Currently, you can reschedule the exam as long as you call one full business day prior to your scheduled time.

You should take full advantage of these features. I don't even think about scheduling until I know I am ready. Also, I am willing to drive a little farther (or fly my plane, for that matter) to a less busy testing center so I can take the exam when I want to take it.

Also, think about the time of day you schedule for taking the exam. At a less busy testing center, you can typically select a time slot from 8 AM to 3 PM. If you are not a morning person, schedule for the afternoon. Also, watch out for days when you have other really important things going on. I once failed a morning exam because I was racing to get out in a short period of time to prepare for an afternoon meeting. Now, I test exclusively on Friday afternoons, when I am typically doing nothing but surfing the Web, anyway.

Get a Good Night's Sleep

Okay, I know you often hear about the importance of getting sufficient sleep. I never paid much attention to this one until I pulled a near all-nighter and then went in to test the next day. You really are better off getting a good night's sleep and then taking the test, rather than staying up all night cramming.

For some of you, getting a good night's sleep also means not getting too much sleep. Getting too much sleep can leave you drowsier than if you got too little rest the night before. Aim to get just the right amount of sleep the night before the exam.

Remember to Breathe

I have encountered MCSE candidates who know the material inside and out but panic during the exam and fail. Please, remember to breathe when you are taking the exam. You will pass every Microsoft test that you set out to pass. Sure, you will run into some exams that take a try or two before you succeed — and that is okay.

Read Carefully

Be sure to read carefully during the exam. You should practice reading carefully using the sample exams included in this book. Even on those seemingly easy standard multiple-choice questions with only one correct answer, you need to be careful. On all Microsoft multiple-choice questions, you must pick the *best* answer. If you do not read carefully and read *all* possible answers, you may choose the second-best response and get no credit. Don't let this happen to you.

You may find help for one question in other questions on the test. For example, a key phrase in one question may jog your memory and help you figure out the answer to another question. However, you can only pick up clues in this way by reading very carefully.

Watch the Clock

Remember, you are taking a timed exam. Use your time wisely. Another sad story involves those that fail because they run out of time. Do not fall into the trap of spending 10 minutes or more on questions that stump you. You just do not have enough time for that!

Use the Scratch Paper

I have taken many exams that I could not have passed without the scratch paper provided by the testing center. Make sure you get plenty and use it. In fact, ask for more than you will ever need. Some centers give you a portable whiteboard thingy. If you get one, ask for some paper towels so you can erase and start over when you need to.

In many cases, you will be creating tables and charts on the scratch paper as soon as you start the exam. I guarantee that you will fill your scratch paper with triangles and circles and all the domain and OU diagramming you'll be doing during this exam.

Know What to Do When You Know the Answer

Congratulations! When you get to a question and you know the answer, choose it and click that Next button. You don't have time to celebrate yet so keep moving. . . .

Know What to Do When You Don't Know the Answer

Oops — you knew this was going to happen. What should you do if you do not know the answer to a question? First, as I suggest earlier in this chapter, remember to breathe. Don't sweat it — you should not expect a perfect score on these exams.

When I run into a question that I cannot answer, I like to go ahead and make my best guess, using everything I know about the subject to help me. I then mark the question. I may return to the question at the end of the test if I have time. I definitely return to the question if another question helps me get the right answer.

Don't get in the habit of changing your guess unless you find help from other questions. Typically, your first guess is the right guess after all.

Don't Cheat

You don't want to even think about cheating. Microsoft has made some pretty big threats about this one lately. Get caught cheating and you immediately lose all Microsoft certifications and you can never apply to get them again. That is probably the ultimate penalty in the certification environment.

What are some classic cheats that you need to avoid? Here are just a few:

- ✔ **Bringing in notes of any kind.** I have seen small pieces of paper smuggled in and I have seen notes written on just about every available body part. My favorites are the subnetting T-shirts that many have created. Only wear these as a joke around the office.

- ✔ **Recording the exam.** This includes smuggling out your scratch paper. My favorite story here involves one creative individual who actually dictated the exam into a recorder.

- ✔ **Calling a friend during the test.** Most testing centers are sure to take cell phones these days.

- ✔ **Posting exam questions on the Web.** Stay away from so-called "brain dump" sites. They are bad news and really hurt the credibility of the certification program. Microsoft has already shut down and penalized the owners of seven sites and claims more will go before next quarter.

Don't Panic

Please, remember to breathe and don't panic. Have fun with the exam — you'll do fine. Please remember that everyone fails one sometime, and it is not a big deal.

Also, as far as this exam goes, you are bound to be successful! After all, you bought this book and used it — didn't you?

Chapter 18

Ten Common Questions and Answers about the Administering ADS Exam

*T*his chapter answers ten common questions that candidates ask me about the administering ADS exam. Use this information to make sure you are ready.

What Is the Exam Format?

At the time of this writing, the exam uses a standard multiple-choice format with a few drag-and-drop type questions here or there. You will see some questions that tell you to "Choose the best answer," and others that say "Choose all the correct answers." Microsoft also uses a new scenario-style question that has the following format:

Here is some background information to set up the problem.

Here is a list of what you want to accomplish:

- ✔ Accomplish item 1
- ✔ Accomplish item 2
- ✔ Accomplish item 3
- ✔ Accomplish item 4
- ✔ Accomplish item 5
- ✔ Accomplish item 6

Here are the steps you take:

- ✔ Step 1
- ✔ Step 2
- ✔ Step 3
- ✔ Step 4
- ✔ Step 5

What have you accomplished? Choose all that apply.

A ○ Accomplish item 1
B ○ Accomplish item 2
C ○ Accomplish item 3
D ○ Accomplish item 4
E ○ Accomplish item 5
F ○ Accomplish item 6

What Is the Passing Score?

At the time of this writing, the minimum required passing score is 651 points out of 1,000.

How Much Time Will I Have?

At the time of this writing, you have 110 minutes to complete the exam.

How Many Questions Will I Get?

At the time of this writing, the exam has 43 questions.

How Hard Is the Test — Really?

Interestingly, you hear many different responses to questions about the difficulty of the exam. Some people will say the exam is impossible to pass. These folks did not study or they studied the wrong materials. Others who have studied hard and read the best materials (like this book, of course) will find the exam simple.

Okay, so I am avoiding the question. If I were to rate this exam against the two dozen or so other professional certification exams I have taken, I would call it a nice, comfortable 6 (if 1 is simple, and 10 is nearly impossible).

What Online Resources Will Help Me Prepare?

The CD-ROM that comes with this book has a great listing of links that will help you prepare. At the very least, be sure to use the Microsoft Certification site (www.microsoft.com/trainingandservices). There, you will find the official page dedicated to this exam. And as always, answer as many reputable practice questions as you can obtain.

What If I Fail?

Hey, no big deal if you fail the exam. The worst parts are probably going to be the expense and the delay you experience before you move on to your next exam. If you studied hard and still fail, you will definitely know what you don't know following the experience. Brush up on your weak areas and go after it again.

If you fail twice within the same week, Microsoft makes you wait at least two weeks before you can try again.

I Heard There Are No More Score Reports — Is That True?

For most new Microsoft exams, you do not get a score report to help you identify your weak areas. You need to know the material really well going in so you can at least identify your weak areas because you no longer get a score breakdown. The new report only lists your score and the passing score.

What Should I Take to the Testing Center?

You need to have two forms of identification with you, one with a picture. That's it. If you take a phone or Personal Data Assistant (PDA) or any other nifty gadget with you, get ready to surrender it at check-in.

How Do I Schedule the Exam?

To schedule your exam day, contact Sylvan-Prometric or Virtual University Enterprises (VUE). You can call Sylvan-Prometric at 800-755-EXAM (from the U.S or Canada) or 410-843-8000 (from anywhere), or register via Sylvan's new and nifty Web site at www.2test.com. Contact VUE by calling 888-837-8616 (from the U.S. and Canada) or 612-995-8800 (from anywhere), or via VUE's Web site at www.vue.com/ms.

Part IX
Appendixes

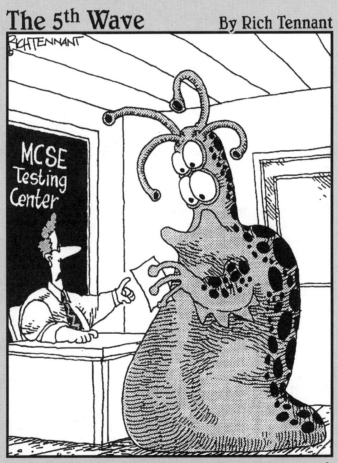

The 5th Wave   By Rich Tennant

"...and it doesn't appear that you'll have much trouble grasping some of the more 'alien' configuration concepts on this MCSE exam."

In this part . . .

Are you ready to do some more practice for the real exam? I can think of no better way to get ready than to take a couple of practice exams.

In this part, you can take two full-length practice exams. This part also includes a glossary of terms you should know and an appendix with installation instructions and information about the contents of the CD-ROM that ships with this book.

Appendix A

Practice Exam 1

· ·

Practice Exam Rules

▶ 90 minutes to complete the exam

▶ 43 questions

▶ At least 30 correct answers to pass

▶ Don't cheat!

· ·

*H*ere's an opportunity to make sure you are ready for exam day: a full-length practice exam that covers topics from throughout the book. If you do well on this test and the second practice test in Appendix B, you should be ready for the real thing.

Use the information provided in the Part of Tens to simulate the testing environment as closely as possible. Be sure to read carefully, just as you would on the real exam. And remember that my rules for time and your passing score are probably a bit more stringent than those you will encounter on the real exam.

Questions

1 How do you install a new domain controller in your Windows 2000 Active Directory-based network?

  A ○ Use Remote Installation Services.
  B ○ Use an ISS script to automate the installation.
  C ○ Use the Active Directory Installation wizard.
  D ○ Use imaging technology.

2 Your Active Directory network has two sites, and the site link connecting the two sites has the default cost assigned. You add a new site link to the implementation and you want to ensure that this new site link gets priority and is used most frequently. What cost should you assign to the new site link?

  A ○ 50
  B ○ 100
  C ○ 150
  D ○ 200

3 Which utility do you use to seize a Windows 2000 FSMO role?

  A ○ MOVETREE
  B ○ REPLMON
  C ○ SIDWALKER
  D ○ NTDSUTIL

4 Which Flexible Single-Master Operations Role is responsible for servicing password operations for Windows NT 4.0 clients?

  A ○ RID Master
  B ○ PDC Emulator
  C ○ Schema Master
  D ○ Infrastructure Master

5 Your Windows 2000 Active Directory forest consists of two domain trees: acme.com and abc.com. Users in the domain sales.acme.com need to access resources in the marketing.abc.com domain. What should you do as an Enterprise Administrator for this forest?

A ○ Create an explicit trust between the two domains.
B ○ Create two forests and place a domain in each forest.
C ○ Do nothing. A trust relationship already exists between the two domains.
D ○ Create a tree root trust between the two domains.

6 You are implementing a Windows 2000 Active Directory domain in your organization. You have not created the sites and subnets that define your physical topology. In Active Directory Sites and Services, where can you locate all the domain controllers you have created?

A ○ Default-First-Site-Name
B ○ FirstSite
C ○ Default-Site-Name
D ○ They do not exist in Active Directory Sites and Services. You must move them from the Active Directory Users and Computers console.

7 Which component of an Active Directory domain controller must be installed on an NTFS partition?

A ○ The Active Directory logs
B ○ SYSVOL
C ○ NTDS.DIT
D ○ The system directory

8 Which of the following choices represent benefits that you can realize by using an Active Directory-integrated zone in your Windows 2000 network? Choose all that apply.

A ❑ Increased Windows 2000 stability
B ❑ Increased fault tolerance
C ❑ Increased DNS stability
D ❑ Enhanced security for your DNS implementation

9 You cannot configure secure dynamic updates in your Windows network. What is the most likely reason?

A ○ DHCP is not properly configured.
B ○ Your DHCP server is not authorized in Active Directory.
C ○ Your DNS zone is not stored on an NTFS volume.
D ○ Your DNS zone is not Active Directory-integrated.

10 You installed DNS using the Active Directory Installation wizard. While using NSLOOKUP to test your DNS installation, you see error messages. What is the most likely problem?

A ○ A reverse lookup zone does not exist.

B ○ There is no forward lookup zone.

C ○ The zone is not Active Directory-integrated.

D ○ The zone is not configured for dynamic updates.

11 You are responsible for implementing Active Directory Services in your network. You are interested in using Microsoft's DNS service for creating the infrastructure required by ADS.

You want to accomplish the following:
• Support Active Directory Services.
• Enable applications to resolve for FQDNs using IP addresses.
• Use incremental zone transfers.
• Use secure dynamic updates.

You take the following steps:
• Install Microsoft's DNS service.
• Configure a standard forward lookup zone.
• Configure the zones for dynamic updates.
• Configure incremental zone transfers.

What have you accomplished? Choose all that apply.

A ❑ Support Active Directory Services.

B ❑ Enable applications to resolve for FQDNs using IP addresses.

C ❑ Use incremental zone transfers.

D ❑ Use secure dynamic updates.

12 Jim is responsible for the Active Directory implementation in his Windows 2000 domain. He wants to provide for fault tolerance in his design and ensure that only authorized updates occur to the dynamic DNS database. What should he do? Choose all that apply.

A ❑ Convert the domain to native mode.

B ❑ Convert the domain to mixed mode.

C ❑ Ensure that he has at least one secondary DNS server configured in the network.

D ❑ Configure an Active Directory-integrated zone.

E ❑ Ensure that the Allow Dynamic Updates option for the zone is set to Yes.

F ❑ Ensure that the Allow Dynamic Updates option for the zone is set to Only Secure Updates.

13 You are concerned that a very restrictive Group Policy that you have linked to the domain will affect the Managers security group in your Windows network. What should you do?

A ○ Do nothing. Group Policy settings do not affect security groups.

B ○ Remove the Read permission on the GPO for the security group.

C ○ Remove the users of the security group from the Authenticated Users group.

D ○ Remove the users from the domain and place them in a subdomain.

14 Steven has configured a password policy for his domain so that all users must have passwords with a minimum length of four characters. These passwords are also set to expire every 60 days. Steven has also created an organizational unit (OU) in the domain named East Branch. This OU contains shares and printers that are constantly hosting extremely confidential information. Steven wants the members of the East Branch OU to have their passwords expire every 30 days, and he wants to force them into a minimum password length of eight characters.

To achieve these design requirements, Steven creates a Group Policy object at the organizational unit level for the East Branch OU. This GPO includes a password policy so that all accounts within Accounting must have a password of at least eight characters, and passwords expire every 30 days. To test the policy, he logs on as a user from the East Branch OU and attempts to change the password to a password of less than eight characters. Unfortunately, the system permits him to change the password to one of less than eight characters.

What is the most likely problem?

A ○ Group Policies for password settings can only be set at the domain level.

B ○ Group Policies do not refresh until a user logs off and logs back on.

C ○ Group Policies cannot be applied to OUs.

D ○ Group Policies do not refresh until the system is restarted.

15 You want some other administrators in your Windows 2000 network to help you administer your Group Policy objects. What should you do?

A ○ Place these administrators in the Domain Admins group.

B ○ Place these administrators in the Enterprise Admins group.

C ○ Assign these administrators the appropriate permissions.

D ○ Assign these administrators the appropriate logon rights.

16 Which of the following can be accomplished in a Windows 2000 forest if all of the domains are running in native mode? Choose all that apply.

A ❑ Global groups can contain global groups from the same domain.

B ❑ Local groups can contain universal groups from any domain.

C ❑ Universal groups can contain universal groups from any domain.

D ❑ Universal groups can contain domain local groups from any domain.

E ❑ Global groups can contain user accounts from the same domain.

F ❑ Local groups can contain local groups from the same domain.

G ❑ Global groups can contain global groups from any domain.

H ❑ Local groups can contain local groups from any domain.

17 Bill is new to your IT organization. One afternoon, Bill deletes several objects from Active Directory, including an entire organizational unit.

Fortunately, you recently backed up your Active Directory installation. You must restore this deleted information as soon as possible.

What is the correct order for restoring Active Directory in this case?

A ○ Use Backup to restore Active Directory; restart the domain controller; select Directory Services Restore Mode; run NTDSUTIL; restart the domain controller.

B ○ Restart the domain controller; select Directory Services Restore Mode; run NTDSUTIL; restart the domain controller; use Backup to restore Active Directory.

C ○ Restart the domain controller; select Directory Services Restore Mode; use Backup to restore Active Directory; run NTDSUTIL; restart the domain controller.

D ○ Run NTDSUTIL; restart the domain controller; use Backup to restore Active Directory; restart the domain controller; select Directory Services Restore Mode.

18 You need to restrict a user account from accessing the Accounting Data share. You want to ensure that this user account cannot access the share regardless of other group memberships the use may have. What should you do?

A ○ Remove the user from the Domain Admins group.

B ○ Remove the user from the Authenticated Users group.

C ○ Explicitly deny the user permissions on the resource.

D ○ Place the user in a group that does not have access to the resource implicitly.

19 Bob has delegated administrative controls to a user account in an OU in his network. He needs to prevent these permissions from flowing down via inheritance to a child OU.

He prevents permission inheritance on the child OU using the Active Directory Users and Computers console. What will happen to the previously inherited permissions for objects in the child OU?

A ○ The permissions will remain until he manually removes them.

B ○ He will be prompted to remove the permissions or retain them.

C ○ The permissions will be removed.

D ○ None of the above.

20 You need to force replication in your Windows 2000 domain between several domain controllers. What tool should you use?

A ○ REPLMON

B ○ NTDSUTIL

C ○ MOVETREE

D ○ NETDOM

21 Several OUs in your Active Directory domain were maliciously deleted. You want to restore these OUs as quickly as possible. Which type of restore should you perform?

A ○ A nonauthoritative restore

B ○ A restore of a full backup of a domain controller

C ○ An authoritative restore

D ○ A restore of a full backup of the infrastructure master

22 How do you backup Active Directory?

A ○ Back up the entire server.

B ○ Back up the registry.

C ○ Back up SYSVOL.

D ○ Back up the system state data.

23 Tim is troubleshooting failed logons in a Windows 2000 multiple domain environment. The root domain is running in native mode, and the client in question is running Windows 2000 Professional. What services are typically required for logon? Choose all that apply.

A ❑ DNS

B ❑ Global catalog

C ❑ Certificate services

D ❑ Index services

24 You want to have an application install automatically when a user chooses its icon on the Start menu. How should you deploy the application?

A ○ Publish the application using a Group Policy object.

B ○ Assign the application using a Group Policy object.

C ○ Distribute the application using a logon script.

D ○ Use a third-party utility to deploy the application.

25 How can you refresh Group Policy in your Windows 2000 network? Choose all that apply.

A ❑ Using the SECEDIT utility

B ❑ Rebooting

C ❑ Waiting a specified interval

D ❑ Using REPLMON

26 You plan to deploy 2,000 client systems using RIS, and you have only three RIS servers configured. You are concerned about overloading the RIS servers in your Windows 2000 network. You also want to ensure that the RIS process is as efficient as possible. What should you do? Choose all that apply.

A ❑ Prestage client computers to use specific RIS servers.

B ❑ Use an Active Directory-integrated DNS zone.

C ❑ Use DHCP to load balance the clients across the multiple RIS servers.

D ❑ Place the RIS servers as close as possible to the appropriate client systems.

27 You are interested in prestaging your client systems in order to use RIS. How can you find the GUID of your client systems? Choose all that apply.

A ❑ Check the system BIOS.

B ❑ Check the GUID.TXT file in the root of the drive.

C ❑ Use Network Monitor and analyze the DHCPDiscover packets.

D ❑ Check the GUID section of HKEY_LOCAL_MACHINE in the Registry.

28 You want to enable several users to install hundreds of client systems using the RIPrep images on your RIS server. You do not want to give these users more rights or permissions than necessary. What should you do?

A ○ Place the users in the Domain Admins group.

B ○ Assign the users RIPrep user rights.

C ○ Use the Delegation of Control wizard to grant the users the appropriate permissions in the necessary OUs.

D ○ Do nothing. All users can install RIS images by default.

29 You have configured a RIS server to deploy Windows 2000 Professional clients in your network. You are testing the RIS server from a client system, and it does not appear to be functioning properly. What should you check?

A ○ Ensure that you have permissions to access the RIS server.

B ○ Ensure that the RIS server is authorized in Active Directory.

C ○ Ensure that your domain is in native mode.

D ○ Ensure that the RIS service is started on the RIS server.

30 Which utility is best for moving a computer account from one domain to another?

A ○ NTDSUTIL

B ○ MOVETREE

C ○ NETDOM

D ○ SECEDIT

31 Which of the following choices represent true statements about Flexible Single-Master Operations placement in a Windows 2000 network? Choose all that apply.

A ❑ The infrastructure master always should be placed on a global catalog server.

B ❑ The schema master always should be placed on the same machine as the domain naming master.

C ❑ The schema master never should be the same machine as the domain naming master.

D ❑ The infrastructure master never should be placed on a global catalog server.

E ❑ The PDC emulator never should be a global catalog server.

32 Which tool do you use to move the Active Directory database?

A ○ NTDSUTIL

B ○ MOVETREE

C ○ NETDOM

D ○ REPLMON

33 You want to use the Security Configuration and Analysis console in your Windows 2000 domain to ensure that you have configured security to meet a certain level of compliance with your corporate security policies. What should be your first step?

A ○ Specify the database to be used by the console.

B ○ Import the appropriate security template.

C ○ Choose the Analyze command.

D ○ Enable auditing in your domain.

34 What auditing event category do you use to track resource access?

A ○ Process tracking

B ○ System events

C ○ Directory object access

D ○ Object access

35 What is the best way to use the security groups of Active Directory?

A ○ Assign permissions to universal groups, place domain local groups in universal groups, and do not use global groups.

B ○ Assign permissions to domain local groups, place users in global groups, place global groups in universal groups, and place universal groups in domain local groups.

C ○ Place users in domain local groups, assign permissions to domain local groups, place domain local groups in global groups, and place global groups in universal groups.

D ○ Assign permissions to global groups, place users in global groups, gather global groups in universal groups, and do not use domain local groups.

36 Which tool do you use to view the results of auditing in Windows 2000?

A ○ Active Directory Users and Computers

B ○ Active Directory Sites and Services

C ○ Active Directory Domains and Trusts

D ○ Event Viewer

37 Your security policy specifies that no temporary Internet files can be left on the browsers of clients in your network. Your network is a pure Windows 2000 environment running Internet Explorer exclusively. What steps should you perform? Choose two.

A ❏ Configure the Internet Explorer option for emptying the Temporary Internet Files folder upon browser shutdown.

B ❏ Configure folder redirection for the Temporary Internet Files folder.

C ❏ Configure a GPO for emptying the Temporary Internet Files folder upon browser shutdown.

D ❏ Configure a GPO that prevents Internet Explorer options from being manipulated by clients.

38 You want medium security levels throughout your Windows 2000 network. What is the easiest way to ensure consistent security settings for the clients in your network?

A ○ Export a configured Registry and import it on the various systems.

B ○ Manually configure a Group Policy object for assignment to the systems.

C ○ Use SECEDIT to modify the settings on each system.

D ○ Import a security template into a GPO.

39 You are concerned that a user in your Windows 2000 network is attempting to access sensitive information stored in one of your organizational units. How can you attempt to catch this individual? Choose all that apply.

A ❑ Create an audit policy for your domain that includes Object Access.

B ❑ Create an audit policy for your domain that includes Directory Service Access.

C ❑ Configure auditing on the specific ADOs you are interested in.

D ❑ Monitor the Event Viewer's security log.

40 You are responsible for security in your Windows 2000 network. You want to ensure that a new server that you installed attempts to use encrypted communications whenever possible. However, this system should still communicate when encrypted communications are not possible. What IPSec policy should you choose?

A ○ None

B ○ Client

C ○ Server

D ○ Secure Server

41 You want to ensure that a system in your Finance department uses IPSec at all times during network communications. What policy should you set?

A ○ Client

B ○ Server

C ○ Secure Server

D ○ Optional

42 Many users throughout John's organization need access to a specific printer. John's network consists of several Active Directory domains in a very large forest. All domains are running in native mode.

What is the best way to permit these users throughout the Active Directory forest to access the printer?

A ○ Assign the appropriate printer permissions to the appropriate universal groups; ensure that the universal groups contain the appropriate domain global groups.

B ○ Assign the appropriate printer permissions to the appropriate user accounts.

C ○ Assign the appropriate printer permissions to the appropriate universal groups; ensure that the universal groups contain the appropriate user accounts.

D ○ Assign the appropriate printer permissions to the appropriate universal groups; ensure that the universal groups contain the appropriate domain local groups.

43 You have configured an audit policy that includes auditing for failed access attempts for Object Access. You have a confidential share named Data1. To test auditing, you log on as a user account that does not have permissions on the share and you repeatedly attempt to access the contents of the share. When you check the security log, it has no record of your security breach attempts. What is the most likely problem?

A ○ You did not configure auditing on the resource.

B ○ You failed to audit for Success with Object Access.

C ○ You failed to audit SYSVOL.

D ○ You do not have the appropriate permissions to view the entries in the security log.

Answers

1 **C.** Use the Active Directory Installation wizard. The Active Directory Installation wizard can perform various tasks, including creating domains and adding domain controllers to existing domains. *See Chapter 3.*

2 **A.** 50. Windows 2000 always tries to use the site link with the lowest cost. The default cost is 100. Here, you need to configure the site link with a cost less than 100. *See Chapter 14.*

3 **D.** NTDSUTIL. This utility just about does it all when it comes to Active Directory. Thanks to the roles mode, NTDSUTIL can help manage the Flexible Single-Master Operations Roles. *See Chapter 3.*

4 **B.** PDC emulator. The PDC emulator's primary job is to service the replication requests of down-level backup domain controllers (BDCs). It also handles password changes for down-level clients. *See Chapter 3.*

5 **C.** Do nothing. *A trust relationship already exists between the two domains.* Trusts in Windows 2000 are two-way and transitive by default. In effect, you have a complete trust model automatically implemented between all Windows 2000 domains in a forest. *See Chapter 3.*

6 **A.** Default-First-Site-Name. You should create your site and subnet objects as soon as possible in your Active Directory installation process. When you do this, systems are automatically placed in the appropriate sites as they are created. Otherwise, you must manually move the objects out of Default-First-Site-Name. *See Chapter 3.*

7 **B.** SYSVOL. The System Volume is the only component of a domain controller that must be installed on an NTFS 5 volume. *See Chapter 3.*

8 **B and D.** Increased fault tolerance and enhanced security for your DNS implementation. You achieve many benefits from storing the DNS zone information in Active Directory. These benefits include multimaster updates, enhanced security, automatic replication and synchronization of zones to new domain controllers, simplified planning and administration for both DNS and Active Directory, and faster and more efficient replication. *See Chapter 6.*

9 **D.** Your DNS zone is not Active Directory-integrated. Secure dynamic updates are only possible in an active Directory-integrated DNS environment. *See Chapter 6.*

10 **A.** A reverse lookup zone does not exist. The Active Directory Installation wizard does not install and configure a reverse lookup zone. *See Chapter 5.*

11 **A** and **C.** Support Active Directory Services and use incremental zone transfers. No reverse lookup zone was created in this case to support reverse lookups, and secure dynamic updates are not possible because the zone is not Active Directory-integrated. *See Chapters 5 and 6.*

12 **D** and **F.** Configure an Active Directory-integrated zone and ensure that the Allow Dynamic Updates option for the zone is set to Only Secure Updates. Remember that Active Directory-integrated zones provide fault tolerance and permit secure dynamic update capabilities. *See Chapter 6.*

13 **B.** Remove the Read permission on the GPO for the security group. This is referred to as filtering of Group Policy and is the recommended strategy for restricting a Group Policy from affecting certain user accounts. *See Chapter 7.*

14 **A.** Group Policies for password settings can only be set at the domain level. Several Group Policy settings can only be applied at the domain level — for example, Password Policies. *See Chapter 7.*

15 **C.** Assign these administrators the appropriate permissions. You can easily grant users the rights necessary to assist with GPO management by simply assigning them the appropriate rights in the Active Directory. *See Chapter 7.*

16 **A, B, C, E,** and **F.** Global groups can contain global groups from the same domain; local groups can contain universal groups from any domain; universal groups can contain universal groups from any domain; global groups can contain user accounts from the same domain; local groups can contain local groups from the same domain. Group nesting is possible in domains running in native mode. Universal groups are also possible in domains running in this mode. *See Chapter 12.*

17 **C.** Restart the domain controller; select Directory Services Restore Mode; use Backup to restore Active Directory; run NTDSUTIL; restart the domain controller. In this case, an authoritative restore is needed. An authoritative restore is the method you use to restore individual Active Directory objects in a domain with multiple domain controllers. The steps involved are restarting the domain controller, selecting Directory Services Restore Mode, using Backup to restore Active Directory, running NTDSUTIL, and then restarting. *See Chapter 4.*

18 **C.** Explicitly deny the user permissions on the resource. When you explicitly deny a user or group resource access, the user or group cannot access the resource regardless of other group memberships. *See Chapter 12.*

19 **B.** He will be prompted to remove the permissions or retain them. When you prevent permission inheritance, you will be promoted to copy or remove the previously inherited permissions. *See Chapter 7.*

20 **A.** REPLMON. Use the Active Directory Replication Monitor to force replication in a Windows 2000 domain. *See Chapter 14.*

21 **C.** An authoritative restore. If you have more than one domain controller in your organization, and the Active Directory service is replicated to any of these other servers, you may have to authoritatively restore any Active Directory data that you want to restore. To do this, you need to run the NTDSUTIL utility after you have restored the system state data but before you restart the server on the network. The NTDSUTIL utility enables you to mark Active Directory objects for authoritative restore. In this way, you can ensure that any replicated or distributed data that you restore is properly replicated or distributed throughout your organization. *See Chapter 4.*

22 **D.** Back up the system state data. Backing up the system state data forces a back up of Active Directory. *See Chapter 4.*

23 **A** and **B.** Both the DNS service and global catalog services are required for logon. The DNS service is used at logon to find a domain controller. The global catalog server provides universal group membership information. *See Chapter 3.*

24 **B.** Assign the application using a Group Policy object. Application assignment causes applications to automatically appear on the Start menu. Installation begins when the user clicks the shortcut. *See Chapter 9.*

25 **A, B,** and **C.** Using the SECEDIT utility; rebooting; waiting a specified interval. Group policy can be refreshed using several methods in Windows 2000. Perhaps the simplest is to use the SECEDIT utility. *See Chapter 15.*

26 **A** and **D.** Prestage client computers to use specific RIS servers; place the RIS servers as close as possible to the appropriate client systems. Prestaging systems enables you to load-balance them across multiple RIS servers. You should also place these servers as close as possible to the servers for the best response times. *See Chapter 11.*

27 **A** and **C.** Check the system BIOS; use Network Monitor and analyze the DHCPDiscover packets. To prestage client systems, you need their GUIDs. To locate the GUID for these systems, check the system BIOS or analyze the DHCPDiscover packets using Network Monitor. *See Chapter 11.*

28 **C.** Use the Delegation of Control wizard to grant the users the appropriate permissions in the necessary OUs. These users need Create Computer account permissions for the appropriate OUs. The easiest way to assign these permissions is by using the Delegation of Control wizard. *See Chapter 10.*

29 **B.** Ensure that the RIS server is authorized in Active Directory. RIS servers must be authorized in Active Directory before they can be used. *See Chapter 11.*

30 **C.** NETDOM. You should use the NETDOM utility in this case because it is more efficient at moving computer accounts. You could also use MOVETREE but it does not disjoin and join the computer account like NETDOM can. *See Chapter 12.*

31 **B** and **D.** The schema master always should be placed on the same machine as the domain naming master. The infrastructure master never should be placed on a global catalog server. Assign the infrastructure master role to any domain controller in the domain that is not a global catalog server, but that is well connected to a global catalog server (from any domain) in the same site. The schema master and the domain naming master roles always should be assigned to the same domain controller. *See Chapter 3.*

32 **A.** NTDSUTIL. The NTDSUTIL utility can accomplish many things, including moving the Active Directory database. *See Chapter 12.*

33 **A.** Specify the database to be used by the console. The first step in using the Security Configuration and Analysis tool is to create or open an existing database for the tool to use. *See Chapter 15.*

34 **D.** Object access. You must create an audit policy that includes Object Access auditing if you want to track resource usage in your Windows 2000 network. *See Chapter 16.*

35 **B.** Assign permissions to domain local groups, place users in global groups, place global groups in universal groups, place universal groups in domain local groups. Although you can use Windows 2000 security groups in many ways, Microsoft recommends using the strategy described here. *See Chapter 12.*

36 **D.** Event Viewer. Use the Event Viewer's security log to view auditing results. *See Chapter 16.*

37 **A** and **D.** Configure the Internet Explorer option for emptying the Temporary Internet Files folder upon browser shutdown; configure a GPO that prevents Internet Explorer options from being manipulated by clients. *See Chapter 8.*

38 **D.** Import a security template into a GPO. You can use security templates to standardize the security settings of your Windows 2000 computers. You can easily import a security template into a Group Policy object. *See Chapter 8.*

39 **B, C,** and **D.** Create an audit policy for your domain that includes Directory Service Access; configure auditing on the specific ADOs you are interested in; monitor the Event Viewer's security log. *See Chapter 16.*

40 **C.** Server. The Server policy option causes the system to secure IP whenever possible, but still permits the system to communicate with clients that cannot support IP. *See Chapter 15.*

41 **C.** Secure Server. Your system better be able to use IPSec to communicate with a server using this policy. This is the strongest policy setting you can have. *See Chapter 15.*

42 **A.** Assign the appropriate printer permissions to the appropriate universal groups; ensure the universal groups contain the appropriate domain global groups. Universal groups should contain global groups that will contain the user accounts. Placing user accounts directly in universal groups is not recommended due to network traffic considerations. *See Chapter 12.*

43 **A.** You did not configure auditing on the resource. Auditing is a two-step process. First, you must create an audit policy. Then, you must configure auditing on the resources you intend to audit. *See Chapter 16.*

Appendix B

Practice Exam 2

● ●

Practice Exam Rules

▶ 90 minutes to complete the exam

▶ 43 questions

▶ At least 30 correct answers to pass

▶ Don't cheat!

● ●

*H*ere's another opportunity to make sure you are ready for exam day: a second full-length practice exam that covers topics from throughout the book. If you do well on both practice exams in this book's appendixes, you should be ready for the real thing.

Use the information provided in the Part of Tens to simulate the testing environment as closely as possible. Be sure to read carefully, just as you would on the real exam. And remember that my rules for time and your passing score are probably a bit more stringent than those you will encounter on the real exam.

Questions

1 Sara has installed and configured a Windows 2000 domain controller in her network. When she installed Active Directory Services, she relied on the Active Directory Installation wizard to complete the installation and configuration of DNS. Which of the following choices represents a step that the Active Directory Installation wizard does not perform during the installation and configuration of DNS?

A ○ Installation of the DNS Server service

B ○ Creation of the forward lookup zone

C ○ Creation of the reverse lookup zone

D ○ Configuration of the SOA record

2 You want to use a certain domain controller for replication purposes between sites in Active Directory. What should you do?

A ○ Configure a new site link.

B ○ Configure a new site link bridge.

C ○ Configure a mandatory connection object.

D ○ Configure a preferred bridgehead server.

3 You want to employ a Microsoft DNS service in your Windows 2000 network. You want to provide secure dynamic update capabilities and avoid having a single point of failure in your DNS system.

You take the following steps:
• Install the DNS Server service.
• Configure a forward lookup zone for your desired Active Directory domain.
• Permit dynamic updates functionality for the forward lookup zone.
• Install Active Directory Services using the Active Directory Installation wizard.

Using the DNS Manager snap-in, you attempt to configure secure updates only for the DNS service. Unfortunately, this option is not available. What is the most likely reason?

A ○ You did not create a reverse lookup zone.

B ○ You are not using DHCP in your network.

C ○ You did not permit the Active Directory Installation wizard to install and configure DNS.

D ○ Your DNS zone is not Active Directory–integrated.

4 Bill is trying to install Active Directory Services in his Windows 2000 network. He is using a domain name of sales.internationalventures.com. Which statements are true regarding this installation? Choose all that apply.

A ❑ This domain name is too long and cannot be used.

B ❑ The default NetBIOS name for the domain is the first 15 characters.

C ❑ His domain name is an example of a Fully Qualified Domain Name.

D ❑ This domain cannot be the root domain of the forest.

5 You are interested in configuring replication between your Active Directory sites. What options do you have for configuring the replication across a site link? Choose all that apply.

A ❑ Time of day

B ❑ Interval

C ❑ Category of data

D ❑ Cost

6 You want to demote a Windows 2000 domain controller to the role of a member server in your network. How should you do this?

A ○ Use the Active Directory Installation wizard.

B ○ Reinstall Windows 2000 Server.

C ○ Restore a previous version of the server from backup.

D ○ Use the Demote command in Active Directory Domains and Trusts.

7 You have two domains located in two different sites in your Active Directory implementation. What are your options for transport protocol on a site link that connects these two sites? Choose all that apply.

A ❑ RPC

B ❑ SNMP

C ❑ IPX

D ❑ AppleTalk

E ❑ SMTP

8 As a member of the Enterprise Admins group, you try unsuccessfully to add a new domain to your Windows 2000 Active Directory implementation. What is the most likely reason for the failure?

A ○ The schema master is not available.

B ○ The domain naming master is not available.

C ○ You do not have the necessary permissions to add the domain.

D ○ The RID master is not available.

9 Several users in your network have special administrative requirements. Compared to the rest of the company, they need special restrictions on their systems as well as custom applications. What should you do to accommodate these individuals?

A ○ Create a child domain for the users.

B ○ Create a separate forest for the users.

C ○ Create an OU for the users.

D ○ Create a new tree for the users.

10 Which of the following choices are part of the system state data in Windows 2000? Choose all that apply.

A ❑ The Registry

B ❑ SYSVOL

C ❑ Active Directory

D ❑ The SYSTEM directory

11 One of your domain controllers has failed. You are not too concerned about it because you have two other domain controllers servicing your Active Directory domain. However, you want to restore the domain controller from backup. The domain controller has been down for several days. What type of restore operation should you perform?

A ○ A full restore

B ○ A nonauthoritative restore

C ○ An authoritative restore

D ○ A partial restore

12 You need to perform an authoritative restore of one of your domain controllers. Which utility do you use?

A ○ NETDOM

B ○ REPLMON

C ○ NETDIAG

D ○ PATHPING

E ○ NTDSUTIL

13 In a traditional DNS implementation, what is the name of the server that maintains a read/write copy of the DNS database?

A ○ Caching-only name server

B ○ Secondary name server

C ○ Primary name server

D ○ Forwarding server

14 To host Active Directory in your network, you must have a DNS implementation that supports which record type?

  A ○ PTR
  B ○ CNAME
  C ○ MX
  D ○ SRV

15 You want to configure the DHCP service to assist in the registration of Windows 2000 and non-Windows 2000 client systems. What must you do?

  A ○ Nothing. No additional configuration is necessary.
  B ○ You must be running the DHCP service on Windows 2000 Advanced Server.
  C ○ You must register the DHCP service with the DNS server.
  D ○ You cannot configure this setup in Windows 2000.

16 What is the key to secure dynamic updates in Windows 2000 DNS?

  A ○ Only administrators can update the DNS database.
  B ○ Only the DHCP service can update the DNS database.
  C ○ Only Enterprise Administrators can update the DNS database.
  D ○ Security restrictions can be placed on the DNS database using Access Control Lists.

17 Your boss claims that because you installed an Active Directory–integrated DNS zone, you cannot integrate with the existing BIND DNS servers in the organization. What should you tell your boss?

  A ○ You should admit that the boss is correct and then submit your resignation.
  B ○ The boss is incorrect. The Active Directory–integrated zone appears as a standard DNS zone to traditional DNS systems.
  C ○ The boss is incorrect. Active Directory–integrated zones can interoperate with BIND version 8.2 or higher.
  D ○ The boss is incorrect. Active Directory–integrated zones can interoperate with BIND version 4.1 or higher.

18 Which statements are true regarding Group Policy objects? Choose all that apply.

  A ❏ Group Policy objects that have been created in Active Directory can be linked to additional objects, as needed.
  B ❏ GPOs can be linked to domains, sites, forests, and OUs.
  C ❏ You use the Group Policy snap-in to modify GPOs.
  D ❏ By default, child OUs inherit the GPO settings applied to parent objects.

19 In which order are GPOs processed?

A ○ Local, domain, site, OU

B ○ Local, site, domain, OU

C ○ Local, OU, domain, Site

D ○ OU, domain, site, local

20 You are making configuration changes to the desktops of several users in your network using a Group Policy object. You want these changes to stop taking effect. What should you do?

A ○ Manually reconfigure the Registries on the affected machines.

B ○ Disable or unlink the GPO.

C ○ Remove the systems from the organizational unit.

D ○ Remove the systems from the domain.

21 Which FSMO role provides for support for a mixed mode network containing both Windows 2000 and Windows NT 4 servers?

A ○ Schema master

B ○ Infrastructure master

C ○ PDC emulator

D ○ RID master

22 You want to have a particular application installed when a system reboots. How should you deploy the application?

A ○ Publish the application using User Configuration.

B ○ Publish the application using Computer Configuration.

C ○ Assign the application using User Configuration.

D ○ Assign the application using Computer Configuration.

23 You want to exclude certain types of files from automatic and manual caching for offline use. How can you do this?

A ○ Using an Administrative Template setting in Group Policy.

B ○ By manually configuring the Registries on the client systems.

C ○ By configuring the Properties of Offline Files on the share.

D ○ You cannot configure this setup in Windows 2000.

24 You want to upgrade an application that has been deployed in your network using a GPO. Before the installation of the upgrade, you want to uninstall the previous version. How should you do this?

  A ○ Manually uninstall the previous version and then use the GPO to perform the upgrade.

  B ○ Configure the GPO to uninstall the previous version and then install the new version.

  C ○ Use the GPO to remove the previous version and manually install the upgrade.

  D ○ Manually uninstall the previous version and then manually install the upgrade.

25 What name is given to the Site object automatically created when you install Active Directory in your network?

  A ○ Default-First-Site-Name

  B ○ Default-Site

  C ○ First-Site

  D ○ Default-Site-Name

26 After backing up your RIS installation, you are forced to restore it. Unfortunately, after you restore the RIS server, RIS does not function properly. What is the most likely reason?

  A ○ You did not back up the WINNT\RIS directory.

  B ○ You cannot restore RIS from a backup.

  C ○ You did not restore the RIPrep images properly.

  D ○ You did not restore the SIS directory.

27 You want to ensure that RIS does not respond to client systems that are not specified for Windows 2000 Professional installations in your network. What should you do?

  A ○ Use a more secure alternative for client deployments.

  B ○ Authorize the RIS server in Active Directory.

  C ○ Authorize the clients in Active Directory.

  D ○ Use the Do Not Respond to Unknown Client Computers option.

28 You need to authorize your RIS server in Active Directory. Which administrative console should you use?

  A ○ Configure Your Server

  B ○ Active Directory Users and Computers

  C ○ DNS

  D ○ DHCP

29 You want to prevent some users from installing certain RIS images on client systems, but they need to be able to install others. What should you do?

A ○ Nothing. You cannot configure this setup.

B ○ Set permissions on the various images.

C ○ Prestage the client systems.

D ○ Preconfigure the client Registries.

30 A group of managers needs to have selected administrative controls over a department of users and resources in your company. You want to ensure that the managers do not end up with administrative controls for more than just this department, however. What should you do?

A ○ Move the users to their own domain and delegate administrative controls to the managers for this domain.

B ○ Move the users to their own OU and delegate administrative controls to the managers for this OU.

C ○ Move the users to their own site and delegate administrative controls to the managers for this site.

D ○ Move the users into their own security group and delegate administrative controls to the managers for this security group.

31 You need to prevent a specific user from having access to a resource in your network. You remove the user from the Managers group. This group has Full Control permission on the resource. Much to your surprise, the user still has access. What is the most likely problem?

A ○ The user is a member of the administrators group.

B ○ The user is a member of another group that has permissions on the resource.

C ○ The user created the resource.

D ○ The user is the manager of the resource.

32 You have just configured a new domain-based Group Policy object that ensures Windows 2000 passwords must be eight characters in length. However, one of your peers can still use a six character password. What should you do to correct the problem? Choose all that apply.

A ❑ Run NTDSUTIL /update.

B ❑ Use SECEDIT to refresh Group Policy.

C ❑ Force replication in the domain.

D ❑ Use gpresult on each client system.

33 You need to move a security group from one domain to another in your Windows 2000 forest. What utility should you use?

A ○ NTDSUTIL

B ○ NETDOM

C ○ MOVETREE

D ○ REPLMON

34 What is the name of the attribute available only in native mode that makes moving objects from one domain to another more efficient?

A ○ SIDList

B ○ SIDHistory

C ○ DistinguishedName

D ○ DN

35 You have shared a printer installed on a Windows 2000 Advanced Server. This server is a member of your Windows 2000 domain. What steps do you take to publish this printer in Active Directory?

A ○ Do nothing. The printer is published automatically.

B ○ Publish the printer using the Active Directory Users and Computers console.

C ○ Publish the printer using the Active Directory Sites and Services console.

D ○ Publish the printer using a Group Policy object.

36 You are concerned that your Active Directory database is not functioning properly. You recently deleted thousands of objects from the database and you continually monitor the size of the Active Directory database. Much to your surprise, the database is not getting any smaller. What should you do?

A ○ Copy NTDS.DIT from the system and then copy it back.

B ○ Use the NTDSUTIL utility with the COMPACT switch.

C ○ Adjust the tombstone lifetime on the system.

D ○ Use the JETPACK utility.

37 You need to assign Full Control permissions to a group of managers in your corporate network for a shared folder that is located on your Windows 2000 Server. You are in an Active Directory domain environment running in native mode. Where should you place the user accounts?

A ○ In a universal group

B ○ In a domain local group

C ○ In a global group

D ○ In a nested domain local group

38 You have your Windows 2000 user accounts defined in an Excel spreadsheet. How can you use this information to create the accounts in the Active Directory database?

   A ○ Using the LDIFDE utility.

   B ○ Using the CSVDE utility.

   C ○ Using the MOVETREE utility.

   D ○ This is not possible in Windows 2000.

39 How can you automate the process of analyzing security settings for your domain controllers and adjusting these settings if needed?

   A ○ Use the SECEDIT utility.

   B ○ Schedule the Security Configuration and Analysis tool using the Task Manager.

   C ○ Use the Alerts feature of Performance Monitor.

   D ○ Use the logging capabilities of Performance Monitor.

40 You want to audit for virus outbreaks on your domain controller. What audit category should you use?

   A ○ Directory service access

   B ○ Account management

   C ○ Privilege use

   D ○ Process tracking

41 You want to audit for unauthorized resource access for a sensitive shared folder in your network. For which group should you set up auditing?

   A ○ Authenticated Users

   B ○ Everyone

   C ○ Users

   D ○ Guests

42 At what level should you assign an IPSec policy in your Windows 2000 network?

   A ○ At the highest possible container level

   B ○ At the lowest possible container level

   C ○ Always at the site level

   D ○ Anywhere but the domain level

43 Auditing is a critical component for your security plan in your network. How can you configure your domain controller to shut down if the security log becomes full?

   A ○ Use a custom VBScript.

   B ○ Configure this setting in a Group Policy object.

   C ○ Use the HISEC.INF security template.

   D ○ You cannot configure this setup.

Answers

1 **C.** Creation of the reverse lookup zone. Using the wizard for the DNS configuration has this drawback: A reverse lookup zone is not created. *See Chapter 5.*

2 **D.** Configure a preferred bridgehead server. If you need to specify which domain controllers replicate information between sites, you can specify a preferred bridgehead server in Active Directory Sites and Services. *See Chapter 3.*

3 **D.** Your DNS zone is not Active Directory–integrated. One of the main benefits provided by Active Directory–integrated zones in Windows 2000 is the fact that secure dynamic updates can be enforced. You can set permissions within these zones to control which computers can update their own records. *See Chapter 6.*

4 **B and C.** The default NetBIOS name for the domain is the first 15 characters; his domain name is an example of a Fully Qualified Domain Name. The name sales.internationalventures.com is an example of a fully qualified domain name, and is perfectly acceptable for a Windows 2000 domain — even a root domain. The default down-level NetBIOS name is the first 15 characters of this FQDN. *See Chapter 3.*

5 **A, B, and D.** Time of day; interval; cost. You cannot schedule replication based on the category of data to be replicated. However, you can assign costs, intervals, and schedules in order to configure this traffic. *See Chapter 14.*

6 **A.** Using the Active Directory Installation wizard. Believe it or not, this wizard can also demote a system to the role of member server. This process does not require a reinstall — just a reboot. *See Chapter 3.*

7 **A and E.** RPC and SMTP. RPC is the default protocol for site links. You can use SMTP as a transport protocol, but only between different domains located in different sites. *See Chapter 14.*

8 **B.** The domain naming master is not available. The domain naming master is responsible for carrying out major changes to the Active Directory structure, such as adding and removing domains. *See Chapter 3.*

9 **C.** Create an OU for the users. You typically should use OUs to group users that have special administrative needs. Thanks to OUs, you can easily delegate authority, assign Group Policies, and partition your Active Directory namespace. *See Chapter 3.*

10 **A, B, and C.** The Registry; SYSVOL; Active Directory. The system state data backup option includes the Registry, SYSVOL, and Active Directory. It does not include the SYSTEM directory. *See Chapter 4.*

11 **B.** A nonauthoritative restore. This restore process ensures that the restored domain controller receives the updates to Active Directory that have occurred since the system failed. *See Chapter 4.*

12 **E.** NTDSUTIL. The NTDSUTIL utility performs many tasks in Windows 2000 Active Directory. One of its main functions is permitting you to perform authoritative restores of Active Directory in your network. *See Chapter 4.*

13 **C.** Primary name server. This server maintains a read/write copy of the DNS database in a traditional DNS implementation. *See Chapter 5.*

14 **D.** SRV. Service (SRV) records are required by Active Directory. These records are used to locate services in the Windows 2000 network. *See Chapter 5.*

15 **C.** You must register the DHCP service with the DNS server. DHCP can assist in the dynamic registration process in DDNS. You must register the DHCP servers with DNS. *See Chapter 5.*

16 **D.** Security restrictions can be placed on the DNS database using Access Control Lists. Secure dynamic update functionality requires Active Directory–integrated zones. When you configure your zone in this way, you can then place security restrictions on database access using Access Control Lists. *See Chapter 6.*

17 **B.** The boss is incorrect. The Active Directory–integrated zone appears as a standard DNS zone to traditional DNS systems. Here is another advantage to Active Directory–integrated zones: They appear as standard DNS zones for integration with other DNS systems. *See Chapter 6.*

18 **A, C, and D.** Group Policy objects that have been created in Active Directory can be linked to additional objects as needed. You use the Group Policy snap-in to modify GPOs. By default, child OUs inherit the GPO settings applied to parent objects. All these statements are correct. However, you cannot link GPOs to forest objects. *See Chapter 7.*

19 **B.** Local, site, domain, OU. The processing order for GPOs is the local system GPO, then the site, domain, and OU GPOs. If you have multiple GPOs at any of these levels, you control the order using the container's properties. *See Chapter 7.*

20 **B.** Disable or unlink the GPO. Here is another nice feature of using GPOs to control your users' environments: If you want to reverse the settings, simply disable or unlink the GPO from the container. *See Chapter 7.*

21 **C.** PDC emulator. The PDC emulator enables your Windows 2000 Active Directory implementation to support a mix of server systems — a critical feature during a gradual migration from Windows NT 4.0 to Windows 2000. *See Chapter 3.*

22 **D.** Assign the application using Computer Configuration. Assigning an application using the Computer Configuration node of the Group Policy snap-in causes the application to install upon the next reboot of the system — a great way to force an application's deployment. *See Chapter 9.*

23 **A.** Using an Administrative Template setting in Group Policy. This is one of the many Administrative Template settings to be found in the Group Policy snap-in. *See Chapter 8.*

24 **B.** Configure the GPO to uninstall the previous version and then install the new version. GPOs are very powerful for maintaining and upgrading software deployments. To upgrade an application, you can have the GPO remove the old application and install a new one. *See Chapter 9.*

25 **A.** Default-First-Site-Name. This object is created automatically for you when you install Windows 2000 Active Directory. You should quickly rename and configure this object and create the additional sites you need for your network. *See Chapter 14.*

26 **D.** You did not restore the SIS directory. A very common issue with RIS restores involves the SIS directory. If this folder is not restored, RIS does not function properly. *See Chapter 10.*

27 **D.** Use the Do Not Respond to Unknown Client Computers option. Using this option forces RIS to respond only to prestaged client systems. This secure option also can be used for load balancing between different RIS servers. *See Chapter 10.*

28 **D.** DHCP. RIS servers need to be authorized in Active Directory before they can begin servicing client requests. You use the DHCP console to authorize your RIS servers. *See Chapter 11.*

29 **B.** Set permissions on the various images. You can easily control installation capabilities for client images using RIS by setting permissions on the RIS images. *See Chapter 11.*

30 **B.** Move the users to their own OU and delegate administrative controls to the managers for this OU. This question points out how OUs can assist with administration in a network. You should use OUs as a basis for the delegation of administrative controls. *See Chapter 12.*

31 **B.** The user is a member of another group that has permissions on the resource. Remember that permissions are cumulative for users who belong to multiple Windows 2000 security groups. *See Chapter 12.*

32 **B and C.** Use SECEDIT to refresh Group Policy; force replication in the domain. Two different issues could be causing this problem. Either replication has not updated all domain controllers with this change, or Group Policy is not refreshed. *See Chapter 7.*

33 **C.** MOVETREE. You use MOVETREE to move most Active Directory objects (including nonempty containers) from one domain to another in the same forest. *See Chapter 12.*

34 **B.** SIDHistory. As you move a user from domain to domain, SIDHistory is populated so you do not have to reset permissions to objects each time you perform the move operation. *See Chapter 12.*

35 **A.** Do nothing. The printer is published automatically. By default, printers that are shared on Windows 2000 Servers participating in the domain are automatically published in Active Directory. *See Chapter 12.*

36 **B.** Use the NTDSUTIL utility with the COMPACT switch. Offline defragmentation is used to reduce the size of the Active Directory database. You perform offline defragmentation using the NTDSUTIL command. *See Chapter 13.*

37 **C.** In a global group. User accounts should be placed in a global group in the security model of Windows 2000. *See Chapter 12.*

38 **B.** Using the CSVDE utility. The CSVDE utility can import comma-separated files to create user accounts for you. In this case, use Excel to create the file. *See Chapter 12.*

39 **A.** Use the SECEDIT utility. The SECEDIT command-line tool can be used to automatically assign security templates to computers. *See Chapter 15.*

40 **D.** Process tracking. Process tracking is typically reserved for programmers when testing applications. It can also be useful for tracking down viruses in your network, however. See *Chapter 16.*

41 **B.** Everyone. Auditing using the Everyone groups enables you to catch external users who are not part of your network. *See Chapter 16.*

42 **A.** At the highest possible container level. To ease your administrative workload, set your IPSec policy at the highest possible container level. In this way, you can assign the policy to many systems in one easy step. *See Chapter 15.*

43 **B.** Configure this setting in a Group Policy object. This setting can be configured using the Default Domain Controllers GPO. *See Chapter 8.*

Appendix C

Glossary

● ●

A Record (Host Record): A DNS resource record used to map host names to IP addresses in your computer network.

Access control entry (ACE): An entry in a Discretionary Access Control List (DACL). The entry provides permissions for a user account or group to interact with the resource that has the DACL.

Active Directory: The directory service for Windows 2000, it provides storage for the objects that define a network, including users, groups, computers, printers, and shares.

Active Directory Services Interface (ADSI): A proprietary programming interface from Microsoft that simplifies access and manipulation of information in Active Directory using a wide variety of programming and scripting languages.

Active Directory Users and Computers: A Microsoft Management Console snap-in used to manage users, groups, computers, shares, printers, and other objects that can be stored in Windows 2000's Active Directory. This tool is roughly the equivalent of User Manager for Domains from previous NT versions.

Attribute: In Active Directory, a property of an object that can be stored in Active Directory. Attributes are mandatory or optional. For example, Telephone Number is an example of an optional attribute that is associated with User objects.

Audit policy: A policy you create that dictates which events can be audited in your Windows 2000 network. For example, you should enable Object Access auditing if you intend to audit resource access in your network.

Auditing: The process of monitoring specific events in your Windows 2000 network. When auditing resource access, you can also specify which users or groups are audited.

Authoritative restore: One of two ways you can restore Active Directory. When you choose to restore using this method, the restore is marked as authoritative, meaning it is treated as the most recent copy of Active Directory and thus overwrites copies stored on other domain controllers.

Backup Domain Controller (BDC): A Windows NT server type that stores a read-only copy of the domain database. It is used in NT networks to add fault tolerance and load-balancing.

Backup operator: A member of the Backup Operators group. These users can back up and restore files regardless of permissions that may exist on the files.

Berkeley Internet Name Domain (BIND): A version of DNS that runs on most UNIX implementations. It is the most popular version of DNS in use.

Built-in groups: Default groups that provide a basis to begin assigning user rights and permissions.

Caching resolver: A DNS service that caches recently resolved name-to-IP-address mappings. The service uses this cache to resolve the same lookups for other clients.

Canonical (CNAME) resource record: A DNS resource record that enables you to map additional aliases to a host (A) record.

Child domain: A type of domain that exists below another in an Active Directory domain tree. It shares a contiguous namespace with its parent. For example, sales.fordummies.com is a child domain of the fordummies.com domain.

Child object: In Active Directory, an object located inside another object. The host object is called the parent object.

Computer account: Accounts created by administrators to identify computers in the Active Directory database.

Console tree: A common way to reference the left pane in the Microsoft Management Console.

Container object: Any object in Active Directory that can contain other objects.

DACL (Discretionary Access Control List): Associated with an object, this list contains Access Control Entries (ACEs). These entries detail which users or groups have permissions for the resource and the extent of these permissions.

Delegation: Refers to your ability to assign specific administrative privileges to select users or groups over limited areas of Active Directory.

Details pane: Common term for the right-hand pane in the Microsoft Management Console.

Directory: A shorthand method for referring to the full-blown Active Directory Services of Windows 2000. When not talking about Microsoft's Windows 2000 specifically, it refers to any information store that contains information about specific objects such as users.

Directory database: Refers to the physical data store for Active Directory Services. The file is NTDS.DIT.

Directory replication: Refers to the transfer of Active Directory database changes to domain controllers throughout the network.

Distinguished name: A name that is used to uniquely identify an object stored in a directory system. The distinguished name identifies the name of the object as well as its location in the directory tree. The distinguished name for an Active Directory object is always unique in the forest.

Distribution group: A Windows 2000 group type used primarily for e-mail purposes.

DNS: An Internet service that translates Fully Qualified Domain Names (FQDNs) into TCP/IP numeric addresses. Active Directory relies upon DNS for name resolution and service location functionality.

DNS Dynamic Update Protocol: A new update to the DNS standard that permits clients to dynamically update their own DNS information. Previously, these updates had to be performed manually.

DNS name server: A server responsible for assisting in the resolution of Fully Qualified Domain Names to TCP/IP addresses.

Domain: In Windows 2000 Active Directory, a collection of computers defined by an administrator. These systems all share the same directory database.

Domain controller: A system hosting Active Directory Services of Windows 2000.

Domain local group: A Windows 2000 security group designed to contain global groups or universal groups. You should assign resource permissions to the appropriate domain local groups that you create.

Domain name: In Windows 2000 Active Directory, the name given to a collection of computers all sharing the same directory database.

Domain namespace: The database structure used by the DNS system.

Domain naming master: A Flexible Single-Master Operations role system responsible for the addition and removal of domains from an Active Directory forest. You have only one of these systems per forest.

Event: Any significant occurrence on a system or in an application that can be logged to a file or used as the trigger for user notification.

Event log service: A Windows 2000 service that maintains security, application, and system logs in Event Viewer to benefit administrators.

Event logging: The Windows 2000 process of recording entries in the logs of Event Viewer for certain occurrences on the Windows 2000 system. For example, an administrator can log how many times a user logs on and off the system in a given time period.

Explicit permissions: Permissions on an object that are either inherited when the object is created, or specifically assigned by an administrator or someone with administrative privileges.

Fault tolerance: The ability of a system or grouping of systems to continue to provide data after a failure has occurred.

Forest: A collection of one or more Windows 2000 Active Directory domains. These domains in a forest share a common schema, global catalog, and configuration, and are linked by transitive, two-way Kerberos trusts.

Forward lookup: A type of DNS query in which a client asks the DNS server for the TCP/IP address of the system, given the system's Fully Qualified Domain Name. Certainly the most common type of query.

Forwarder: A DNS server that resolves DNS queries that have been forwarded to it from other DNS servers.

Fully Qualified Domain Name (FQDN): A DNS-style name for a network object. This name defines the object's location in the DNS system.

Global catalog: A domain controller that contains a partial replica of selected attributes of all objects contained in Active Directory. This partial replica represents the portion of Active Directory most likely to be searched upon by users.

Global group: A security group of Active Directory that can contain users from a single domain and can be assigned resource access throughout the entire forest. You should typically create global groups that mirror the organizational roles of the users.

Group Policy: Used in Windows 2000 to configure and control the desktops of users, as well as configure critical network settings.

Group Policy object (GPO): An object that stores a collection of Group Policy settings. You assign these objects to Active Directory containers in order to apply the settings to the user accounts and computers.

Incremental zone transfer (IXFR): A DNS technology that replicates changes made to the database, as those changes occur, and thus provides much more efficient replication of this information.

Infrastructure master: Responsible for updating references from objects in its domain to objects in other domains. The infrastructure master compares its data with that of a global catalog server.

Inheritance: Default security behavior in which permissions that you assign to a parent container flow down to child objects of the container.

Interactive logon: Refers to logging on to a system from a keyboard that is physically at the system.

Internet Engineering Task Force (IETF): An open community of very bright people in charge of new developments for the Internet. It is also responsible for keeping the Internet running as smoothly as possible.

Iterative query: A query to DNS in which the client indicates it expects the best answer possible from the server without the DNS server going to other servers for assistance.

Kerberos: An Internet standard that controls security measures in your network. Specifically, one of the tasks of Kerberos is to handle user authentication.

Key Distribution Center (KDC): A Kerberos service that runs in your Windows 2000 network. This service is responsible for issuing tickets to permit clients access to domain controllers for authentication and other network services.

LDAP Data Interchange Format (LDIF): An LDAP file format that enables you to modify directory information using a simple text file.

Lightweight Directory Access Protocol (LDAP): A protocol that defines how a directory client can access a directory server and how the client can perform directory operations and share directory data. LDAP standards are established by working groups of the Internet Engineering Task Force (IETF).

Load balancing: A strategy for distributing traffic across multiple network components. In Active Directory, you often add domain controllers to help load-balance logon traffic.

Logon rights: Rights assigned to user accounts to designate how a user can log on to an Active Directory domain.

Member server: A Windows 2000 Server system that is participating in Active Directory, but is not a domain controller.

Multimaster replication: The replication system in Windows 2000. Under this system, any domain controller can accept changes to Active Directory. This domain controller then replicates these changes to other domain controllers in the network.

Name resolution: The process in which a so-called "friendly" name is translated to a TCP/IP address. Windows 2000 relies upon DNS for this purpose.

Name server (NS) resource record: A DNS record that indicates the DNS server's Fully Qualified Domain Name for the network.

Namespace: A set of unique names for computing resources in a shared computer environment.

Naming context: Any contiguous section of the Active Directory tree.

Native mode: A mode your Windows 2000 network can be switched to when all domain controllers have been upgraded to Windows 2000. Native mode permits additional benefits like nesting of groups and universal group usage.

Nonauthoritative restore: A restore of the Active Directory that is not marked as the most current. Therefore, any changes to Active Directory that have occurred since the backup will be written to the domain controller's restored copy.

Noncontainer object: Any object in Active Directory that cannot contain another object. An example is a printer object.

Nontransitive trust: A trust relationship that does not extend beyond the two domains it relates.

Notify list: A list maintained in the primary zone of DNS. This list indicates which other servers should be notified of zone changes.

Novell Directory Services (NDS): Novell's directory service product found in Novell networks.

NSLOOKUP: A command-line utility that specializes in testing and maintaining DNS.

NTFS V5: The file system used in Windows 2000. This file system has many benefits beyond those provided by the File Allocation Table (FAT) system.

Object: An entity stored in Active Directory. These entities are defined by a set of optional or mandatory attributes.

One-way trust: A trust relationship such that if Domain A trusts Domain B, Domain B does not automatically trust Domain A.

Operations master: A Windows 2000 domain controller that has been assigned one of the five special roles for domain management.

Organizational unit: A container object used within Active Directory domains. OUs are used as a basis for delegating authority and assigning group policies.

Owner: The user account responsible for setting permissions on an object.

Parent domain: In DNS, a domain that exists directly above another domain in the DNS namespace. For example, sales.nwtraders.msft is the parent domain for nwtraders.msft.

Parent object: The container object directly above an object in the Active Directory tree.

Performance alert: A feature of Windows 2000 Performance Monitor and Alerts that notifies a user when a counter rises above or falls below a certain threshold.

Performance counter: Objects found in the System Monitor that enable you to monitor specific resource values in your Windows 2000 network.

Performance object: A collection of counters for monitoring network resources.

Permissions: Rules associated with objects that govern which users can interact with the object and what level of interaction they can perform.

Pointer resource record: A DNS record used in the reverse lookup zone to resolves for a name given a TCP/IP address.

Policy: Shorthand for Group Policy. The way you manage and control your network in Windows 2000.

Primary domain controller (PDC): A Windows NT 4.0 domain controller that maintains the only read and write copy of the directory database in the domain.

Primary master: The DNS server responsible for the updates to its zone information.

Privileges: User rights that assign specific capabilities within the network. For example, backing up files is a privilege that can be granted on the network.

Recursive query: A DNS query in which the client requests name resolution from the DNS server and expects the DNS server to provide an answer regardless of the workload required, including checking with other DNS servers.

Relative distinguished name: The part of a distinguished name in Active Directory that is an attribute of the object itself. For example, John Smith is an example of the relative distinguished name for a user account.

Relative ID master: The operations master responsible for issuing RIDs to domains so the domains can create SIDs as appropriate.

Remote Installation Services (RIS): A service that enables administrators to install client systems remotely — in many instances, without having to visit the client systems at all.

Remote Procedure Calls (RPC): A protocol that facilitates Active Directory replication in and between Active Directory sites.

Replication: The process of updating database systems on multiple systems in order to synchronize data.

Replication topology: A description of the path replication takes throughout a network.

Reverse lookup: In DNS, the process of resolving from a TCP/IP address to a name (the opposite of "normal" name resolution).

Schema: The description of the objects and their attributes that can be stored in the Active Directory.

Schema master: The operations master role responsible for any updates to the Active Directory schema. You have one of these systems per forest.

Secondary master: A DNS server that receives DNS updates only from other DNS systems. Specifically, it receives updates from the primary zone. Its copy of the DNS zone information is read-only.

Security log: An Event Viewer log that contains information regarding the results of security auditing in Windows 2000 networks.

Service (SRV) resource record: The DNS records that helps clients locate network services on the network.

Simple Mail Transfer Protocol (SMTP): An alternative protocol that can be used for Active Directory replication between sites and domains.

Site: One or more well-connected TCP/IP subnets in your physical Windows 2000 network. These objects are used to help control the replication of Active Directory.

Snap-in: A tool imported into the Microsoft Management Console that enables you to manage a particular aspect of Windows 2000.

Standalone server: A Windows 2000 Server that is not participating in a Windows 2000 domain.

Start of authority (SOA) resource record: A resource record that indicates the starting point of authority for a particular zone of DNS information.

SYSVOL: A shared folder in a Windows 2000 domain that stores the server copy of the domain's public files. These files are replicated among all domain controllers.

Transitive trust: A standard type of trust in Windows 2000. In this relationship, if Domain A trusts Domain B, and Domain B trusts Domain C, then Domain A also trusts Domain C.

Two-way trust: Also a standard feature of trusts in Windows 2000. If Domain A trusts Domain B, Domain B also trusts Domain A.

Universal group: A Windows 2000 security group designed to store global groups from around the forest. Universal groups are typically placed in domain local groups in order to assign access permissions to resources.

X.500: A set of standards that define a distributed directory service.

Zone: In DNS, a section of the overall DNS namespace that is managed by a single DNS entity: a DNS server.

Zone transfer: The process by which DNS servers interact to update each other's zone data.

Appendix D

About the CD

● ●

*H*ere's some of the great stuff on the CD-ROM:

- ✔ The QuickLearn game, a fun way to study for the test
- ✔ Practice and Self-Assessment tests, to make sure you are ready for the real thing
- ✔ Practice test demos from Transcender, Specialized Solutions, and Self Test Software

System Requirements

Make sure your computer meets the minimum system requirements listed in this section. If your computer doesn't match up to most of these requirements, you may have problems using the contents of the CD:

- ✔ A PC with a 486 or faster processor.
- ✔ Microsoft Windows 95 or later.
- ✔ At least 16MB of total RAM installed on your computer. For best performance, we recommend at least 32MB of RAM installed.
- ✔ A CD-ROM drive — double-speed (2x) or faster.
- ✔ A sound card for PCs.
- ✔ A monitor capable of displaying at least 256 colors or grayscale.
- ✔ A modem with a speed of at least 14,400 bps.

Important Note: To play the QuickLearn game, you must have a 166 or faster computer running Windows 95 or 98 with SVGA graphics. You must also have Microsoft DirectX 5.0 or later installed. If you do not have DirectX, you can install it from the CD. Just run D:\Directx\dxinstall.exe. Unfortunately, DirectX 5.0 does not run on Windows NT 4.0, so you cannot play the QuickLearn Game on a Windows NT 4.0 or earlier machine.

Using the CD with Microsoft Windows

To install the items from the CD to your hard drive, follow these steps:

1. **Insert the CD into your computer's CD-ROM drive.**

2. **Click Start⇨Run.**

3. **In the dialog box that appears, type** D:\IDG.EXE.

   Replace *D* with the proper drive letter if your CD-ROM drive uses a different letter. (If you don't know the letter, see how your CD-ROM drive is listed under My Computer.)

4. **Click OK.**

   A license agreement window appears.

5. **Read through the license agreement, nod your head, and then click the Accept button if you want to use the CD. After you click Accept, you'll never be bothered by the License Agreement window again.**

   The CD interface Welcome screen appears. The interface is a little program that shows you what's on the CD and coordinates installing the programs and running the demos. The interface basically enables you to click a button or two to make things happen.

6. **Click anywhere on the Welcome screen to enter the interface.**

   Now you are getting to the action. This next screen lists categories for the software on the CD.

7. **To view the items within a category, just click the category's name.**

   A list of programs in the category appears.

8. **For more information about a program, click the program's name.**

   Be sure to read the information that appears. Sometimes a program has its own system requirements or requires you to do a few tricks on your computer before you can install or run the program, and this screen tells you what you might need to do.

9. **If you don't want to install the program, click the Back button to return to the previous screen.**

   You can always return to the previous screen by clicking the Back button. This feature enables you to browse the different categories and products and decide what you want to install.

10. **To install a program, click the appropriate Install button.**

    The CD interface drops to the background while the CD installs the program you chose.

11. **To install other items, repeat Steps 7–10.**

12. **When you've finished installing programs, click the Quit button to close the interface.**

    You can eject the CD now. Carefully place it back in the plastic jacket of the book for safekeeping.

In order to run some of the programs on this *MCSE Windows 2000 Directory Services For Dummies* CD-ROM, you may need to keep the CD inside your CD-ROM drive. This is a Good Thing. Otherwise, the installed program would have required you to install a very large chunk of the program to your hard drive, which may have kept you from installing other software.

What You'll Find

Shareware programs are fully functional, free trial versions of copyrighted programs. If you like particular programs, register with their authors for a nominal fee and receive licenses, enhanced versions, and technical support. Freeware programs are free, copyrighted games, applications, and utilities. You can copy them to as many PCs as you like — free — but they have no technical support. GNU software is governed by its own license, which is included inside the folder of the GNU software. There are no restrictions on distribution of this software. See the GNU license for more details. Trial, demo, or evaluation versions are usually limited either by time or functionality (such as being unable to save projects).

Here's a summary of the software on this CD.

Dummies test-prep tools

QuickLearn Game

The QuickLearn Game is the *For Dummies* way of making studying for the Certification exam fun. Well, okay, less painful. OutPost is a DirectX, high-resolution, fast-paced arcade game.

Answer questions to defuse dimensional disrupters and save the universe from a rift in space-time. (The questions come from the same set of questions that the Self-Assessment and Practice Test use, but isn't this way more fun?) Missing a few questions on the real exam almost never results in a rip in the fabric of the universe, so just think how easy it'll be when you get there!

Please note: QUIKLERN.EXE on the CD is just a self-extractor, to simplify the process of copying the game files to your computer. It will not create any shortcuts on your computer's desktop or Start menu.

You need to have DirectX 5.0 or later installed to play the QuickLearn game; and it does not run on Windows NT 4.0.

Practice Test

The Practice test is designed to help you get comfortable with the certification testing situation and pinpoint your strengths and weaknesses on the topic. You can choose the number of questions, the amount of time, and even decide which objectives you want to focus on.

After you answer the questions, the Practice test gives you plenty of feedback. You can find out which questions you answered correctly and incorrectly and get statistics on how you did, broken down by objective. Then you can review the questions — all of them, all the ones you missed, all the ones you marked, or a combination of the ones you marked and the ones you missed.

Self-Assessment Test

The Self-Assessment test is designed to simulate the actual certification testing situation. After you answer all the questions, you find out your score and whether you pass or fail — but that's all the feedback you get. If you can pass the Self-Assessment test regularly, you're ready to tackle the real thing.

Links Page

I've also created a Links Page, a handy starting place for accessing the huge amounts of information on the Internet about the certification tests. You can find the page at D:\Links.htm.

Screen Saver

A spiffy little screen saver that the Dummies team created. Maybe, like sleeping with the book under your pillow, this can help you learn subliminally! Screen shots of test questions will fill your screen, so when your computer is not doing anything else, it can still be quizzing you! And if you'd like to visit the *Certification For Dummies* Web site, all you have to do is press the space bar while the screen saver is running — your default browser will be launched and send you there! (You might want to keep this in mind if you're the kind of person who hits the space bar to get rid of your screen saver. . . .)

Commercial demos

bv-Admin for Migration and bv-Admin, from BindView Corporation

These trial versions show you how easily you can manage and migrate Active Directory structures and objects by using third-party tools.

QuickCert, from Specialized Solutions

This package from Specialized Solutions offers QuickCert practice tests for several Certification exams. Run the QuickCert IDG Demo to choose the practice test you want to work on. For more information about QuickCert, visit the Specialized Solutions Web site at www.specializedsolutions.com.

Self Test Software for MCSE Windows 2000, from Self Test Software

More practice exams for the MCSE Windows 2000 track. These demos cover all the core exams.

Storage CeNTral 4.1 and FileScreen 2000, from W Quinn

These trial versions give you a peek at the incredible third-party utilities available for Windows 2000.

Transcender Certification Sampler, from Transcender Corporation

Transcender's demo tests are some of the more popular practice tests available. The Certification Sampler offers demos of many of the exams that Transcender offers.

Transcender Windows 2000 Directory Services Flash, from Transcender Corporation

Another demo from the good folks at Transcender, this one is designed to help you learn the fundamental concepts and terminology behind ADS. You provide short-answer-type explanations to questions presented in a flash card format, and grade yourself as you go.

W2000 Security MCSEprep and W2000 Directory Services MCSEprep, from Super Software

More great demo test prep products!

If You've Got Problems (Of the CD Kind)

I tried my best to compile programs that work on most computers with the minimum system requirements. Alas, your computer may differ, and some programs may not work properly for some reason.

The two likeliest problems are that you don't have enough memory (RAM) for the programs you want to use, or you have other programs running that are affecting installation or running of a program. If you get error messages like Not enough memory or Setup cannot continue, try one or more of these methods and then try using the software again:

✔ **Turn off any antivirus software that you have on your computer.** Installers sometimes mimic virus activity and may make your computer incorrectly believe that it is being infected by a virus.

✔ **Close all running programs.** The more programs you're running, the less memory is available to other programs. Installers also typically update files and programs; if you keep other programs running, installation may not work properly.

✔ **In Windows, close the CD interface and run demos or installations directly from Windows Explorer.** The interface itself can tie up system memory, or even conflict with certain kinds of interactive demos. Use Windows Explorer to browse the files on the CD and launch installers or demos.

✔ **Have your local computer store add more RAM to your computer.** This is, admittedly, a drastic and somewhat expensive step. However, adding more memory can really help the speed of your computer and enable more programs to run at the same time.

If you still have trouble installing the items from the CD, please call the IDG Books Worldwide Customer Service phone number: 800-762-2974 (outside the U.S.: 317-572-3342).

Index

Notes

Notes

Notes

Notes

IDG Books Worldwide, Inc., End-User License Agreement

READ THIS. You should carefully read these terms and conditions before opening the software packet(s) included with this book ("Book"). This is a license agreement ("Agreement") between you and IDG Books Worldwide, Inc. ("IDGB"). By opening the accompanying software packet(s), you acknowledge that you have read and accept the following terms and conditions. If you do not agree and do not want to be bound by such terms and conditions, promptly return the Book and the unopened software packet(s) to the place you obtained them for a full refund.

1. **License Grant.** IDGB grants to you (either an individual or entity) a nonexclusive license to use one copy of the enclosed software program(s) (collectively, the "Software") solely for your own personal or business purposes on a single computer (whether a standard computer or a workstation component of a multiuser network). The Software is in use on a computer when it is loaded into temporary memory (RAM) or installed into permanent memory (hard disk, CD-ROM, or other storage device). IDGB reserves all rights not expressly granted herein.

2. **Ownership.** IDGB is the owner of all right, title, and interest, including copyright, in and to the compilation of the Software recorded on the disk(s) or CD-ROM ("Software Media"). Copyright to the individual programs recorded on the Software Media is owned by the author or other authorized copyright owner of each program. Ownership of the Software and all proprietary rights relating thereto remain with IDGB and its licensers.

3. **Restrictions on Use and Transfer.**

   (a) You may only (i) make one copy of the Software for backup or archival purposes, or (ii) transfer the Software to a single hard disk, provided that you keep the original for backup or archival purposes. You may not (i) rent or lease the Software, (ii) copy or reproduce the Software through a LAN or other network system or through any computer subscriber system or bulletin-board system, or (iii) modify, adapt, or create derivative works based on the Software.

   (b) You may not reverse engineer, decompile, or disassemble the Software. You may transfer the Software and user documentation on a permanent basis, provided that the transferee agrees to accept the terms and conditions of this Agreement and you retain no copies. If the Software is an update or has been updated, any transfer must include the most recent update and all prior versions.

4. **Restrictions on Use of Individual Programs.** You must follow the individual requirements and restrictions detailed for each individual program in the "About the CD" section of this Book. These limitations are also contained in the individual license agreements recorded on the Software Media. These limitations may include a requirement that after using the program for a specified period of time, the user must pay a registration fee or discontinue use. By opening the Software packet(s), you will be agreeing to abide by the licenses and restrictions for these individual programs that are detailed in the "About the CD" section and on the Software Media. None of the material on this Software Media or listed in this Book may ever be redistributed, in original or modified form, for commercial purposes.

5. **Limited Warranty.**

   (a) IDGB warrants that the Software and Software Media are free from defects in materials and workmanship under normal use for a period of sixty (60) days from the date of purchase of this Book. If IDGB receives notification within the warranty period of defects in materials or workmanship, IDGB will replace the defective Software Media.

   (b) IDGB AND THE AUTHOR OF THE BOOK DISCLAIM ALL OTHER WARRANTIES, EXPRESS OR IMPLIED, INCLUDING WITHOUT LIMITATION IMPLIED WARRANTIES OF MERCHANTABILITY AND FITNESS FOR A PARTICULAR PURPOSE, WITH RESPECT TO THE SOFTWARE, THE PROGRAMS, THE SOURCE CODE CONTAINED THEREIN, AND/OR THE TECHNIQUES DESCRIBED IN THIS BOOK. IDGB DOES NOT WARRANT THAT THE FUNCTIONS CONTAINED IN THE SOFTWARE WILL MEET YOUR REQUIRE-MENTS OR THAT THE OPERATION OF THE SOFTWARE WILL BE ERROR FREE.

   (c) This limited warranty gives you specific legal rights, and you may have other rights that vary from jurisdiction to jurisdiction.

6. **Remedies.**

   (a) IDGB's entire liability and your exclusive remedy for defects in materials and workmanship shall be limited to replacement of the Software Media, which may be returned to IDGB with a copy of your receipt at the following address: Software Media Fulfillment Department, Attn.: *MCSE Windows® 2000 Directory Services For Dummies®*, IDG Books Worldwide, Inc., 10475 Crosspoint Blvd., Indianapolis, IN 46256, or call 800-762-2974. Please allow three to four weeks for delivery. This Limited Warranty is void if failure of the Software Media has resulted from accident, abuse, or misapplication. Any replacement Software Media will be warranted for the remainder of the original warranty period or thirty (30) days, whichever is longer.

   (b) In no event shall IDGB or the author be liable for any damages whatsoever (including without limitation damages for loss of business profits, business interruption, loss of business information, or any other pecuniary loss) arising from the use of or inability to use the Book or the Software, even if IDGB has been advised of the possibility of such damages.

   (c) Because some jurisdictions do not allow the exclusion or limitation of liability for consequential or incidental damages, the above limitation or exclusion may not apply to you.

7. **U.S. Government Restricted Rights.** Use, duplication, or disclosure of the Software for or on behalf of the United States of America, its agencies and/or instrumentalities (the "U.S. Government") is subject to restrictions as stated in paragraph (c)(1)(ii) of the Rights in Technical Data and Computer Software clause of DFARS 252.227-7013, or subparagraphs (c)(1) and (2) of the Commercial Computer Software - Restricted Rights clause at FAR 52.227-19, and in similar clauses in the NASA FAR supplement, as applicable.

8. **General.** This Agreement constitutes the entire understanding of the parties and revokes and supersedes all prior agreements, oral or written, between them and may not be modified or amended except in a writing signed by both parties hereto that specifically refers to this Agreement. This Agreement shall take precedence over any other documents that may be in conflict herewith. If any one or more provisions contained in this Agreement are held by any court or tribunal to be invalid, illegal, or otherwise unenforceable, each and every other provision shall remain in full force and effect.

Installation Instructions

To install the items from the CD to your hard drive, follow these steps:

1. **Insert the CD into your computer's CD-ROM drive.**

2. **Click Start⇨Run.**

3. **In the dialog box that appears, type** D:\IDG.EXE.

   Replace *D* with the proper drive letter if your CD-ROM drive uses a different letter.

4. **Click OK.**

5. **Read through the license agreement that's displayed and then click the Accept button if you want to use the CD. After you click Accept, you'll never be bothered by the License Agreement window again.**

   The CD interface Welcome screen appears.

6. **Click anywhere on the Welcome screen to enter the interface.**

   The interface displays a list of categories for the software on the CD.

7. **To view the items within a category, just click the category's name.**

   A list of programs in the category appears.

8. **For more information about a program, click the program's name.**

9. **To install a program, click the appropriate Install button. (If you don't want to install the program, click the Back button to return to the previous screen.)**

   The CD interface drops to the background while the CD installs the program you chose.

10. **To install other items, repeat Steps 7 – 9.**

11. **After you install the programs you want, click the Quit button and then eject the CD.**

    For more information, see the "About the CD" appendix.

IDG BOOKS WORLDWIDE
BOOK REGISTRATION

Register This Book and Win!

We want to hear from you!

Visit **dummies.com** to register this book and tell us how you liked it!

✔ Get entered in our monthly prize giveaway.

✔ Give us feedback about this book — tell us what you like best, what you like least, or maybe what you'd like to ask the author and us to change!

✔ Let us know any other *For Dummies*® topics that interest you.

Your feedback helps us determine what books to publish, tells us what coverage to add as we revise our books, and lets us know whether we're meeting your needs as a *For Dummies* reader. You're our most valuable resource, and what you have to say is important to us!

Not on the Web yet? It's easy to get started with *Dummies 101*®: *The Internet For Windows*® *98* or *The Internet For Dummies*® at local retailers everywhere.

Or let us know what you think by sending us a letter at the following address:

For Dummies Book Registration
Dummies Press
10475 Crosspoint Blvd.
Indianapolis, IN 46256

™

BESTSELLING BOOK SERIES